Podcasting Now! Audio Your Way

Andrew J. Dagys

with John Hedtke

THOMSON

COURSE TECHNOLOGY

Professional ■ Technical ■ Reference

ISBN: 1-59863-076-8

Library of Congress Catalog Card Number: 2005931885

Printed in the United States of America

06 07 08 09 10 PH 10 9 8 7 6 5 4 3 2 1

Publisher and General Manager, Thomson Course Technology PTR:
Stacy L. Hiquet

Associate Director of Marketing:
Sarah O'Donnell

Manager of Editorial Services:
Heather Talbot

Marketing Manager:
Cathleen Snyder

Acquisitions Editor:
Mitzi Koontz

Marketing Coordinator:
Jordan Casey

Project Editor:
Kate Shoup Welsh

Technical Reviewer:
Arlie Hartman

PTR Editorial Services Coordinator:
Elizabeth Furbish

Copy Editor:
Kate Shoup Welsh

Interior Layout Tech:
Susan Honeywell

Cover Designer:
Mike Tanamachi

Indexer:
Kelly Talbot

Proofreader:
Sandi Wilson

THOMSON

COURSE TECHNOLOGY ™
Professional ■ Technical ■ Reference

Thomson Course Technology PTR, a division of Thomson Course Technology
25 Thomson Place ■ Boston, MA 02210 ■ http://www.courseptr.com

I dedicate this book to my patient and loving wife,
Dawn-Ava, and our children—
Brendan, Megan, and Jordan.
I love you all.

—Andrew J. Dagys

To Gael Stirler, one of my oldest friends,
who combines artistic talent, business acumen,
good looks, and boundless optimism into
a single dynamic package.

—John Hedtke

Preface

Every once in a while, a major and exciting technological shift occurs that radically changes how people can do things. Podcasting is one of those shifts. This book is poised to take you on a journey that shows you how podcasting can entertain, inform, and fulfill you. The podcasting phenomenon is growing in leaps and bounds, and this book provides insights as to *why*.

Podcasting lets you, the individual, *broadcast* audio programs on the Internet. That in itself represents a new paradigm in the way "radio" is delivered. Podcasting also lets you subscribe to a "feed" of one or more podcast files (usually in MP3 format) that you can *listen* to. Put more simply, with podcasting you can both create and listen to content. Podcast content may consist of a combination of voice with music, video, text, and other media formats. The underlying technology is easy to learn, and this book shows you *how*.

Podcasting represents a shift in three fundamental areas:

- **Time.** As podcast listener, you can use special tools called *aggregators* to schedule a search for new podcasts to which you have subscribed. You can then listen to them whenever you want to.

- **Place.** As either a listener or creator of podcasts, you can use a wide array of mobile devices to retrieve or post podcasts on-the-go.

- **The media of your message.** Although the precise meaning of terms I throw at you in this book (like *podcasting*, *weblogging*, and *video weblogging*) may at times be blurry, they are always secondary. Words and definitions simply don't matter all that much. What does matter is what you want to do with that technology. Do you want to be an individual radio broadcaster? Fine. Podcasting alone may suffice. Do you want to be an individual TV broadcaster? Also fine. Vlogging (essentially podcasting with video) may be the way to go. Do you just want to be an individual print publisher? Sure. Weblogging alone may do. Perhaps all three? That's possible too.

After you read this book, you will not only have knowledge of available podcasting tools—and when and why to use them—but also of weblogging and vlogging. This is a key value proposition of this book—one that recognizes that podcasting is highly interrelated with both weblogging and vlogging. Any other view sells you short.

As its title suggests, *Podcasting Now! Audio Your Way* aims to get you up and running fast, but effectively. Podcasting is a craft that is simple and fairly quick to learn, as long as you understand *what* the process is and some key fundamentals, which this book explains. If you stray from this process or from the fundamentals, you may waste valuable time. This book keeps you on track and focused on what is important. In that regard, it won't take you long as to *when* you'll be podcasting!

In the next few years, indeed months, podcasting will continue to evolve rapidly. Fortunately, this book captures the essentials that will not change by much, and discusses what are likely to remain the key players in the podosphere. I trust that this book will provide you with an interesting and compelling glimpse into the present and the future of podcasting.

Acknowledgments

Andrew J. Dagys

The book-writing process is very rewarding from a personal standpoint, but it is also a tremendous collaborative effort that requires acknowledgement of the important contributions of others. Without these dedicated and insightful individuals, this book would not have been possible.

First, I wish to thank Mitzi Koontz, my acquisitions editor, who believed in my ability to complete this book. She remained supportive of me even during some of the bumps, hiccups, and tight deadlines that often line the path to a finished book. She was patient with my endless stream of questions, and placed much value on a good working relationship, which was also important to me. I thank her for her faith and confidence in me.

One of the most rewarding experiences associated with writing this book was the privilege of working with my editor. My heartfelt gratitude goes to Kate Shoup Welsh for her tremendous effort on this title. At every corner, she was focused on the pursuit of excellence. The flow and art in this title is due to her masterful ability to see the big picture from afar, and her powerful writing skills. I have learned tremendously from her always-justified edits. Thank you, Kate, for your hard work. It really shows in this book.

I also wish to thank John Hedtke, who, as a very experienced author, did a tremendous job throughout this book. His knowledge of audio technology in particular has made this a particularly professional work. Thank you for your critical contributions!

This book would never have been written had it not been for the insight of Stacy Hiquet, Publisher and General Manager of Thomson Course Technology PTR. Thank you for allowing me the privilege of working with this first-class publishing house.

Starting a book is one matter, but *Podcasting Now! Audio Your Way* would not have been completed had it not been for the "all clear" signals provided by the valuable technical editing of

Arlie Hartman. Thank you for your efforts. As for the middle piece of the book-writing process, and for chasing down people and parcels, I thank Elizabeth Furbish for her assistance with my endless stream of correspondence—at least the correspondence that made it to home base. On the periphery are all the others listed in the credits. Thank you for your contributions.

Finally, I wish to thank Robert Harris, Jack David, Joan Whitman, and Robert Hickey for shepherding me through the exciting world of writing. There is no other like it.

John Hedtke

It's a rare book that's done by only a few people. I'd like to take a moment to acknowledge the many contributions from a variety of sources, without whose invaluable assistance, this book would not be what it is. First, thanks to Neil Salkind and Laura Lewin of Studio B, my agents and wonderful people. Thanks to Mitzi Koontz, of Thomson Course PTR, for wanting to do a book on podcasting, and to Kate Welsh, an exceptional editor, who put a high polish on my writing. Thanks, Kate. Other Thomson pros whose contributions were invaluable include Sue Honeywell, Sandi Wilson, and Kelly Talbot. Thanks to Dave Winer, for inventing podcasting in the first place (and thereby giving us yet another way to spend our time online), and to Andrew Grumet and the iPodder team for inventing iPodder, a cross-platform podcast receiver. Everyone should download a copy right away! Thanks to Dominic Mazzoni of Audacity, the best software I've found for podcast editing. (Go download this, too!) Thanks to Scott Logan, for many contributions, including a wealth of material and research, and to John Iasiuolo of the Computer Outlook Radio Talk Show, for information and background about podcasting and how cool it is. Thanks to Charlie Halbrook, old friend and audio expert, who explained about noise and how to filter it, and to Jason Scott, technology historian and documentary filmmaker. Thanks to Marilyn Mauer, for too many things to mention, and to Susan Wahlberg, for general office work.

The following contributors of time, products, and invaluable information also deserve thanks: the folks at PodcastAlley.com, PodcastBunker.com, and PodNova.com, all great places to go to look for more podcasts; John McKenna at CoffeeCup Software for his assistance and for producing a broad range of software that's pleasurable to look at, as well as fun and easy to work with; Jason Litchford at Griffin Technology for his help with equipment and terminology in noise elimination; Mark Prince and the folks at Forte, Inc., makers of Agent and Free Agent, my favorite newsgroup program; Alex Neihaus and Laurie Klausner of Ipswitch, Inc., makers of WS_FTP Pro (my favorite FTP program), for their help with FTP processes and software documentation; Steve Humphrey and Rodney Rumford of Podblaze.com for their visions of the future of podcasting; Ryan Sommer of A&R Partners (for Palm, Inc.) for his insight on how podcasting is changing handheld computing; Bill Keyser of GoodCans.com (and the Listening Station) for his expertise in headphone technology; and Lucy Chung of Edelman.com, working with Cowon America, for her invaluable assistance. To all of these people and companies, I offer my heartfelt thanks.

About the Author

As a Canadian-based writer, **ANDREW J. DAGYS** has authored and co-authored 10 books, including the best-selling *The Internet for 50+* (2e) and *The Financial Planner for 50+* (both with Prentice Hall Canada). He also authored best-selling and flagship titles, namely *The Internet for Canadians for Dummies* (2e), *Investing Online for Canadians for Dummies* (2e), and *Stock Investing for Canadians for Dummies*, which recently attained bestseller and second-edition status (Wiley Canada). He has also revised *Money Management All-in-One for Canadians for Dummies*.

Andrew's professional expertise includes identifying opportunities for business and technology process improvement. His writing expertise includes discussion of how technology can be harnessed to enhance personal lifestyle. Following technology trends and innovations is one of his passions. He is also an avid but careful investor in technology and other stocks that show promise.

Andrew has written many technology-related columns in leading lifestyle magazines. These publications include *Canadian Living Magazine* and *Forever Young*. He is a frequent guest on TV and radio shows to discuss important technologies, and how they can help people become more effective and productive in their areas of interest. He also enjoys providing seminars on topics within his expertise, and has spoken many times in public forums to share his knowledge of important technological and financial trends and issues.

Andrew lives in Toronto with his wife Dawn-Ava, and three children—Brendan, Megan, and Jordan. He can be reached at aj-dagys@rogers.com.

About the Contributing Author

JOHN HEDTKE has written 24 books, nearly 100 magazine articles, and hundreds of manuals and online help systems for technical and non-technical documentation for all levels of readers. He owns and operates JVH Communications, a company that provides writing, consulting, and training services to private and government clients. He also speaks to professional groups on subjects such as career planning, time management, and writing books and magazine articles. John is a Fellow of the Society for Technical Communication and was elected to the Board of Directors in 2005.

CONTENTS

INTRODUCTION

Welcome to *Podcasting Now! Audio Your Way*. Although books on technology abound, all too many assume you have a degree in the high arts of technology, and that you are interested in knowing about every piece of technological minutiae. Other books go too far the other way and don't cover enough, leaving gaps for you to fill on your own. I hope that you find this book to be different.

Podcasting Now! Audio Your Way shows you everything you need to know to listen to and create podcasts—and everything in between. This book is as complete as can be at the time of this writing, and covers some very important—and recent—developments in the world of podcasting. It is written to get you motivated and excited about the entertainment, information-gathering, and other lifestyle-enhancing possibilities that podcasting can provide.

This book was also written to show you just how easy it really is to podcast, and that there are many ways you can get started. It is my hope that this book will inspire you to dabble in podcasting and, more importantly, reveal to you the revolution that is happening in self-expression and networking.

I throw out just enough technical jargon (and briefly explain it) to position you to embrace these terms with confidence. If you wish to dig deeper into a subject area, I show you resources that may help. After reading this book, you'll be able to talk like a techno-geek without actually being one! I discuss how podcasting stuff works in plain and lighthearted English.

Podcasting Now! Audio Your Way had to be written because there is so much to say about podcasting that can't be covered in other media formats. Also, there were many very significant developments that occurred in just the few months that led to the release of this book. I was thrilled to be able to have captured all these developments and felt very fortu-nate that they occurred when they did. In the meantime, podcasting continues to evolve and I try to predict its new directions throughout.

Too many publications get absorbed in terminology and forget the simple fact that pod-casting is highly related to other technologies as well. In this book, instead of ignoring these peripheral technologies, such as video weblogging (podcasting with video) and moblog-ging (podcasting on-the-go), I squarely deal with them, completely but succinctly. In other words, I did not ignore these technologies just because they didn't have the word "podcast" in them. I also give you a flavor of some of the exciting, entertaining, and informative things others are broadcasting in the podosphere.

In this book, I assumed that you were interested in listening to podcasts, creating them, or both. I also assumed that although you enjoy and see the benefits of the technology lifestyle, you don't have the time or inclination to troll through disjointed instructions and excessive babble that often comes with online manuals and other sources. You want immediate gratification and an organized and complete approach. Most of all, I assumed that you are courageous and enough of a pioneer to delve into the world of podcasting!

About This Book

This book is about listening to podcasts as well as creating them. I describe the process you need to follow to do both, and to do it with rich multimedia. It is also about the many podcasting software and hardware options you have, and the criteria to help you select from those options. Discussion is mostly geared toward the affordable but also delves into state-of-the-art toys that cost a bit more.

I saved some of the best discussion for last. Near the end of the book I provide you with a glimpse into the future of podcasting. In fact, many of the resources I talk about were in beta testing at the time of this writing. I also take you from glimpse mode to "how-to" mode and show you exactly how to create (and listen to) video weblogs, which are essen-tially podcasts with integrated visual multimedia. (Again, I never get you hung up on def-initions.) I also walk you through some of the most interesting podcasts in the podosphere.

How This Book Is Organized

Podcasting Now! Audio Your Way has three stand-alone parts. The good news is that you can begin Part II before embarking on Part I. You can even first browse some of the pod-casts listed in Appendix A, "Resources," to get a feel for what you are getting into.

Here is how the book is organized:

In Part I, "Listening to Podcasts," I introduce you to the basics of podcasting. You'll learn how it works. You'll also be asked to install a full-featured and easy-to-use podcasting application to listen to your first podcast. You'll learn your way around the software application, including how to add subscriptions, schedule downloads, and download podcasts to your MP3 player so you can listen to the latest episodes on-the-go. Once you have mastered the fundamentals—which is easy and not time-consuming to do—I'll show you how to extend your reach to access podcasts that live in many places on the Internet.

In Part II, "Creating Podcasts," I introduce you to some key concepts about digital audio, how to plan your podcasts, and how to select the hardware and software you need to record and edit your podcasts. Once this planning stage is set, I walk you through the podcast-production process, including configuring recording software, recording a podcast, editing what you've captured, and converting it to MP3 or another format. I also show you some software to help you create the information feeds or code that will let others locate your podcast. Part II also raises the bar by taking you into a few uncharted waters. These waters include the many ways you can package podcasts with multimedia like video, music, and pictures. Podcasts may reside on different types of web sites and weblogs, so I discuss your various podcast hosting options; the one you choose will depend on how you wish to present your podcast. This part of the book closes with how you can get your podcast promoted—a key objective for anyone who creates them.

In Part III, "Podcast Software, Hardware, and Video Weblogging," you are taken for an important walk through the growing world of podcast aggregators, which help you find and listen to podcasts. I present some of the most common freeware and other software available for most computers and MP3 devices. I provide you with the important criteria you need to help you decide which aggregator is for you, even if you are a Mac or Linux user. I ask you to wear the hat of podcast listener and introduce you to some of today's hottest MP3 players and peripherals. Finally, I take you to the leading edge of podcasting, including video weblogging, or *vlogging*. You'll see that there are a couple ways to create vlogs; both the "do-it-yourself" and "commercial online services" routes are discussed fully. You will also learn about aggregators to help you find the vlogs of others. I also show you how some of the hottest applications and trends in the new generation "Web 2.0" integrate with podcasting. These apps and trends include Google searches, social networks, voice-over-Internet, satellite radio, and advertising models that may help you make money from your podcasts.

Appendix A, "Resources," and the glossary round things out by providing at-a-glance reference points to relevant additional resources and key definitions.

How to Use This Book

As you read this book, don't get too hung up on the technology or terminology. Whether something is technically a podcast, weblog, or vlog is entirely beside the point. What is important is what your personal objective is. For example, do you just want to podcast with voice only, or do you prefer a jazzed-up experience replete with music, video, and other multimedia? It is the answer to that question that determines what part of the book you'll find most satisfying.

In addition to general text, you'll see helpful screenshots to take a bit of the mystery away and show you what you can expect to see on your own computer. I peppered the book with brief notes that are important and relate to certain discussion points. I also salted this discussion with sidebars which are sort of like "did you know" blurbs about cool developments related to the section you are reading.

Most importantly, be sure to use this book with a fun frame of mind!

PART ONE

LISTENING TO PODCASTS

CHAPTER 1

GETTING STARTED WITH PODCASTING

This chapter introduces you to the basics of podcasting. You'll learn what podcasting is and how it works. You'll also see how to install iPodder (a popular podcasting application) and listen to your first podcast.

Podcasting Described Really Quickly

Podcasting—a term created from "iPod" and "broadcasting"—is a way of automatically downloading MP3 and other audio files that you can listen to on your computer or on an MP3 player or an MP3-capable cell phone. Podcasting isn't just downloading music files, though; you're downloading prepared programs (radio-style programs, not computer programs) from the Internet. It's a lot like TiVo for the Internet: you tell your podcasting software what you'd like to listen to, and the software will download the programs you specify.

One thing that makes podcasting different is that it's a two-way street. If you're not finding a podcast with your favorite music or topics, there are probably other people on the net who share your frustration. You can create your own podcasts and share them with other people almost as easily as downloading podcasts. (Chapter 4, "Getting Ready to Do It Yourself," begins to show you how to start a brilliant career as a podcaster.)

Do You Need an iPod to Listen to Podcasts?

The word "podcasting" implies that you're going to be listening to podcasts on an Apple iPod. Although I'm sure that Apple would like this to be true, you can actually listen to podcasts on anything that will play an MP3 file, including digital music players from Rio, Sony, Toshiba, Creative, or any of a dozen other companies. You can also play podcasts on a laptop, a Palm Pilot or other handheld computer, and some of the newer cell phones (which have MP3 capabilities). You can expect wristwatches that play MP3s, portable CD/radio units with MP3 features, car stereos, and probably everything except microwave ovens that you can play podcasts on. Or you can figure that you're going to listen to this at work or your home-office location and just play podcasts on your computer and never worry about downloading podcasts to a digital music player at all. Chapter 2, "Listening to Podcasts," describes how to use a digital music player with your podcasting software.

Podcasting Described More Slowly and in More Detail

Although you don't *have* to know anything about how the elements of podcasting work in order to use it, you'll soon find that you can get more enjoyment out of it if you have an understanding of the basics that go into podcasting. Podcasting is actually the result of several different tools and technologies that all came together on the Internet:

- MP3 files
- Blogs
- RSS (short for "Really Simple Syndication") and desktop aggregators
- iPods and MP3 players

What Is MP3?

MPEG (pronounced "EM-peg") is an acronym for Moving (or Motion) Pictures Experts Group. MPEG is a group of standards for compressing and storing audio and video in files. MP3 is actually short for "MPEG 1, layer 3," the portion of the MPEG standard that specifies how audio files are stored.

What makes MP3 files special is that they give CD-quality sound in a file that requires only about one megabyte for every minute of sound. (By comparison, the format used on CDs for recording requires about 11 megabytes for every minute.) This, combined with their high quality of sound reproduction, has made MP3 files enormously popular for distributing and exchanging songs and music. Many search engines list MP3 as the second-most-popular search topic.

To play an MP3 file on your computer, you need MP3 software. Most computers come with some variety of MP3 software built in; if yours does not suffice, you can download a variety of MP3 players to suit your needs. Chapter 2 identifies some popular MP3 software programs and places to find them.

Podcasting relies on MP3 files as the basic audio format. If recorded at near-CD quality, a one-hour podcast can be downloaded in as little as 10 minutes with a good cable modem connection. Even better, some podcasts (such as talk-show formats) aren't recorded at near-CD quality, so you may get two or three minutes of sound for each megabyte. A full hour show could then be downloaded in just a few minutes.

What Is RSS?

You're already familiar with favorites (if you use Internet Explorer) or bookmarks (if you use Firefox, Netscape, Opera, or some other web browser), which store the URL, or web site address. When you click the favorite or bookmark, the browser goes to the web site address.

This works fine, but there's no way of determining whether the web site has changed since you last looked at it. Most web sites are relatively static, but some web sites—news or job web sites, for example—change constantly. The only way to see if anything's changed is to go to the web site and actually look. This can become time-consuming; moreover, you may overlook something or even miss an opportunity entirely if the web site was updated shortly after you checked it.

RSS, an acronym for "Really Simple Syndication," lets web sites syndicate content and information they want to share. You can check RSS feeds through your web browser by creating an RSS link. Whenever there's an update to the web site's content, the RSS information is updated as well. Checking the RSS link for the web site will then show the latest information in the form of a headline and possibly a line or two about whatever's been posted. You can click the link to go see the whole thing or not, but the big trick is that *you didn't have to go to the web site to find out if there is anything new.*

The best part about RSS is that it's not necessary to check for new RSS content with a web browser. Many other applications can also read RSS feeds, including *news aggregators,* programs that check RSS feeds from news web sites and the like and let you get a digest of the news you're interested in from any of several thousand different sources. Check out RSSOwl (http://www.rssowl.org), FeedReader (http://www.feedreader.com), or BottomFeeder (http://www.cincomsmalltalk.com/BottomFeeder) if you'd like to try a straight news aggregator.

ATOM and Other Syndication Formats

RSS is a standard for syndicating web content—well, seven or eight different standards that tend to look fairly similar, actually—but RSS is not the only format for syndicating web content. If you look at news aggregators, you'll see some that read ATOM feeds. ATOM is another popular syndication format that grew out of RSS. There are other formats to syndicate information as well, such as OPML (Outline Processor Markup Language), OML (Outline Markup Language), ICE (Information Content Exchange), and SyncML (Synchronization Markup Language). For example, the Firefox browser (http://www.mozilla.com) has a number of free extensions available that handle both RSS and ATOM formats.

Most syndication is currently done with RSS and ATOM, but each of these formats has its advantages. All you need to worry about is that your podcasting software knows how to use the format in which the podcast is being distributed. Unless you're setting up a podcasting distribution web site of your own and get involved with the technical details, you can let the web sites and your computer handle the details.

RSS became a popular technology with the growth in blogging, or weblogging (described next). Trying to monitor even a few weblogs by going to the individual web sites is a pest; monitoring a dozen or more is just not practical. RSS was the perfect solution for tracking new entries on weblogs. Many news aggregators and online aggregators now track weblogs as well as news sources; some of them, such as SharpReader (http://www.sharpreader.com), Bloglines (http://www.bloglines.com), and Kinja (http://www.kinja.com), focus exclusively on weblogs. Almost every weblogging site provides some form of RSS support so you can track the weblogs you're interested in.

RSS is good for more than just weblogs, though. You can use RSS to track news stories that you're interested in. Some web sites, such as NewsIsFree (http://www.newsisfree.com) and the Nearest Neighbor News Network (http://www.nearestneighbor.net), provide *online aggregators* that do the filtering for you on the web site side of things. This lets you set up your news preferences on the web site without having to install and learn how to use a news aggregator. Online aggregators are a boon for those who need to switch between work and home locations or who are on the road frequently.

The information you get from RSS doesn't have to be just text or even just audio files. RSS can package just about anything: text, documents, audio files, video/multimedia, or any combination of downloadable data you can think of. What all this boils down to is that you can identify the kinds of information you want to look for and then have your computer romp around on the Internet and check for it as often as you like—a few times a week, a day, or even an hour if something major is breaking. RSS also speeds things up for you by filtering information: You'll only get the things you're after. As a result, you can follow a lot more news without a lot of distractions.

RSS is an essential part of podcasting. When you listen to an Internet radio station such as Whole Wheat Radio (http://www.wholewheatradio.com), you go to the web site and then start the radio feed. You use RSS to *subscribe* to a podcast, and then your podcast software takes care of the mechanics of looking for new podcasts and downloading them. You make the computer do the work for you (which is what they're for, after all). Without syndication, there'd be no podcasting.

Weblogs and Blogging

A *blog* (short for *weblog*) in its simplest form is an online diary or journal. People write their thoughts, experiences, and opinions online, and other people read them. Weblogs, like diaries, can be about literally anything: what's happening in your life, with your relationship, with your health, and with your job are all examples of weblog topics, but these only scratch the surface. Weblogs can include many different formats, too: text (naturally), pictures, links to other sites, audio, video, or any combination of these. (Not surprisingly, the fastest way to find out about weblogs if you're not already familiar with them is to look at some. Check out the large weblog sites such as http://www.livejournal.com, http://www.blogger.com, http://www.bloglines.com, and any of a few dozen others.) You could just post a bunch of information on your web site, but it wouldn't really be a weblog. Weblogs are different because of the following:

- **Weblogs look uncluttered.** Personal and business web sites (or *standard* web sites) typically have a main page and a bunch of links that take you to other pages that also frequently have links, and so on. By contrast, weblogs typically have a main page with the most current entries displayed in reverse chronological order as well as links to other weblogs. The weblog entries can have links to pictures, audio or video files, or other weblogs or web sites, but everything you tend to want is right there in front of you.

- **Weblogs are easy to maintain.** I used to post a lot of things on my web site as a way to keep friends informed about the things that were happening in my life. It was a lot of fun, but it was an awful lot of work: I had to actually build a new web page, code all the links, add formatting, and then update the links between all the other topics I'd posted. I had complete control, but it was really getting in the way of the relatively simple process of telling people what had happened. In contrast, weblogs make the process of posting very simple: Once you set up the weblog (which is a pretty simple process itself), you just go to the weblog site and enter the post's title and text and *voilà!* You've updated your weblog! The weblog site takes care of all the messy little details like formatting the text you've entered, adding date and time stamps, displaying any links or pictures in the post, archiving past entries, and all the rest. You can even have your new posts in draft form so you can work on them, preview them, and then polish them before you publish them for everyone to see.

- **Weblogs can be reformatted easily.** If you're running a personal web site, changing the format for the pages is a particularly messy process. Even if you've got all the necessary technical skills in HTML (hypertext markup language) and web design and so on, it's a real pest. Weblog sites usually have a stack of preformatted design templates for you to choose from; you can modify them or even choose something entirely different whenever you want to change your look and then (here's the cool part) just republish your weblog in one operation. Once again, the weblog site does the work for you.

- **Weblogs let readers post comments or feedback.** When you post the latest news that's going on in your life on a personal web site, it's pretty much a "read-only" sort of affair. Sure, people can email you with their thoughts, but it's private and can't really become a conversation triggered by your post or someone's feedback. Moreover, the feedback—and your replies and other replies to your replies—all are tied to the specific weblog posting that triggered them. While some weblogs restrict who can enter comments or keep comments private, most of them have built-in comment features that make it easy for folks to tell you what they think about whatever you've added.

  - **Weblogs have a lot of tools to make weblogging easier.** Besides the basic features for creating and updating weblogs, there are zillions of tools for weblogging. For example, weblog sites usually have built-in profile search features, so people can find weblogs with similar focuses and interests. There are also a number of browser bookmarklets and add-ons that let you click a button and add the web site you're currently looking at (along with any comments you care to add) to a new post in your weblog so you can share it with your readers. Another great weblogging tool is a *blogroll*, a list of weblogs displayed off to the side of your weblog posts that lists whatever weblogs or web sites you want to tell people about.

note

Bookmarklets are nifty little downloadable applications that you can add to your favorites or book- marks lists. When you click them, they do some simple task like show you the links on a web page, change the font colors or size to something you like better, or zoom in on the first image on a page. Check out web sites like http://www.bookmarklets.com or http://www.squarefree.com/ bookmarklets if you'd like to try them for yourself.

- **Weblogs have RSS features.** The most important part of weblogs is that blog sites support RSS (or some other syndication format). You can set up an RSS link and have your web browser or news aggregator monitor the weblog for any new entries. Anyone can post information about themselves or post their opinions, but syndication makes it easy to track what's happening on your favorite weblogs.

You can have weblogs—and podcasts, for that matter—on absolutely any subject. Most weblogs are personal diaries of the daily trivia of some aspect of a person's life, but they can also be aimed at disseminating information on a specific technical, professional, or business goal. Businesses, corporations, churches, and political parties have weblogs and use them for outreach, marketing, and discussion. There are also group weblogs, where members of a group can all post entries to the same weblog. Just as the browsable part of the Internet has come to be known as "the Web," the collection of all weblogs (and weblog hosting sites) is referred to as the "blogosphere."

Weblogs helped break ground for podcasting in a few ways. First, weblogs got people used to the idea of going to weblog sites for any topic imaginable. Second, weblogs helped popularize the idea of using RSS to check in on the latest "episode" of a given weblog. Finally, and very significantly, podcasts are kissing cousins to weblogs. In other words, weblogs are the home of choice to most podcasts today. While podcasts can "live" in other online places, as you'll learn in Chapter 7, "Hosting and Promoting Your Podcasts," podcasts are most often found within weblogs.

Putting It All Together

When all these elements came together, podcasting was the result. MP3 files provide a convenient way of recording audio in a compact and highly efficient format, RSS makes it easy to distribute podcasting files, and weblogging provides the tools and formats (and, not infrequently, a lot of the content).

note

Audio blogging—weblogging with audio files rather than text—has been around for quite a while longer than podcasting, but it's just about the same thing. Both audio blogs and podcasts can be about any subject in the world. In addition, both can be any length from 15 seconds to the better part of a day. A number of weblog sites let you telephone in an audio blog entry, and virtually all of them have options for you to post a link to an audio file. Third-party services, such as Audblog (short for "audio blogging") at audblog.com, provide a way to get audio to your weblog or email from phone or other sources. The things that differentiate podcasting from audio blogging are that you can subscribe to a podcast to automatically get the latest entries and you can set things up to automatically transfer the received MP3 file to an MP3 player for listening to later. In addition, you can have podcasts without a weblog (although as I mentioned many podcasts do have a related weblog), but you can't have audio blogs without a weblog. Don't worry too much about which is which, though, because the dividing line between the two is pretty thin. If you can download files and play them where and when you want, just figure it's podcasting and be happy with it.

Like weblogs, you can find podcasts on any subject you can think of, from cooking to maintaining your ham radio to the problems of being an adult child of alien abductees. I recently heard about a person who found information on how to hack the computer read-outs on his Cadillac from a podcast. It's all out there; all you need to do is look for it.

Choosing Podcast Software

There are a number of excellent programs for listening to podcasts, including Doppler Radio, jPodder, and Now Playing for Windows, and BashPodder, PoddumFeeder, and Podcast Tuner for the Mac. Chapter 8, "Podcasting Software," shows you these and a number of other programs that are available and describes their features. All these programs have something to recommend them, and you may want to try several of them out to see which you prefer. Appendix A, "Resources," also lists additional podcasting software not discussed in the chapters.

note

Programs that receive podcasts are sometimes known as "podcatching software." This definition is a bit narrow, however, because most software captures, or *aggregates*, are more than just podcast feeds, as noted earlier. Hence, the term "podcast aggregator" is a more descriptive and commonly used term.

I've chosen to focus on iPodder in this book for a number of reasons:

- **iPodder is free.** That's right, iPodder is totally free. It's cheap at twice the price. It is an open source product licensed under the GPL (GNU Public License), which means that the source code is available and the product can be freely redistributed. (You can donate to the development effort, though, and doing so is a good idea if you find you really like the product.)

- **iPodder is cross-platform.** iPodder runs on Windows, Mac, and Linux platforms. It's also available in 15 languages including the usual suspects (English, Chinese, French, German, and Italian)and others such as Hungarian, Polish, Swedish, and even Esperanto—with more coming all the time.

- **iPodder is popular.** The product has been downloaded by almost a million people so far. If you want to share your experiences with or ask questions of other iPodder users, you won't have to look far.

iPodder has a distinguished (if relatively short) history. It was originally developed by Adam Curry and Dave Winer. Adam is a former MTV VJ who coined the term "podcasting" and who is also largely responsible for the development of podcasting. Adam's podcast, "The Daily Source Code," is one of the podcasts used as a default subscription.

iPodder is an *open source* product. This means that the source code is available and that anyone can work on the software provided they follow a similar set of rules about source availability. Open source software has many advantages over proprietary software

(Microsoft Windows is one example of proprietary software). Open source products are usually free, and even the ones that cost money are invariably quite inexpensive compared to their proprietary counterparts. Open source products also don't leave you at the mercy of a software company. If the company goes out of business, the source code is still available, and you or someone else could pick it up and carry on. You can also customize open source products or build add-on products if you're so inclined because you can modify the source code. Perhaps most importantly, open source products, especially popular open source products like iPodder, are frequently more stable and bug-free because they tend to have a large following of users who like poking at the internals of the program to see if anything breaks and then coming up with a way of fixing it.

Installing iPodder

Installing iPodder is a simple process: Start by going to the iPodder web site (http://www.iPodder.sourceforge.net) and downloading the iPodder installation file for your computer. After the software is downloaded, install it on your Windows, Mac, or Linux computer per the instructions on the iPodder download page.

Learning Your Way Around

Now that you have iPodder loaded on your computer, you need to learn your way around the software. The first time you run iPodder, you see a screen like the one shown in Figure 1.1.

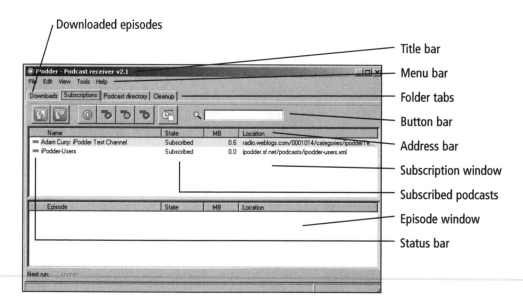

Figure 1.1 The iPodder 2.1 main screen.

note

iPodder is amazingly cool software that runs on a variety of operating systems. The screen shots in this book focus primarily on the Windows version, but there are only minor look-and-feel differences between the Windows, Mac, and Linux versions.

The iPodder screen is simple and uncluttered. Below the menu bar are four folder tabs; clicking each one of these tabs displays a particular screen:

- **Downloads.** The Downloads screen displays the various podcasts (also known as *podcast episodes*) you've downloaded.
- **Subscriptions.** The Subscriptions screen (the default) displays the podcasts to which you are currently subscribed.
- **Podcast Directory.** The Podcast Directory screen shows a list of podcast directories from which you can select podcast feeds to subscribe to.
- **Cleanup.** The Cleanup screen lets you delete downloaded podcasts that you've already listened to or otherwise don't want to save.

You'll see how to use each of these screens in Chapter 2.

Menus and Commands

iPodder has five menus: File, Edit, View, Tools, and Help, as shown in Table 1.1.

Table 1.1 Menus and Commands

Menu	Command	Description
File	Import Feeds from OPML	Imports podcast feeds from an *OPML* (Outline Processor Markup Language) file. (OPML is a convenient way of transferring information about podcast feeds; you probably won't ever need to say what OPML stands for on a test, however.)
	Export Feeds as OPML	Exports podcast feeds from iPodder to an OPML file so you can then share your preferences in podcast feeds with other iPodder users, for example.
	Preferences	Lets you set options for a wide variety of iPodder commands and operations.
	Close Window	Closes the iPodder window but leaves iPodder running in the background so you can download podcasts using the iPodder scheduler.
	Quit	Exits iPodder completely.

Menu	Command	Description
Edit	Select All	Selects all the downloads in the Download tab at once.
View	Downloads	Jumps to the Downloads tab, where you can view, listen to, and manage the downloads. (Selecting this command is the same as clicking the Downloads folder tab.)
	Subscriptions	Jumps to the Subscriptions tab, where you can view your subscriptions, check for episodes, add or remove feeds, view the properties of selected subscriptions, check selected feeds, and adjust your scheduler. (Selecting this command is the same as clicking the Subscriptions folder tab.)
	Podcast Directory	Jumps to the Podcast DIrectory tab, a preset list of podcast directories from which you can choose podcast feeds. You can also add your own podcasting sites to the list. (Selecting this command is the same as clicking the Podcast Directory folder tab.)
	Cleanup	Jumps to the Cleanup tab, where you can manage and delete downloaded podcasts. (Selecting this command is the same as clicking the Cleanup folder tab.)
Tools	Check all	Checks every subscription for new episodes.
	Catchup	Checks every subscription you have for the newest episode available, and then displays the episodes in the Subscriptions folder when you select the individual feed. (You can change your preferences to have Catchup ignore the other available episodes permanently, or for just one time only.)
	Check Selected	Checks only those subscriptions you've selected in the Subscriptions window.
	Add a Feed	Displays the Add a Feed screen to let you manually add a podcast feed. (Adding a podcast feed manually is described in Chapter 2.)
	Remove a Feed	Removes the feed(s) you've selected in the Subscriptions window, as well as any saved episodes.
	Scheduler	Displays the Scheduler screen so you can set scheduling options. (Scheduling is described in Chapter 2.)
	Select Language	Lets you choose a language other than the one you're currently using. iPodder currently supports 15 languages, with more added frequently.

(continued on next page)

Table 1.1 Menus and Commands (continued)

Menu	Command	Description
Help	Online Help	Opens your default browser to the iPodder online help page.
	FAQ	Opens your default browser to the iPodder Frequently Asked Questions page. This is a useful site for any general questions you may have concerning iPodder.
	Check for Update	Checks your version of iPodder against the latest version available on the iPodder web site. If there's a newer version available, you can then download and install it.
	Report a Problem	Opens your default browser to a bug-tracking page where you can report a problem you've encountered. You can also check the previous posts and see if anyone else has had the same problem and if there's a corresponding solution or workaround.
	Go to the Website	Opens your default browser to the iPodder home page.
	Make a Donation	Opens your default browser to a web page where you can donate anywhere from $5 to $250 to the iPodder development team. (If you find iPodder helpful, it's a good idea to do this.)
	License	Displays the iPodder software license.
	About	Displays the About iPodder screen, where you can find basic information about iPodder and development credits.

Coming Up Next...

After learning what podcasting is, the technology behind it, and how it got here, and after installing iPodder, you can see that it's pretty easy to find your way around the program. But don't confuse simplicity with a lack of power: As you'll see in the next chapter, iPodder can do everything you're likely to want in the way of downloading podcasts and subscribing to podcast feeds.

CHAPTER 2

LISTENING TO PODCASTS

Now that you have iPodder loaded on your computer, you need to learn your way around the software. This chapter shows you how to listen to your first podcast, how to add subscriptions, and how to set up iPodder options. You'll also see how to use the iPodder scheduler to download podcasts automatically.

Listening to Your First Podcast

Now that you have iPodder installed, it's time to listen to your first podcast. Start iPodder on your computer and, if it's not already displayed, click the Subscriptions tab.

The Subscriptions screen shown in Figure 2.1 contains a *Subscription window* on top, showing the podcasts, also known as *podcast feeds* to which you're currently subscribed, and an *Episode window* below, showing the downloaded podcast episodes of the selected subscription, which you can listen to.

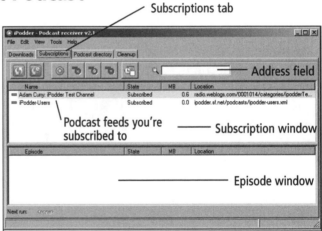

Figure 2.1 The Subscriptions screen with the default subscriptions.

As you can see in Figure 2.1, you're already subscribed to a couple of podcasts—namely *Adam Curry: iPodder Test Channel* and *iPodder-Users*. Click the first podcast entry in the Subscription window. iPodder checks the subscription to see if there are new episodes to download. If there are, iPodder downloads and displays them in the Episode window, as shown in Figure 2.2.

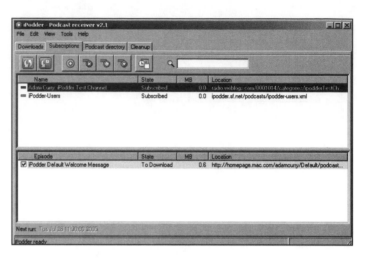

Figure 2.2 The main screen showing a new episode.

Any episodes displayed in the Episode window are checked by default, signifying that iPodder should download them. (If you have a subscription with a lot of episodes available, you can click to uncheck any episodes you do not want to download.) When you've made your selections, you can download the selected episodes in one of several ways. In this example, click the Check Selected button (🔲) or open the Tools menu and choose Check

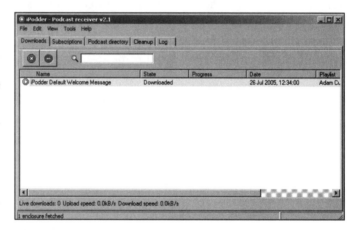

Figure 2.3 The Downloads screen showing a downloaded new episode.

Selected. iPodder displays the Downloads screen and downloads the episode, as shown in Figure 2.3.

As the iPodder is downloading, it shows you the progress of each episode being downloaded. Click on the green arrow to the left of the episode's name and *voilá!* The podcast starts playing on your computer. Congratulations—you're listening to your first podcast!

You can download episodes for each of your subscriptions individually, but this would be tedious even with only a handful of podcasts. Fortunately, you can check all of your subscriptions at once by clicking the Check for New Podcasts button (🔲). iPodder scans all the podcast feeds you're subscribed to for new episodes, downloads new episodes, and displays the downloaded information in the Downloads screen. An example of this appears in Figure 2.4.

After you've downloaded episodes, they also appear in the Episode window in the lower half of the Subscriptions screen, as shown in Figure 2.5. If you prefer, you can play downloaded episodes directly from the Subscriptions screen by clicking the episode's green arrow.

You already saw how to use Check for New Podcasts button to get all the podcasts for your subscriptions that you haven't already downloaded. If, however, you have a lot of subscriptions or, say, you were on vacation, you may find yourself drowning in episodes by the time everything's been downloaded. Clicking the Catchup button (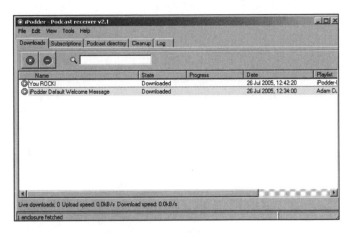) or opening the Tools menu and

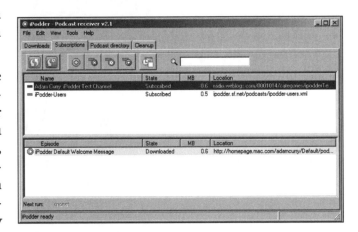

Figure 2.4 The Downloads screen showing multiple downloaded new episodes.

Figure 2.5 The Subscriptions screen showing downloaded episodes for a subscription.

choosing Catchup scans for outstanding episodes for each of your subscriptions, but skips all but the most recent. When you run Catchup, iPodder asks you if want to skip all but the top item in the podcast feed permanently or just this time. The default setting is for iPodder to skip them permanently, but you'll see how to change this option later in this chapter.

Adding a New Podcast Feed

iPodder comes with two podcast feeds already subscribed. Even as cool as it is to hear Adam Curry's welcome podcast, there are a lot more podcasts out there to listen to.

iPodder comes with a number of directories of podcast feeds already set up for you. You can start exploring some of the available podcast feeds by selecting podcasts from the directories on file, and then expand your choices to other podcasts you find yourself. (Chapter 3, "Extending Your Reach," shows you how to find new podcast feeds on the web and add them to iPodder.)

1. Click the Podcast Directory tab. The Podcast Directory screen appears, as shown in Figure 2.6.

2. The Podcast Directory screen has a selection of podcast directories from which to choose podcasts. Click the plus sign next to one of the folders. The folder opens to show several subfolders, as shown in Figure 2.7.

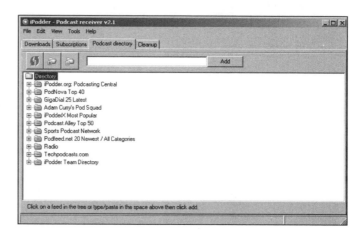

Figure 2.6 The Podcast Directory screen.

note

As the podcast directory opens, you may notice that it says "downloading" for an instant. What's happening is that iPodder is checking the directory's RSS link and updating the information that's available.

3. Each of the items with an orange bar by it is a podcast feed to which you can subscribe. Some of the categories contain subcategories as well. (There are a *lot*

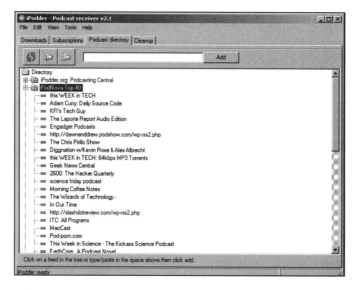

Figure 2.7 The Podcast Directory screen with a podcast directory expanded.

of podcast feeds available in the Podcast Directory screen.) Double-click the podcast feed you want to add. The Add a Feed dialog box appears (as shown in Figure 2.8).

4. Click Save to save the podcast feed and then go to the Subscriptions screen. The first time you add a podcast feed to your subscriptions, iPodder automatically scans for the available episodes and shows them in the Episode window, as shown in Figure 2.9.

5. At this point, you can download the selected podcasts by clicking the Check Selected button or by opening the Tools menu and choosing Check Selected. The episodes are downloaded and appear on the Downloads screen.

6. You can play the down-loaded podcasts by clicking the green arrow as you did before.

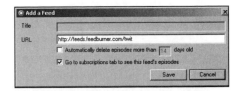

Figure 2.8 The Add a Feed dialog box.

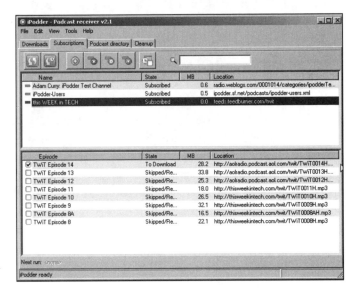

Figure 2.9 The Subscriptions screen with a new podcast.

There are hundreds of podcast feeds in the Podcast Directory screen worth exploring. In addition, Chapter 3 shows you how to find thousands of new podcast feeds on the web and add them to iPodder. There is no real limit to the number of podcast feeds you can subscribe to in iPodder, so feel free to experiment.

Tips for Playing Podcasts on Your Computer

Although you'll likely be playing podcasts on a digital music player of some kind, there's no reason you can't play them on your computer. Indeed, playing podcasts on your computer is a great way to get started listening to podcasts. You don't have to worry about downloading information to an MP3 player, and you don't have to synchronize hardware and software; it's just downloading and clicking. In fact, it's very likely you'll end up playing podcasts on your computer much of the time; after all, you're there and they're there and the Internet's there, so what the heck? Here are some tips for playing podcasts on your computer with the best results:

- Podcasts are MP3 files—really cool MP3 files, maybe, but MP3 files nevertheless—so if you're playing them on your computer, you need a good MP3 player installed. The default Windows and Mac players are acceptable but they're not dazzling. If you're using a Windows computer, try Winamp (http://www.winamp.com), MusicMatch Jukebox (http://www.musicmatchjukebox.com), or Real Player (http://www.real.com). Macintosh users should look at QuickTime (http://www.quicktime.com) or VLC Media Player (http://www.videolan.org). You can also use Apple's iTunes (www.itunes.com) on Windows and Mac computers. Linux systems can use Xaudio (http://www.xaudio.com) or Mpg123 (http://www.mpg123.de).

- Any time you're doing something on the computer other than playing a podcast, you're going to be taking the computer's attention away from the podcast you're playing. Depending on what you're doing, you may hear a brief dropout in the sound. This doesn't hurt the file you're playing, but it can be annoying if you're trying to listen to a musical podcast and you then have to start large applications or defragment a hard disk or do anything else that requires a lot of computer power that should otherwise be spent entertaining you. (That said, I listened to a lot of podcasts while I was writing this book and I can attest that word processing by itself will not affect your sound output one whit.)

- You can play podcasts with cheap generic speakers, but who'd want to? Oh, sure, the standard cheap little speakers that come with most computers will give you adequate sound, particularly if you're mostly listening to podcasts of people talking. But if you're spending a lot of time listening to podcasts on your computer, you may want to invest in a good set of computer speakers with some bass response or in a good set of headphones if you're in an office or other setting where you can't just crank up the volume. For the best sound output, you should give serious consideration to plugging your computer into your sound system as described in Chapter 4, "Getting Ready to Do It Yourself."

- The default sound card that comes with your computer is going to work fine for podcasts, even musical or symphonic podcasts. If you buy a really expensive sound card, you may notice a very slight improvement, but there's no real difference in playing podcasts on an average sound card compared to one of the very best. Invest your money in much better speakers and you'll get a far greater return on your investment.

If you don't like a podcast feed for some reason, removing it from your subscriptions is even quicker than adding it. Simply highlight the feed in the Subscriptions screen and click the Remove Feed button ( ) or open the Tools menu and choose Remove Feed. iPodder will delete the subscription for that feed, along with any downloaded podcasts.

Playing Podcasts on an MP3 Player

You've read about how podcasting is not dependent on iPods and that you can play podcasts on your computer just fine. Now you're going to see how to transfer and play podcasts on your portable MP3 player.

Actually, it's not hard at all to play podcasts on any MP3 player you like. (*MP3 player* here refers to any device (piece of hardware) that plays MP3 files: iPods, Creative Zen players, Palm Pilots, and even the Timex TMX2 MP3 wristwatch.) Most MP3 players use some kind of program that lets you download MP3 files directly into the player as well as do maintenance tasks like clearing the player's memory or hard disk. (For example, the iPod uses the free iTunes software.)

After you install the necessary software and/or drivers for your MP3 player on your computer, follow this general procedure for downloading podcasts into your player:

1. If necessary, copy the podcast MP3 files into the software. (Many programs need you to bring MP3 files in to the program's library so it knows where to find them.)
2. Connect the MP3 player to your computer. This can be through a USB port, a serial cable, or by putting the MP3 player into a cute little cradle that connects to your computer through an infrared link.
3. Download the podcast files into the MP3 player.

You now have a bunch of podcasts on your MP3 player to play whenever you like. It's not any challenge at all.

note

Some MP3 players are even easier to work with. When you connect the MP3 player to the computer, it looks like a flash memory drive. All you need to do is copy the podcast MP3 files to the MP3 player just like any other hard disk location. In other words, it's often like copying files from your computer to a jump drive, which is a very small memory device that connects to a USB port. (Jump drives have replaced floppy disks as a popular storage medium.)

Setting Options in iPodder

You can customize iPodder in a lot of ways to make the process of downloading, listening to, and managing your podcast feeds and podcasts as easy as possible. To set options in iPodder, start by selecting Preferences from the File menu. The Preferences dialog box (shown in Figure 2.10) appears with the General screen displayed by default. The General screen lets you set general options for downloading and saving podcasts:

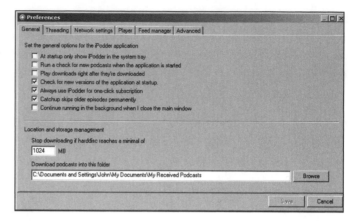

Figure 2.10 The General screen in the Preferences dialog box.

- **At startup only show iPodder in the system tray.** Check this box to open iPodder in the system tray rather than as a full application window. This is useful if you add iPodder to the startup folder so that iPodder starts automatically when the system starts, but you just want it running in the background, downloading podcasts. You can always click the icon in the system tray and open iPodder to add subscriptions or do other tasks.

- **Run a check for new podcasts when the application is started.** Check this box if you want iPodder to automatically check for new podcasts when it starts. This option works well with the preceding option by automating the download process.

- **Play downloads right after they're downloaded.** Check this box to play downloads as soon as they're downloaded. Combined with the two preceding options, you can configure iPodder to run automatically in the background, check for new podcasts, and play them as part of your morning startup routine.

- **Check for new versions of the application at startup.** By default, iPodder checks for a new version of the software whenever you start the program. Uncheck this box to prevent this. Leaving it checked is a good idea, as you never know when there's going to be an update to the software.

- **Always use iPodder for one-click subscription.** Check this box to establish iPodder as the default application for RSS files. This is useful if you have multiple applications on your system that can use RSS files and you want to make sure that iPodder is the application you use to open and process RSS files. (You probably won't want to do this unless you're an RSS whiz, so don't worry about it.)

- **Catchup skips older episodes permanently.** The Tools, Catchup command checks every subscription for the newest episode available. When this box is checked, iPodder skips the older episodes permanently. Uncheck this box to give yourself the option of skipping older episodes just that time or permanently when you use the Tools, Catchup command.

- **Continue running in the background when I close the main window.** Check this box to automatically keep iPodder running in the background when you close the main window. (This has the same effect as executing the File, Close Window command.)

- **Stop downloading if hard disc reaches a minimal of _____ MB.** Enter the amount of disk space in megabytes to reserve for podcasts. The default is 1024 megabytes, which is a *lot* of podcasts—probably several solid days of playing time! If you exceed this amount, iPodder starts deleting the oldest podcasts first to make room.

- **Download podcasts into this folder.** You can use the default setting, which downloads podcasts to the My Received Podcasts folder, or you can click Browse and select a different drive and directory.

When you're satisfied with your entries, click the Threading tab in the Preferences dialog box. The Threading screen appears, as shown in Figure 2.11.

The Threading screen displays information about how you scan for and download podcasts. You can set both the number of subscriptions to scan and the number of podcasts to download at one time. For example, with the default settings shown in Figure 2.11, if you have 15 subscriptions, iPodder scans the first four of them for new podcasts. As it finishes scanning each one, it scans another, and then another, but no more than four at one time. In the same fashion, each time iPodder finishes

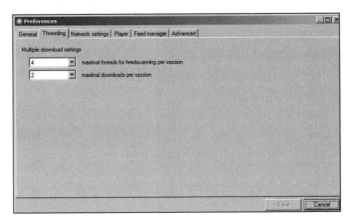

Figure 2.11 The Threading screen in the Preferences dialog box.

downloading one podcast from a list, it starts downloading another, with a maximum of two podcast downloads going at once.

The purpose behind this is to avoid overloading your Internet connection. If you have a really fast connection, like a T3 connection in an office, you may be able to raise these numbers significantly without getting in your own way when scanning and downloading. Similarly, if you're using a dial-up connection, you may want to drop these numbers somewhat.

tip

If everything looks like it's going fine, don't change these numbers. You probably need to have a lot of subscriptions or a really slow connection before this becomes an issue.

Enter information in the Threading screen as follows:

- **___ maximal threads for feedscanning per session.** Enter the maximum number of podcast feeds that iPodder can simultaneously scan at once.

- **___ maximal downloads per session.** Enter the maximum number of podcasts that iPodder can simultaneously download at once.

When you're satisfied with your entries, click the Network Settings tab. The Network Settings screen appears, as shown in Figure 2.12.

Enter information in the Network Settings screen as follows:

- **Use a proxyserver.** Check this box to use a proxy server for downloading. When you check this box, you need to enter the proxy server's address and port number in the fields.

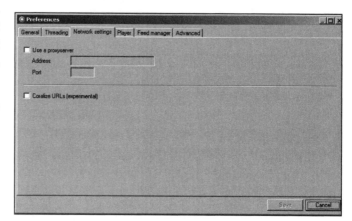

Figure 2.12 The Network Settings screen in the Preferences dialog box.

- **Coralize URLs.** Check this box to "coralize" the URL by adding .nyud.net:8090 to the end of the URL. This routes the request for the URL through the Coral network.

What's Coral?

Coral ("You make it fun; we'll make it run") is one of those really cool networking ideas that pop up regularly on the Internet. Coral is a volunteer peer-to-peer network for distributing content that lets users with low-bandwidth web sites respond to high-bandwidth requests. For example, suppose you released a video clip of Mt. St. Helens blowing up that suddenly became wildly popular because of media coverage. Normally, your web site would get clobbered by the demand, and you'd have to hock your living room furniture to pay for the bandwidth charges. Instead, Coral redirects browsers to proxy servers that will soak up the load for you so you don't have the bandwidth problem. It's all transparent to the people being rerouted, so everybody wins. It's worth trying out, but be aware that it's a volunteer network and it may not work all the time. For more information on how to use Coral, check out their web site at http://www.coralcdn.org.

When you're satisfied with your entries, click the Player tab. The Player screen appears, as shown in Figure 2.13.

Enter information in the Player screen as follows:

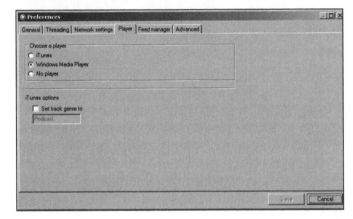

Figure 2.13 The Player screen in the Preferences dialog box.

- **Choose a player.** Select the button for the appropriate MP3 player. iPodder automatically selects iTunes or Windows Media Player depending on what's already installed on your computer. If you have another MP3 player (such as Winamp) set as the default for playing MP3s on your computer, select the No player option. When iPodder tries to play an MP3 file, it will look to the system for information on which MP3 player to use, and all will be well.

- **iTunes options.** If you use iTunes, you can check this box to set the track genre. The default track genre is Podcast, but you can enter any track genre you like.

When you're satisfied with your entries, click the Feed Manager tab. The Feed Manager screen appears, as shown in Figure 2.14.

Enter information in the Feed Manager screen as follows:

- **Synchronize my subscriptions to a remote service.** Check this box to synchronize your subscriptions using an OPML file of subscriptions that is stored at the

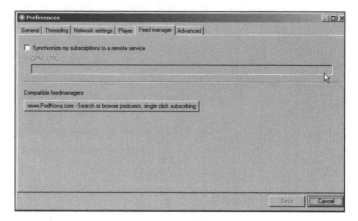

Figure 2.14 The Feed Manager screen in the Preferences dialog box.

URL you enter. You might use this if you are setting up a company podcast feed that has a basic set of company podcasts managed by one person. Everyone would use the OPML file as the source for their subscriptions. (This is covered in more detail in Chapter 3.)

- **Compatible feed managers.** PodNova (http://www.podnova.com) is one feed manager listed in iPodder. PodNova is an Internet site that provides you with a directory of podcasts that you can search using the search engine provided. You have to register to use it but the service is free.

A Word on PodNova

PodNova lets you share your list of podcasts with others quickly and easily. What's cool about PodNova is that you can set up a directory of podcast feeds on a specific topic or for a purpose like a class or group discussion and then tell people to check out that directory. People can get the podcasts from the directory of podcast feeds and listen to them.

PodNova has an advantage over iPodder in that no downloading is necessary to listen to the feed on your computer; however, because you aren't downloading the feed onto your computer, PodNova can't help you if you want to move your feeds to an MP3 player. You can use PodNova to locate podcasts, sample them, and then obtain their RSS URL if you like the feed.

When you're satisfied with your entries, click the Advanced tab. The Advanced screen is displayed, as shown in Figure 2.15.

Enter information in the Advanced screen as follows:

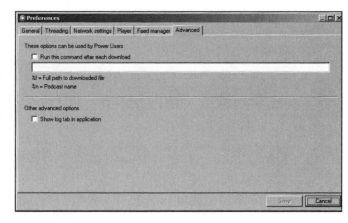

- **Run this command after each download.** Check this box to run the command you enter in the field after you download each podcast. For example, you can copy each

Figure 2.15 The Advanced screen in the Preferences dialog box.

downloaded podcast to a second location such as a network directory or you might rename them with a unique identifier to show that you were the one who downloaded them (as opposed to someone else in your office or workgroup). You could also use this option to automatically send downloaded podcasts to an MP3 player.

- **Show log tab in application.** Check this box to display an additional tab—the Log tab—on the main iPodder screen. Each time iPodder checks for or downloads a new podcast, adds a new subscription, or does almost anything else, an entry is added to the iPodder log. Figure 2.16 shows the Log screen and examples of log entries.

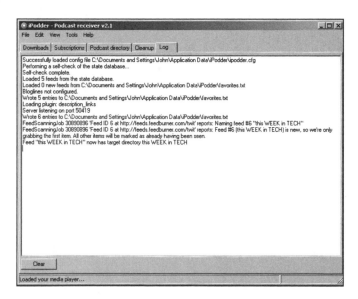

Figure 2.16 The Log screen.

More on the Log Screen

Having the Log screen displayed is mostly helpful when you're troubleshooting a connection or making sure that something downloaded correctly. For example, if you're having trouble getting new podcasts (which in this log are called *enclosures*, the technical term for RSS downloads) from a podcast feed you've subscribed to, the log may show that the URL is no longer working. You can then look for the new URL and update the podcast feed's information so it works again. You can clear the log of old information and start afresh by clicking Clear at the bottom of the Log screen. If everything's working well, however, the log will likely be just one more thing on the iPodder screen. For this reason, you may want to leave it turned off unless you actually need to check something.

When you're satisfied with your entries, click Save at the bottom of the Preferences dialog box to save your settings or click Cancel to discard them and leave things as they are. You can go back and make changes to the iPodder preferences whenever you like.

Using the Scheduler

The Scheduler is a handy feature for downloading podcasts when you're away from the computer. Not only can you start the day with a pile of freshly downloaded podcasts to go with your coffee, the scheduler is a boon to podcast aficionados who use a dial-up connection because you can download podcasts in the middle of the night when it doesn't matter if it takes 20 or 30 minutes.

To schedule iPodder to automatically download podcasts, do the following:

1. From the Tools menu, select Scheduler, or just click the Scheduler button ( ). The Scheduler dialog box appears, as shown in Figure 2.17.

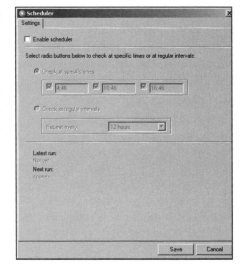

Figure 2.17 The Scheduler dialog box.

2. Enter information in the dialog box as follows:

   ■ **Enable scheduler.** Check this box to use the scheduler.

   ■ **Check at specific times.** Select this option to check for podcasts at specific times. You can enter up to three different times (in 24-hour format) in the fields below. You must check the box for each field to enter a time and, subsequently, for the scheduler to use it.

You can set up times and then only use some of them by unchecking the appropriate boxes. iPodder will remember the times you entered so you can re-enable them later.

- **Check at regular intervals.** Select this option to have iPodder check for podcasts at a regular interval. You can select a range of times from the drop-down list from every 12 hours to every 30 minutes.

3. When you're satisfied with your entries, click Save.

After you have set up the scheduler, the information for the next scheduled run time appears in the bottom of the main iPodder screen. After iPodder checks for new podcasts at the designated times or intervals, it updates the information in the lower half of the Scheduler dialog box like the example in Figure 2.18.

If you keep a fairly regular schedule, you may want to have iPodder download podcasts at specific times, like right before you leave for work and come home so you can have the most up-to-date info. On the other hand, if you are listening to podcasts at home or at your office and you just check in sporadically, you are more likely to want iPodder to download every hour or two. In either case, if you want to check for new podcasts between scheduled download times, you can always click the Check for New Podcasts button to scan for new podcasts.

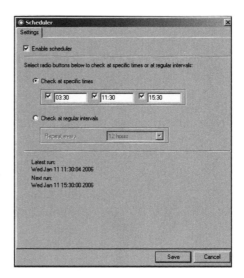

Figure 2.18 The Scheduler dialog box showing updated run information.

If you checked the Play downloads right after they're downloaded check box in the General screen of the Preferences dialog box (refer to Figure 2.10), iPodder will start playing podcasts as soon as it has downloaded them. Depending on how you've set up the scheduler, you may wake yourself from a sound sleep with the latest in BBC techie news coming from your home computer.

Coming Up Next...

This chapter has given you a wealth of information about listening to podcasts on your computer and your MP3 player, adding new podcast feeds, changing iPodder options to suit your particular needs, and using the scheduler to automate the entire process. In the next chapter you'll learn how to find more podcasts than you can imagine. You'll see how to locate just the perfect podcast for your interests using podcast web sites and many other sources.

CHAPTER 3

EXTENDING YOUR REACH

By this time, you've had a chance to explore most of iPodder's features, seen how to manage your subscriptions, and learned how to download podcasts to your MP3 player so you can listen to the latest episodes on the road. The one thing you haven't seen is how to expand your horizons by finding that perfect podcast addressed at You, the collector of stuffed pink carnival elephants or You, the left-handed banjo player. This chapter shows you how to extend your reach through podcasting web sites, podcast directories, newsgroups, and other sources.

Finding Podcasts on the Web

While the iPodder Podcast Directory screen has a lot of feeds to choose from, there are zillions of other places where you can find podcast feeds. Doing a Google search for "podcasting directories" results in a few million hits; just searching for "podcasting" results in over 10 million hits. (This is explosive growth, by the way; in Fall 2004, there were only a few thousand hits on "podcasting.") Many of the web sites you can find are general, covering a wide range of podcasting interests, but others focus on specific interests, such as techie news or sports. There's something for everybody. You should be able to find something you like on the Internet, no matter what you're interested in.

Podcast Alley (http://www.podcastalley.com) is a great place to start your search. Figure 3.1 shows the main Podcast Alley screen.

There are a number of different ways to find podcasts on Podcast Alley. Apart from the featured podcasts and the Top 10 for the month, you can pick a podcast genre (such as business, comedy, food and drink, news, music/radio, and video podcasts) from the drop-down list in the upper-left part of the screen. You can also search for a specific podcast. If you don't know where to start, click Top Podcasts. The Top Podcasts list (shown in Figure 3.2) shows the top 50 podcasts as rated by Podcast Alley visitors.

The list showing the current top 50 podcasts for all genres is the same list you see in iPodder in the Podcast Directory screen, but there are many more options available to you on the Podcast Alley web site. For example, you can search for the top 50 podcasts in a specific genre. You can also select the year and month you want to look at for previous top 50 lists and, if that's not enough, you can click a link at the bottom of each top 50 list to look at the *next* 50 entries in the list. When you see a podcast title that sounds interesting,

Figure 3.1 The Podcast Alley main screen.

Figure 3.2 The Podcast Alley Top 50 screen.

click it; you'll see a short description of the podcast and a few links, as shown in Figure 3.3.

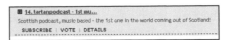

Clicking Details shows you what people have entered in the way of information about the podcast, as shown in Figure 3.4.

Figure 3.3 Selecting a podcast.

You can explore the notes about the podcast or even go to the web site (http://www.tartanpodcast.com), but the fastest way to find out if you like a podcast is to subscribe to it and see for yourself. When you click the link to subscribe, Podcast Alley (and most podcasting web sites) displays the URL link for the podcast feed. To add this podcast feed to your subscriptions in iPodder, open iPodder and go to the Podcast Directory screen. Copy and paste the RSS link into the URL field and then click Add. The Add a Feed dialog box (shown in Figure 3.5) appears with the URL.

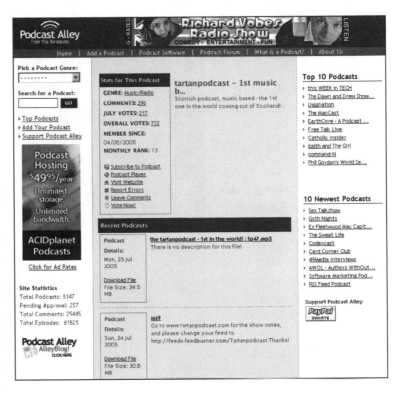

Figure 3.4 Details about a podcast.

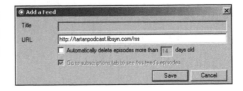

Click Save to subscribe to the podcast feed. iPodder checks the feed and provides the information about the available episodes as usual.

Figure 3.5 The Add a Feed dialog box with the new URL entered.

Manually Adding Podcast Feeds

Another good web site to look at for podcasts is Podcast Bunker (http://www.podcastbunker.com). The main page for Podcast Bunker appears in Figure 3.6.

Podcast Bunker doesn't list just *anybody's* podcast. They listen to all of them to make sure that they're actually worth hearing. They also provide a 30-second preview clip of podcasts so you can hear what they're like before going through the hassle of subscribing—a very handy feature when you have to skim a lot of podcast titles.

Figure 3.6 The Podcast Bunker main screen.

Figure 3.7 shows the preview window for *The Radio Adventures of Dr. Floyd*. While the preview clip is playing, you can read about the podcast.

Figure 3.7 Listening to a 30-second preview.

To subscribe to a podcast feed on Podcast Bunker, you click a small orange RSS *chicklet*, as shown in Figure 3.8. However, instead of seeing a neat little URL, you see something like what's shown in Figure 3.9.

Figure 3.8 Clicking a chicklet to subscribe to a podcast feed.

This is the underlying code that tells your computer how to link to the podcast and process it. It's fairly daunting stuff at first glance. Fortunately, all you need to do to set up the subscription when you see something like this is to copy the URL from your browser's address window—in this case, the URL

```
<?xml version="1.0" encoding="UTF-8" ?>
<!-- generator="iBlog 1.4.5" -->
- <rss xmlns:itunes="http://www.itunes.com/DTDs/Podcast-1.0.dtd" version="2.0">
  - <channel>
    <title>The Radio Adventures Of Dr. Floyd - www.DoctorFloyd.com</title>
    <link>http://www.DoctorFloyd.com</link>
    <description>Official Podcast Of The Radio Adventures Of Dr. Floyd. The Web's First Family Friendly
      Podcast! Updated every week! 5 Minutes Of Family Friendly Fun! Listen to ALL the episodes at
      http://www.DoctorFloyd.com!</description>
    <language>en-us</language>
    <copyright>Copyright 1999-2005 Throwing Toasters</copyright>
    <docs>http://blogs.law.harvard.edu/tech/rss</docs>
    <managingEditor>info@DoctorFLoyd.com (Doctor Floyd)</managingEditor>
    <webMaster>info@DoctorFLoyd.com</webMaster>
    <category>Family Podcast</category>
    <category>Rocky & Bullwinkle</category>
    <category>Podcast</category>
    <category domain="http://www.DoctorFloyd.com">FLOYD</category>
    - <image>
      <url>http://www.DoctorFloyd.com/images/floyd_logo.jpg</url>
      <title>The Radio Adventures Of Dr. Floyd</title>
      <link>http://www.DoctorFloyd.com</link>
      <width>130</width>
      <height>179</height>
    </image>
    <lastBuildDate>Sun, 24 Jul 2005 19:31:41 -0700</lastBuildDate>
    <pubDate>Sun, 24 Jul 2005 19:31:47 -0700</pubDate>
    <generator>iBlog 1.4.5</generator>
```

Figure 3.9 RSS link code for a podcast feed.

is http://www.doctorfloyd.com/blog/rss.xml—and add it to your subscriptions by pasting it into URL field in iPodder like you did earlier.

"Avast, Me Hearties!" Piracy and Copyright Law

There's something you should know about some of the podcasts you're likely to run into online: they may technically be illegal. That's right, if someone creates an MP3 file of a song and posts it to the Internet without the permission of the owner of the music, then that person has committed a crime—specifically, a violation of federal copyright laws and also of the No Electronic Theft, or NET, Act of 1997, which makes it a felony to create or distribute unauthorized digital music. Such felonies aren't cheap, either; even if posting the song yields no financial gain, the potential penalties are up to three years in jail and $250,000 in fines. The penalties don't end there: It is also illegal to *possess* MP3s that are in violation of the NET Act.

The Recording Industry Association of America (RIAA) has been keeping a close eye on what's being distributed online. When MP3 files were first being posted on the net, they were mostly illegal. However, in the last few years, a lot of the MP3 sites have cleaned up their acts and are only distributing authorized MP3 files.

(continued on next page)

"Avast, Me Hearties!" Piracy and Copyright Law (continued)

The issue of creating MP3 files at home and distributing them on the Internet is still under discussion. While the Supreme Court has ruled that you can record your own videos at home for purely personal use without violating the copyright laws relating to the copying of a copyrighted film, there is no clear ruling yet on whether it's legal to create MP3 files from CDs or albums that you own. The RIAA contends that it is illegal to do so—that it is a violation of the Audio Home Recording Act of 1972. They could be right.

Is this like the flap in the early 1970s over people owning cassette recorders that would let them duplicate vinyl albums and distribute cassette copies? No, not really. With your own cassette recorder, you could only make copies by recording the album onto a cassette, which would get you perhaps one cassette every 45 minutes or so. It definitely violated the copyright of the music, but the quantity was relatively small. There was some signal loss, too; a cassette tape you recorded off an album wouldn't be quite as good as a commercial copy of the album on cassette (just like a video you taped off cable wouldn't be quite as crisp as a commercial copy you rented). Moreover, the cassette would fade with time the more you played it. In contrast, you could rip the tracks from a new CD into MP3 format with little or no loss of quality, upload them to a newsgroup or web site, and have thousands of people a day downloading them. Both kinds of piracy are illegal, but the online distribution of MP3 files can do a lot more damage. And this is what's causing concern with the RIAA and regulatory agencies.

A lot of people think that, while the RIAA has the law on its side, it's not the artists who are losing money—it's the record companies, who (they point out) have an unfortunate tendency not to pay the artists, either. While it's a crime to steal, they agree, the RIAA is trying to maximize corporate profits under the banner of helping the starving artists. Moreover, they claim that the greater exposure given to artists by sharing files ("Have you heard this group? Let me send you this great track!") has actually improved the overall sales by letting more people hear artists they like. One such group, Downhill Battle (http://www.downhillbattle.org), has proposed a collective licensing agreement for downloading music that would get money to musicians and music labels according to popularity. And there are a number of web sites that offer downloads from large music catalogs for a small monthly or per-track fee, although that doesn't usually give you the right to redistribute songs yourself.

"So what *is* legal about MP3 files, then?" I hear you cry. Well, a rapidly growing number of musicians and artists are releasing authorized MP3 tracks for distribution on MP3 web sites, newsgroups, FTP sites, and on collections of MP3 files on CD. You can also record and distribute MP3 files of anything you have the rights to, such as music your band has written and recorded. (It's worth noting that making copies of CDs or vinyl that you own onto cassettes that are intended for your own personal, noncommercial use is also legal.) Creating MP3 files from your CDs and albums is still a no-no, but I doubt you'll get busted for doing either one. It's probably going to be just fine to do a weekly radio-show style podcast of bluegrass music or classical guitar, too. But you should think twice before distributing the entire soundtrack to, say, *Chicago* as a podcast for several thousand of your closest friends to download, because you may find yourself in unpleasantly hot water.

Adding Groups of Podcast Feeds

So far, you've seen how to add podcast feeds one at a time using the Podcast Directory screen or through the Add a Feed dialog box. This is effective, but it may not be as efficient as you'd like. In Chapter 1, "Getting Started with Podcasting," you were introduced to OPML (Outline Processor Markup Language) files. These are files that contain (among other things) lists of podcast feeds. You can import these into iPodder and add an entire group of podcast feeds at once.

Many podcasting web sites offer selections of podcast feeds as OPML files. Podcast Alley lets you add the top 10, the top 50, or the 100 newest podcast feeds. To do so, click the OPML icon or link and copy the URL. Then, in iPodder, open the File menu and choose Import Feeds from OPML. iPodder displays a standard File dialog box; paste the URL for the OPML file into the File name field (the file doesn't have to be on your hard disk) and click Open. iPodder grabs the OPML file off the web and starts adding the podcast feeds to your subscriptions list, after which it starts scanning for new episodes. This can take a little while, particularly if you've just added 50 new subscriptions.

You can also use this feature to share groups of your favorite podcast subscriptions with friends. Use the File, Export Feeds as OPML command to create a file. You can then email the file to someone else, who can open the file in iPodder on their end using the File, Import Feeds from OPML command. (If you got a downloaded OPML file instead of a URL from a podcast directory web site, you'd import it with this command.)

Importing and exporting podcast feeds is a great way to get a group listening to the same set of podcasts. For example, you may want to use a podcast file as background material or supplemental information for a seminar. A company that uses podcasts may want its employees to have the same basic set of podcasts on their desktops. Or you may have just discovered half a dozen of the funniest podcast feeds you've ever heard and you want to post these as a downloadable file on your blog so that everyone can have a chance to listen to them.

Every Podcast Ever Made, While They Last!

Jason Scott is a great guy who does fascinating things. He's a computer historian who undertakes really cool projects you wouldn't think possible and then he succeeds wildly. He's got a film degree and created the animation for "Conspiracy Rock," a short film that played on Comedy Central and in the 1999 Sundance film festival. He's also been involved with computers and online communications all his life. He does lots of cool things and is an interesting guy to know.

Several years ago, Jason got the idea to document the history of bulletin board services, or *BBSes* as they were known. BBSes had pretty well died out by the late '90s as the Internet took over, but for almost two decades, they were the way in which a lot of people sent and received messages, downloaded files, and got used to the idea of an interconnected network of computers and what they could do with it. Jason thought that BBSes were an important part of technology history and started filming a documentary in 2001. He figured he might need to film for year and do maybe 100 interviews. By the time he was finished, the project had taken three years and involved 200 interviews, and Jason had logged 25,000 miles of travel. The finished project is eight small documentaries in 5-1/2 hours, each of which focuses on a separate aspect of BBSes and BBSing. It's fascinating stuff and well worth buying ($50 at http://www.bbsdocumentary.com).

Jason is now involved with another fascinating project: He's downloading all the podcasts, every one of them he can find, and he's storing them. He's got over a terabyte of podcasts right now (1 terabyte = 1,000 gigabytes = maybe three years of 24x7 podcast audio). Like I said, he's a historian and he wants a record of this for the future. While you never can tell *now* what's going to be important *then*, saving all the podcasts is not a bad idea at all. Podcasts are still in their infancy, so it's kind of like taking a lot of baby pictures. You can find out more about the whole thing by going to http://www.textfiles.com and http://ascii.textfiles.com (which also has Jason's blog) and looking for links about podcasting.

Managing Your Subscriptions on the Web

All the methods you've seen in this chapter for adding more podcast feeds for your listening pleasure are pretty similar. You find a podcast feed or a group of podcast feeds and you add them to the list in your iPodder. But there's another way to handle your subscriptions: using an online feed manager.

Feed managers are similar to podcast directories. They have lots of podcasts and podcast categories to explore, there are ratings and user comments, and you can search for podcasts in several different ways. What makes feed managers different from podcast directories is that feed managers maintain your subscription list on the web site. You can then dynamically link to your subscription list using iPodder or another aggregator program and the latest episodes are always ready for you to listen to. Feed managers also offer "one-click" subscriptions. Once you've found a podcast feed you want to add to your subscriptions, you just click the subscription icon and you're subscribed. Managing your subscriptions list (deleting subscriptions, checking for episodes, and so on) is pretty easy, too.

The coolest thing about feed managers is that you can access your subscriptions from any-where with different computers and still keep up with your podcasts. Of course, that's because they are online. For example, if you listen to a variety of podcasts at home and work, you'd normally have to filter several podcasts that you had already heard at one place to get to the latest episode. However, if you have the dynamic link to your subscrip-tions list on the feed manager in both locations, the feed manager keeps track of which episodes you've downloaded and you can stay current easily. Depending on the feed man-ager, you may even be able to listen to the episodes online at the web site through your web browser—very helpful if you're on the road and are borrowing someone else's com-puter or using a business center but still want to take a few minutes to hear a couple pod-casts. As a matter of fact, you can be on the road, hear about a podcast, log in to your feed manager account, and add it to the list. When you get back to your computer, you'll have the latest episode ready and waiting.

As I mentioned in Chapter 2, "Listening to Podcasts," PodNova is one feed manager, and is directly support-ed in iPodder. But there are many oth-ers like it, which I list in Appendix A, "Resources." To try PodNova, go to the PodNova web site simply by clicking the PodNova but-ton on the Feed Manager screen of the Preferences dia-log box or by directing your web browser to http:// www.podnova.

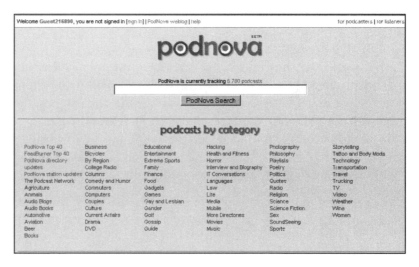

Figure 3.10 The main PodNova screen.

com. When you do, the main PodNova screen (shown in Figure 3.10) appears.

If you haven't been to the PodNova before, you are automatically given a guest ID (visible in the upper-left corner). You can explore and use PodNova as a guest, but guest accounts expire in a month, so it's a good idea to sign up for a user ID (it's free).

There are top 40 lists of podcasts on PodNova just like on many other podcast directory sites, as well as dozens of categories. Clicking any of the categories takes you to a directory of the podcast feeds such as the one shown in Figure 3.11 for the Audio Books category.

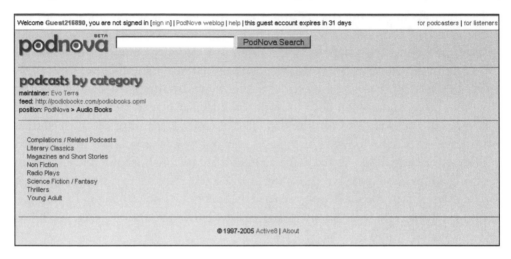

Figure 3.11 A typical podcast category screen in PodNova.

Like the category shown in Figure 3.11, most categories have subcategories. Clicking any of the subcategories takes you down a level and possibly to further subcategories. You can see how far down in the hierarchy you are by the position description near the top of the screen. Another handy feature is that each PodNova category is maintained by someone you can contact directly. Clicking on the maintainer's name brings up a web form that you can use to drop a line to the maintainer, so you can make a suggestion, register a compliment or complaint, or ask about a specific podcast.

When you get to the individual podcast feeds, they look something like the screen shown in Figure 3.12.

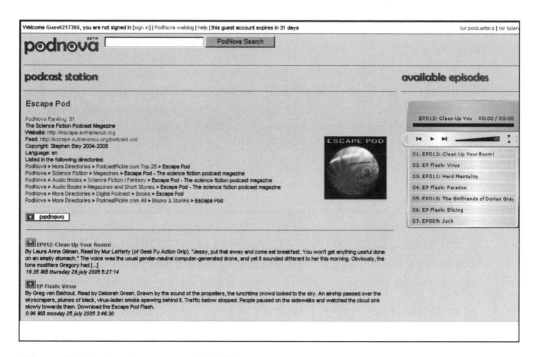

Figure 3.12 A podcast screen in PodNova.

To use PodNova's "one-click subscription" feature, just click on the PodNova chicklet. The pink plus sign changes to a blue minus sign and you're subscribed in PodNova.

There's a lot of information on this screen about the podcast feed and the individual episodes. You can go to the podcast feed's web site by clicking the web link or by clicking the icon. You can also get the URL for the podcast feed directly, see what languages the podcasts are available in, and find out about individual episodes. The chicklets to the left of each episode name let you subscribe directly to that episode (it's a one-time deal that lets you listen to that one episode). However, if you're interested in a quick test-drive of an episode or two, you can use the player in the upper right corner to listen to any of the available episodes. You can also use this to listen to episodes remotely on a computer that doesn't have iPodder or another podcatching program.

You can spend hours romping around the PodNova web site, drilling down from the main page into categories, but you might want to try a different technique. Once you've found a podcast feed that you like, try jumping to some of the other directories in which that podcast feed appears. In this example, Escape Pod was found through the Audio Books/Magazines and Short Stories path, but as you can see in Figure 3.12, the feed appears in several other category directories. If you like this one, you can click the parent category on some other path, such as Books in the More Directories/Digital

Podcast/Books path, and see what else might be in that group. You can skip from one feed to the next this way, finding new podcasts you want to listen to.

As a matter of fact, if you decide you like a whole category or subcategory, you can just subscribe to everything at once by clicking the feed link in the category screen. Copy the URL from the resulting screen full of code (like the one in Figure 3.9) and import the OPML file as was described earlier in this chapter to subscribe to everything in the category.

caution

Make sure that you know how many podcast feeds are in and below the category you're subscribing to or else you may find you've subscribed to a lot more podcasts than you intended!

As you subscribe to the various podcast feeds, PodNova keeps track of them for you. You can see what's in your account at any time by clicking your user ID (or your guest ID if you're not registered yet) and going to the member screen, as shown in Figure 3.13.

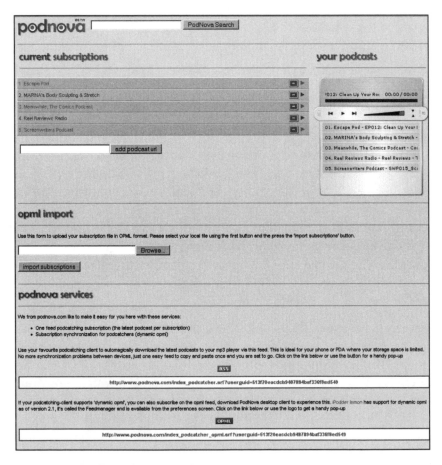

Figure 3.13 The PodNova member screen.

The list of subscriptions is easy to read. You can unsubscribe to a subscription by clicking the blue chicklet at the right side of the subscription line. You can also see the episode list by clicking the arrow for the subscription; the episodes appear in the player to the right, where you can listen to them directly. You can subscribe to individual podcast feeds by entering the URL in the field below the subscription list and clicking the button to the right of the field. You can also import a group of subscriptions from an OPML file (they're handy things, aren't they?) using the OPML Import field.

Although listening to podcasts through the web site is wonderfully convenient, it doesn't get them directly onto your computer or your MP3 player. To do that, click the OPML chicklet on the bottom half of the member screen and copy the URL that PodNova displays. (It's the same URL as the one already displayed directly below the chicklet, but it's easiest to copy it out of the little dialog box.) In iPodder, go to the Feed Manager screen in the Preferences dialog box and check the Synchronize my subscriptions to a remote service check box, and then paste the URL into the OPML URL field. (An example of this appears in Figure 3.14.)

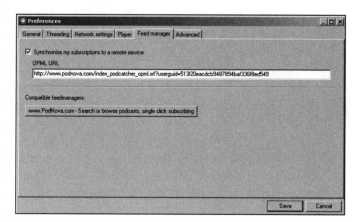

Figure 3.14 The Feed Manager screen with an OPML URL added.

When you click Save, iPodder goes to the URL and synchronizes your subscriptions with the information in the OPML file. All the subscriptions are added to your subscriptions, and the information about which episodes you've downloaded is added to the subscription information in iPodder. At this point, you can download and listen to episodes in iPodder as usual. Like most podcasting web sites, PodNova is growing rapidly. You can expect to see exciting new features and options regularly.

Finding More Podcasts on the Web

The three web sites shown in this chapter are just the beginning. There are hundreds of other web sites you can find, each of which with its own particular focus or preferences and its own look and feel. While each web site is different, the general process for finding podcast directories and podcasts on the web looks like this:

1. Search for "podcasts," "podcast directory," or "lists of podcasts" in your favorite search engine. Include additional search criteria (such as "cooking" or "cats") if you want to narrow your search. (The web sites listed on the iPodder Podcast Directory screen are great places to look for podcasts. But although you'll get a good basic selection on the Podcast Directory screen, there are thousands more podcasts and a wide variety of search options you can use directly from the web sites.)

2. When you find a podcast feed on a podcast directory or a single podcast web site, look for a URL or for a link that says "Subscribe," "RSS," "XML," "URL," "OPML," or something along those lines. The URL should look something like http://rss.rapidfeeds.com/?fid=939 or http://www.ultimathule.info/xml/Ultima_Thule_Ambient_Music_Radio.xml.

3. Copy the URL (including the http:// prefix), open iPodder, and paste the URL into the URL field on the Podcast Directory screen or directly into the Add a Feed dialog box. Save the subscription, and then download episodes as usual.

Appendix A lists several dozen of the best web sites for finding podcasts. Most of the larger web sites also have links to other web sites themselves. It's worth noting that the podcasting web sites aren't just repositories of podcast feeds. Besides podcasts, you can get all sorts of other things, including the following:

- **Software.** You can find every kind of podcasting software imaginable on web sites. Some of them have so much software that it's arranged by type and operating system.

- **Hardware.** Many podcasting sites sell iPods or other MP3 players. Some of them also sell add-on equipment such as mikes, speakers, podcasting headsets, interface cables, and other gadgets.

- **Newsletters.** There are half a dozen email newsletters about podcasts that you can sign up for through the sponsoring web site.

- **Reviews.** Many podcasting web sites have reviews of podcasts, software, and hardware.

- **FAQs and technical info.** Some podcasting sites feature a wealth of background information for all expertise levels, from the beginner to the serious audiophile.

- **Message forums.** Some of the larger web sites have bulletin boards and other message forums where you can post comments, swap opinions, and ask questions.

- **Breaking news.** There are lots of developments in podcasting technology, legislation, and policies. Many sites have some kind of daily news column; others also have regular editorials and feature articles.

tip
___

Web sites change, move, and go extinct all the time. It's a good idea to check your favorite podcasting sites regularly as well as to be on the lookout for new ones.
___

Finding Still More Podcasts

In addition to the variety of podcast directories on the web, there are many other places you can look for new podcast feeds.

Communities, Discussion Groups, and Newsgroups

First, check community web sites such as Yahoo! Groups (http://groups.yahoo.com) or MSN Groups (http://groups.msn.com) or AOL's People Connection for communities (also known as discussion groups or discussion boards) devoted to podcasts and podcasting. Communities are online forums for posting messages, asking questions, and meeting other people with similar interests. You can also download software, files, and other information from them. In the communities that focus on podcasting, you can find discussions about podcasting, podcasting techniques, and podcasting software, announcements of new podcasts, and links to podcasting web sites.

Newsgroups are another venue for sharing information and files. There are more than 30,000 newsgroups on virtually any subject you can imagine (and a lot you probably can't), with new newsgroups being created all the time. Not surprisingly, there are several newsgroups that focus on podcasting.

To explore newsgroups, you'll need a *newsreader*, a program that lets you read newsgroups and post articles to them. One of the best newsreaders out there is Free Agent from Forté (http://www.forteinc.com). In addition to being a very good program, one of Free Agent's major advantages is that it's free. (Agent, the registered version, has more features and options.) Both programs provide extensive options for sorting and filtering to keep you from being overwhelmed by useless or irrelevant information.

tip
___

If you're an AOL user, you can use the AOL newsgroup reader at Keyword: Newsgroups.
___

Podcast Sharing

Many podcasting web sites support OPML file sharing, so that you can offer some of your favorites to other people and see what other folks are listening to as well. You also should look at an amazing web site, at http://del.icio.us (pronounced "delicious," just like it reads). The del.icio.us web site lets people share their favorite web sites with everyone else.

Try searching for "podcasts" and see what comes up. If you get really interested, you can even start submitting your favorite web sites to add to the pool. Be careful, though: Looking at this web site can suck hours out of your day, even if you have a very fast Internet connection.

Coming Up Next...

You've seen in this chapter how to find podcasts on the web and add them to iPodder. You've also seen how to use the PodNova feed manager to create a web-based podcast subscription list that you can use to keep up to date no matter where you are. The next chapter shows you how to go from the role of "listener" to the role of "broadcaster" by introducing you to the basics of creating your own podcasts on your computer. The fun is only beginning!

PART TWO

CREATING PODCASTS

CHAPTER 4

GETTING READY TO DO IT YOURSELF

So far in this book, you've learned how to find podcasts and listen to them. This chapter teaches you how to go from "podcast listener" to "podcast creator." (From there, it's probably only a short step to "internationally known speaker" and then to "ruler of the world." Or not. Really, it's up to you.) You'll learn some important concepts about digital audio, how to plan your podcasts, and how to select the hardware and software you need to record and edit your podcasts.

Before You Begin

You're probably anxious to get right into podcasting, but there's actually some prep work before getting to the nitty-gritty of talking into a mic. For one thing, creating your own podcasts means you get to work with *digital audio files*: files of audio that are stored on your computer in a digital format. If you understand the basics of how digital audio works, you're going to have a much easier time understanding what you need to do and how to make your podcasts sound as good as they can. It's not difficult, but there are a few things you should know.

What Is MP3, Anyway?

MPEG (pronounced "EM-peg") is an acronym for *Moving Pictures Experts Group*. MPEG is a group of standards for compressing and storing audio and video in files. MP3 is actually short for *MPEG 1, layer 3,* the portion of the MPEG standard that specifies how audio files are stored.

What makes MP3 files special is that they give near CD-quality sound in a file that requires only about one megabyte for every minute of sound. (By comparison, the format used on CDs for recording requires about 11 megabytes for every minute.) This means that you can fit 10 to 11 hours of music (or other audio) stored in MP3 format on a single CD, compared to the 74 or 80 minutes you usually get on a CD. Furthermore, at three to five megabytes per track, MP3 files—also referred to as *tracks*—are small enough to download from web sites. This, combined with their high quality of sound reproduction, has made MP3s enormously popular for distributing and exchanging songs and music. Many search engines list *MP3* as the second-most-popular search topic.

What Are Layers, Anyway?

The MPEG standard has several layers. Each of these layers identifies the type of compression used in the files.

- Layer 1 uses frequency masking to strip sounds. For example, if a sound is "hidden" behind another louder sound, Layer 1 will remove the hidden sound, but it won't remove anything else.

- Layer 2 does everything Layer 1 does, but there's additional filtering of the sounds that come in. Layer 2 compression algorithms can "decide" what information to remove. Layer 2 is substantially more compressed than Layer 1.

- Layer 3, the layer used for MP3 files, does everything that Layer 2 does and a lot more. There's a lot of additional filtering and a built-in compression algorithm that squeezes data down even further for a very compact file.

This is probably more than you'll ever need to know about MPEG layers, but you can now dazzle your friends with your technical erudition.

How Are Sounds and Music Stored on Your Computer?

As you doubtless remember from high-school science classes, all sounds are composed of waves. Waves are *analog*: They continuously vary in strength or quantity. An analog wave looks like the one shown in Figure 4.1.

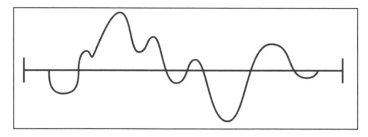

Figure 4.1 A simple analog waveform.

Information stored on computers is in a *digital* format. Digital sounds are stored as a series of bits rather than by a continuously varying signal, as shown in Figure 4.2.

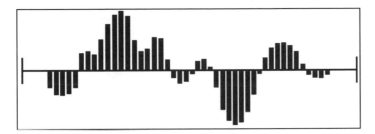

Figure 4.2 The digitized version of the analog wave in Figure 4.1.

Computers can only store sound in a digital format. That means any sound waves you store on the computer must be converted from their analog format (what you hear with your ear) to a digital format (what the computer can understand) using an *analog-to-digital converter*, which is part of your computer's sound card. During the conversion process, the sound card *samples* the sound waves at regular intervals and stores the information from the sample in a digitized file, as shown in Figure 4.3.

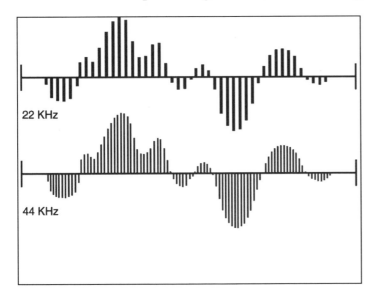

22 KHz

44 KHz

Figure 4.3 Sampling rates as applied to waveforms.

note

Whenever a signal is converted from analog to digital, digital to analog, or from one digital format to another, there will always be some loss of quality.

How accurately the conversion to digital works is determined by two factors:

- **Sampling rate.** The sampling rate is the number of times per second the sound card is sampling the sound being converted. Typical sampling rates for audio are 11 kilohertz, 22 kilohertz, and 44 kilohertz. One hertz (abbreviated Hz) is a single cycle per second, so a sampling rate of 44 kilohertz means that the computer is sampling the sound 44,000 times every second. The more often the computer samples the sound, the more of the sound the computer "hears."

- **Sampling precision.** The sampling precision (also known as the *resolution*) is how much information is stored about the sample. Typical rates are 8 bit and 16 bit. 8-bit sampling will give up to 256 different levels, while 16-bit sampling gives up to 65,536 different levels.

In general, the more frequently you sample and the greater the precision, the more closely the digital version will resemble the analog version.

What Are the Common Types of Digital Music Formats?

There are many different ways to store sound and music digitally. The most basic of these is the old familiar WAV (pronounced "wave") file. To create a WAV file, sounds are converted directly from the analog signal into digital sound and stored as the component waveforms. WAV files are *uncompressed*; that is, the computer doesn't do any additional processing to make the files more compact or to enhance the sound digitally. With WAV files, what you hear is what you get.

note

Macintosh computers don't tend to use WAV files (although they can). Instead, the standard uncompressed audio file format for Macs is *AIFF* (Audio Interchange File Format). The internal structure is somewhat different from a WAV file, but it's all about the same from the outside.

The digital audio files that appear on a CD (known as "CD-DA" files) are a different format from WAV files, but they're the same in a couple of important ways. First, they're digital. Second, they are uncompressed. And like WAV files, the sound you hear is exactly what went into them. When you play either of them, the digital information is converted to an audio signal you can hear after it goes through the speakers.

Because the data is uncompressed, WAV and CD-DA files (which are also known as "raw WAV files") have one other thing in common: They're big...really big. CDs are typically recorded at a sampling rate of 44.1 kilohertz with a bit rate of 16 bits (or 2 bytes) per sample. This means that a CD-quality digital audio file will require 88,200 bytes (a little more than 86 kilobytes) for each second of sound. Wait a minute, though; don't forget that this is only one channel. If you're recording in stereo, you'll need twice that, about 176.25 kilobytes of storage for each second of sound. A typical three-minute CD track in stereo would require slightly over 30 megabytes of storage. CDs hold approximately 650 megabytes of data, so at around 10 megabytes for each minute of sound, a standard audio CD only holds about 74 minutes. (650 megabytes technically works out to only 68 minutes, but there's a little squeezing that can be done to pack the data a little tighter and get a few more minutes of audio on a CD.) Extended play CDs (700 megabytes) can hold up to 80 minutes of audio.

How Do MP3 Files Work?

MP3 files give near CD-quality sound in a file that's only about one-eleventh the size of a WAV or CD-DA file. Where a CD-DA file requires about 10 megabytes for each minute of stereo music, MP3 files require only one megabyte. This massive reduction in file size is because, unlike CD-DA or WAV files, MP3 files do not completely reproduce all the sounds in the original recording. When you convert CD-DA or WAV files to MP3 files using an *encoder*, the encoder saves only the sounds that are important—that is, sounds that the human ear will actually hear—and throws away the rest. For example, an MP3 encoder automatically removes sounds above a predetermined threshold level (most people can't hear sounds above 16 kilohertz). The MP3 encoder also removes sounds that are masked by louder sounds at or near the same frequency. This is done through the use of a collection of principles known as *psychoacoustics* or *neuristic listening*, which are fancy names for identifying how humans hear and noting some of the things they won't miss. People hear from about 20 hertz (low) to 20 kilohertz (high), with the most sensitivity between 2 to 4 kilohertz. Voices range from 500 hertz to 2 kilohertz.

note

Because there is always some audio signal lost in the conversion, MP3 is known as a *lossy* compression method.

Here's how the MP3 encoding process works: When you're talking to someone in a quiet room, you can hear each other easily; if, however, the TV is playing or someone's vacuuming, the additional noise will mask what you can hear. Similarly, when there are loud noises happening in the sound file, quieter noises at or near the same frequency will be masked, and you won't be able to hear them. During the MP3 encoding process, weaker sounds that would be masked by louder sounds are discarded, creating a file that sounds about the same but is smaller than the original CD-DA or WAV file.

Depending on how high the compression ratio is, the encoding process removes more or less of the information. If the compression ratio is very high, you'll create very small files, but you will hear a distinct difference and reduction in quality as compared to the original CD-DA or WAV file. On the other hand, if the compression ratio is low, the resulting MP3 file may be fairly large as MP3 files go, but you won't be able to tell the difference between it and the original CD-DA or WAV file.

note

Different encoders produce different results, depending on the underlying encoding formulas they use.

Depending on what you're encoding, you may be able to get even greater compression ratios than the typical one megabyte per minute of song. For example, speech doesn't require the dynamic range of music, so it's possible for the encoder to remove a lot more information from the original file. A comedy album may require quality only as good as something you might hear on FM radio, which would compress about twice as well as CD-quality music (or about $1/2$ megabyte for each minute of sound). Even better, old 78-rpm records, speeches, newscasts, language practice tapes, and other spoken information could be compressed as much as 96 times from the original, making it possible to store up to eight minutes of information in a one-megabyte file!

Laying the Groundwork

Now that you have a better understanding of how digital audio works, including the important relationship between data compression and sound quality, you're ready to start putting your podcast together. This takes some planning, but it's time well spent. Sure, you might be able to whip out a great podcast on the fly without thinking about it—just like you "might" win the lottery. The odds of getting the podcast you want are much higher if you take a little time to perform the following steps. If you do all of these, your finished podcast is going to be a lot closer to the podcast as you originally envisioned it.

1. Identify the type of podcast you want to do.
2. Plan the show.
3. Rehearse!
4. Set up hardware and software.

You've probably had ideas for programs you'd like to do, which may be why you bought this book in the first place. Before you go out and blow a lot of hard-earned cash on recording equipment and software, however, it will pay to develop a plan.

What Kind of Podcast Do You Want to Do?

There are lots of things to consider before you get near the microphone. Are your podcasts going to follow a theme from show to show, or are they going to be one-off productions of whatever comes up? Are you doing this to have fun or is there a specific goal or purpose? How often do you intend to release podcast episodes: hourly, daily, whenever the next performance is, or when there's breaking news? Is this a one-person effort or a group project? If it is a group project, are you the person in charge?

Give some thought to the kinds of things you want to podcast. Is this podcast going to be an online diary of the day-to-day trivia in your life? Will it be a live show, with whatever happens to hit the mic, or is it going to be scripted? Do you want to have sound effects, background music, or multimedia? Will it even have talking at all? You might put together a podcast of bird calls, wind in the trees, or ocean surf. Here are some directions you might be interested in pursuing:

- **Music.** Share your favorite bluegrass tunes, piano sonatas, operatic highlights, or twelve-string runa pieces.

tip

Don't overlook potential copyright issues. Make sure that you're not trampling someone's copyright by podcasting their music before you potentially cause yourself trouble.

- **Interviews and talk shows.** You can interview celebrities, near-celebrities, or even your next-door neighbor.
- **News.** As an amateur or very small news organization, you're not likely to be sending reporters to remote locations, but you or someone you know may be in a location (such as New Orleans right after Katrina hit) that's newsworthy. You might also be working on a political candidate's campaign as she travels around the country, so podcasting news about the campaign would be a natural outgrowth.
- **Sports shows.** Not only can you podcast sports events ("Hey, the Eugene Emeralds are playing the Everett Aquasox tonight!"), but you can also do sports talk shows that let you rant about how the Seattle Mariners are once again at the bottom of their division.

- **History and documentaries.** There are lots of things that deserve documentary research, big and little. How about a podcast about little-known figures of the Civil War? Interesting landmarks as you explore family trees? Biographical portraits of early Renaissance painters?

- **Poditorials.** As talk radio has shown us, there's always room for another uninformed opinion, whether you're interested in it or not. You can join the ranks of your fellow commentators and express your views on the Way Things Are versus the Way Things Ought to Be.

- **Science and technology.** One of the first things that new Internet technology gets used for is, well, talking about Internet technology. There are already bunches of "tech talk/ask the computer pundit" podcasts available and dozens more on the way.

- **Comedy.** My preference in audio is usually comedy. Fortunately, there's some great podcast comedy to be found, ranging from a simple joke-of-the-day podcast to full-blown comedy productions vaguely reminiscent of the Firesign Theater.

- **Plays.** Got a hankering to share your dramatic productions with the world? Podcasts are a great venue for dramatic productions.

- **Children's programming.** Not only are there podcasts of people reading stories for children, but there are podcasts specifically designed for kids.

As you can see, these ideas only scratch the surface. The list of possible shows is truly endless.

When you're thinking of a theme for your podcast, think about why anyone else might want to listen to it. It's okay to have a podcast of nothing but you complaining about your job, but it needs to be interesting and potentially appealing to someone else. Scott Adams complains about work in "Dilbert," but so does the guy in the cubicle next to yours who is always grousing about how unfairly he's being treated by the boss and/or the company. One of them is probably a whole lot more entertaining than the other.

Give some thought to what your audience is going to be like. Is this a general-interest podcast, or are you focusing on a specific segment of podcast listeners? Because you're not required to have a paying audience to support you, podcasts can be created for any interest group, no matter how small. Podcasts with you wandering around your neighborhood with a voice recorder observing how things look may well not have any commercial potential, but you can probably find at least a few people who're willing to listen to you.

Something else to keep in mind: Regular broadcast radio is regulated by the FCC (or the DOC in Canada) and, as such, there are certain standards of public taste that have to be considered. In contrast, there are no limits on podcasts, which is to say that you can say anything no matter how crude or tasteless and there's nothing to prevent it. (I'm thinking of Howard Stern as I write this; I can*not* imagine why.) By the same token, there's nothing to say that you'll get someone to listen to your production. (Oh, who am I kidding? There'll be *plenty* of people willing to listen to the podcast equivalent of an uncensored *Jerry Springer* show.)

As you think about what you want your podcast to be *now*, also consider where you'd eventually like your podcast to go. Is this going to be a hobby, something you do for the fun of it, or are you looking at the possibility of developing a devoted audience and possible sponsors? (Hey, it can happen!) Also, be ready for the possibility that your podcast may catch the public's attention. You may suddenly find yourself with hundreds or even thousands of fans.

tip

Even if you have really great content, you'll get better audience response if you release episodes on a regular basis. People like to know what to expect. If you have a shiny new episode every Thursday afternoon at 4:00, your listeners are much more likely to be looking forward to it.

Your podcast may actually have no boundaries and no rules, but chances are that there's a theme or format that you're going to want to keep to. Identifying the goals and setting the boundaries for your particular podcast shapes everything else about the podcast, including the frequency of new releases, the length of the individual episodes, how episodes are distributed, and even the kinds of hardware and software you use. If you plan everything out in advance, you'll have far fewer problems making your podcasts happen.

The bottom line is that there's nothing you've ever heard on radio or on an album that you can't also do as a podcast. In the world of podcasting, you can produce virtually any kind of sound-based media.

Nothing Happens Without a Plan!

After you identify the type of podcast you want to do, it's important to develop a plan. Everything in podcasting works better with a plan. Even having a podcast of a live concert is going to require some planning. And while you may like podcasting that involves just you and the mic and whatever sound effects you can generate on the fly while you're talking, anything more complex is easier to envision if you say what's going to happen when.

Start by mapping out the podcast on paper. Think about the length and flow of the piece, whether it will be divided into segments, and whether additional segments—promo pieces, perhaps—will be spliced in. Even for a live show, a simple plan will make your life a little easier. The plan for a simple podcast reading a children's story aloud might look like what's shown in Table 4.1.

Table 4.1 Sample Program Layout for a Children's Story Episode

Start Time	End Time	Event	Description
00:00	00:30	Opening music/credits	Standard episode opening
00:31	EOS	Voice only	Read "The Emperor's New Clothes" (approximately 10 minutes)
EOS+00:01	EOS+00:25	Voice reading closing credits	Add closing background music

As Table 4.1 shows, the sample layout for a children's story show is about as simple as it gets. You have opening and closing segments enclosing an undefined time of reading a story—not much to it. There aren't a lot of production issues to worry about; in fact, if you have the episode opening and closing background music on your computer, you can do this all in a single pass by playing the segments you want at the right time and having the mic pick it up so you don't have to do any sound editing at all. Pretty nifty; you'd be ready to send this puppy out to your admiring throng immediately.

Something else you can see in Table 4.1 is that you have some times defined by when the previous segment ends. The EOS ("end of segment") note says that the segment will take however long it takes. This isn't radio, where you have to have specific time periods and break for commercials and so on; you can be a little more relaxed if you like.

For a simple show like this one, all you really need to play is theme music or some other introduction that you like playing at the start of each episode. You might also have credits or closing music. There aren't going to be sound effects or anything fancy. But suppose you're doing a podcast called "What's New in Local Bluegrass?" that features local artists playing, concert announcements, local music gossip, and maybe even an interview with the new bass player for Grotto de Blotto. You're going to need to map things out much more carefully to make sure you get all the segments in the final episode. You may also know how long your recorded segments are, which makes planning your time slots much easier. You can provide a certain amount of "fill" if you want to create a show of a specific length. A plan for this kind of show might look something like what's shown in Table 4.2.

Table 4.2 Sample Program Layout for a More Complex Show

Start Time	End Time	Event	Description
00:00	00:30	Opening music	Standard episode opening.
00:31	01:45	Voice only	Opening comments. Announce episode content, introduce live musical segment.
01:46	16:12	Live Grotto de Blotto segment	Recording of last Friday's concert.
16:13	18:00	Voice only	Wrap live segment.
18:01	25:00	Voice only	Gossip from local music scene. Be sure to announce the formation of the new summer live music venue; close by introducing new G. de B. bass player, Melvin Morsmere.
25:01	34:47	Recording of phone interview	Tape of interview with Melvin.
34:48	36:50	Voice only	Wrap up interview; announce one more song from G. de B. live show.
36:51	41:20	Voice only	Live Grotto de Blotto segment: Closing number from the G. de B. show.
41:21	43:00	Voice and music	Closing comments, thanks; fade closing music in.

The sample shown in Table 4.2 is a good deal more complex than the one in Table 4.1. It includes recorded segments from a live concert (again, don't forget your copyright permissions!), a phone interview, and canned music, all of which you know the length of already. Right away, you can see one of the advantages of using a plan like this: You can immediately hear in your mind what this kind of podcast and even this episode is going sound like. The plan also provides you with a check list for the things you have to prepare. You won't sit down to record the voice parts and realize you forgot a whole piece you wanted to do. If you want to make your podcasts a certain length, you know where to lengthen or trim segments. Keeping all of this straight without a plan would be difficult.

note

Don't worry if you're envisioning a show that's going to require you to add sound effects or music and you don't know how to edit sound files. In Chapter 5, "Configuring, Recording, and Editing Your Podcast," you're going to learn how to use a great program called Audacity to turn out professional-sounding programs quickly and easily, even if you've never done more than adjust the bass and treble on your car stereo.

Your plans can be as simple or as complex as you like, but they should support the level of complexity of your podcasts. Some podcasts are nothing more than one guy with a microphone and an opinion, but other podcasts are as complex as actual CDs, with lots of sound editing, audio effects, and very careful timing. A good rule of thumb is to make your plans as detailed as necessary and as simple as possible.

Rehearsing Is Mandatory

Lots of people think they would sound good in front of a microphone, but when they actually step up to the mic, they stiffen up and even freeze solid. Unless you're doing a completely live, on-the-fly podcast, you're going to need to a script of some kind, and you're going to need to rehearse.

The brain is an incredible piece of sound-processing equipment, but a large part of it may be occupied with what's happening on the outside at the same time it's trying to process your words in an unfamiliar situation. For this reason, creating a script is a big part of being successful; they're a boon to anyone in podcasting. This isn't stage acting (unless you're taping a podcast of a stage show, of course), so it's okay if you have words written out to refer to.

Suppose you're using the plan shown in Table 4.2. In that case, using a script or an outline would ensure that you hit all the high points of local music gossip. It sounds less professional if you're in the middle of introducing your next segment when you suddenly say "Oh, I forgot to mention, here's something else that you need to know!" Most audio professionals use scripts or outlines to keep them on track.

tip

It's a good idea to double-space and print your scripts in a large font so they're easy to read at a glance, even in a poor light.

Once you have a script, you need to rehearse, rehearse, rehearse. Rehearsing helps you make sure that things flow smoothly and sound good. You need to know where to pause for a breath, how to pace sentences, and get an idea of your timing (this is especially important if you have to match segments to times). You may even go back and modify your script to smooth out phrasing or to improve the flow by shifting the order around. Some of your rehearsal should be done in front of the mic so you get comfortable with it as part of the scenery. To summarize: If your production sounds stilted, choppy, or has a lot of pauses when you listen to it, write out what you want to say and practice saying it.

Setting Up Your Hardware and Software

You have an idea, a plan, and a script. Now you need the tools to make your podcast happen. Here's an introduction to the hardware and software you're going to need.

Hardware

You're going to need the following hardware to record your own podcasts:

- Computer
- Sound card
- Headphones and speakers
- Microphone

Computer

You don't need much computer to create your own podcasts. Although an older model might be a little slow and clunky, almost any basic computer sold in the last five years has enough oomph to do the things you need. That said, you're likely to want something that's a bit more recent so you won't have compatibility problems with the software that you're likely to use. And let's face it: Having a computer that runs quickly and has lots of disk space and a big monitor is just *fun*.

Fortunately, basic computer equipment is absurdly inexpensive these days. Excellent basic computers can be had for as little as a couple hundred dollars from online dealers such as Fry's (http://www.outpost.com) and PC Connection (http://www.pcconnection.com) or Mac Connection (http://www.macconnection.com). Every new computer is going to have a network card, a fair amount of disk space (400-gigabyte drives are available for as little as $120 at the time of this writing), and lots of RAM.

note

> As a general rule, if you can connect to the Internet at an adequate speed, download podcasts or music files, and play them without problems, your computer should work just fine.

Sound Card

The quality of the sound you get out of your computer is largely a function of how good your sound card is. Every computer sold today has some kind of sound card—frequently, the card is built right into the computer's motherboard—but you may want to get a better sound card to improve the sound of the podcasts and MP3 files you're playing.

If your computer is more than a few years old, make sure that your sound card is capable of 16-bit audio at the very least; 24-bit or 32-bit audio is even better. Also check for Dolby Digital 5.1 Surround Sound. You can look all this up in the card's product documentation. (If you don't have the documentation, get the make and model of the card from your computer's system information features and look the card up online.) If your card isn't up to par or you'd like to get something a little snappier than what's there already, there are hundreds of relatively inexpensive options for add-on sound cards.

Headphones and Speakers

Any time you're using a microphone to record anything, you really need headphones to hear what's going into the mic. Speakers alone won't do it. Headphones eliminate outside noise as well as playing back the sound you're recording, so you're not thrown off by anything except the sound actually being recorded.

tip

You can get headsets that plug into your computer's USB port, which may be more convenient than rooting around in the back of the computer to find the headphone jack. In addition, where you've only got one headphone jack on your sound card, it's not uncommon for a computer to have four or more USB ports, so you can plug in multiple sets of headphones.

In addition to headphones, a good set of speakers is desirable for playing back what you've just recorded so everyone in the room can listen and nod approvingly. Most of the speakers that come with home PC units are fairly low quality unless you spring for a configuration that adds a little quality to your sound experience. Fortunately, a few extra dollars can buy a measure of happiness. You can get a decent set of stereo computer speakers that has a subwoofer for as little as $40. For a little more money, you can get a set of speakers for Dolby Digital 4.1 or 5.1. The 4.1 speakers have a subwoofer and four small speakers—two in the front and two in the rear; 5.1 speakers have all of this and a front center-channel speaker. (To get the full effect, your sound card must support Dolby 4.1 or 5.1.) You can deck yourself out with a full set of 5.1 speakers for well under $100. For headphones and speakers, check out Sennheiser, Koss, and Logitech. I've always been partial to Altec equipment, but Creative Labs also has a great line of moderately priced gear.

Microphone

The difference a good mic can make to your podcasts is amazing. As you listen to podcasts, you'll soon discover you can identify who's using a cheap microphone versus those who've gone for something a little more upscale. The quality of the podcasts done with cheap mics is pretty grainy. If you're going to take all the time to plan and record a podcast, you ought to make sure that the quality isn't being undercut by a lousy mic.

A lot of computers come with a generic "stick" microphone, which is designed to attach to your monitor and lean down in front of your face. These are okay, but they're nothing to podcast home about. They're perfectly adequate when you need mic'ing for a web chat session with a friend, but they're fairly shabby for anything else. The biggest problem with the cheap, generic mics is that they're, uh, cheap. They don't have a great dynamic range, they're not very responsive, and they have no filtering capabilities of any kind. They're designed to pick up whatever noise they hear, and they do, including phones ringing in the other room, cars driving by, and even the hum from the fans on your computer and monitor. The shortcomings of cheap mics become even more apparent if you're playing music or singing. Most of the subtlety and color will be lost—sort of like playing something through a telephone.

There are microphones of all shapes and sizes for every conceivable sound-recording application:

- **Cardioid mics.** These are what most people think of when they think of microphones. They tend to be shaped like a... well, like a microphone. Cardioid mics are directional: They don't hear sounds to the sides, but they hear very well straight in front of the business end. Musicians on stage are singing into cardioid mics of some kind or another. You need to point the mic directly at the source of the sound, which is why you have to adjust the mic to be pointed directly at the musician's lips or guitar.

note

One type of cardioid mic that is very directional is known as a *shotgun* mic. Shotgun mics are used in situations where you need to hear only one thing and exclude anything else. Whenever you see a mobile news team holding a big stick-shaped microphone, it's a shotgun mic.

- **Lavaliere mics.** These are small mics that clip on to your clothing or are worn on a small chain around the neck. They're good for picking up voice and have the advantage of having a small pickup range, so they're less likely to hear extraneous sounds from other rooms. They're also inexpensive enough that you can afford several of them if you want multiple people to be able to talk at the same time.
- **Headset mics.** For hands-free operation or the advantage of a mic that can follow you around, you might want to consider getting a headset with both a mic and headphones. The headset keeps your hands free and the microphones are designed to limit background noise. The Shure 512 is an excellent choice for a talk-show or sports-style headset, although it costs a bit more money than you might want to spend at first.

It's important to remember that there is no "best" microphone. A mic that's good at recording your voice is not going to have the same characteristics as a mic designed to be used for recording a football game, and both will be different from the mic you'd use to record a symphony. The location's acoustics make a difference in the requirements, too. For example, sound studios are designed to insulate any outside noise as well as damp echoes from within the room itself, while a home office will have substantially different sound characteristics.

There are hundreds of inexpensive microphones that can work for creating podcasts. For openers, it's probably best to stick with an inexpensive, general-purpose microphone and then get something fancier if you need it. (It's also not a bad idea to avoid investing a bunch of money in equipment until you've been podcasting for a little while.) Shure, Sony, and Electro-Voice all offer an extensive line of mics, but even Radio Shack has some good, inexpensive options you may want to consider.

Accessories

In addition to the basics, there are lots of other pieces of audio hardware you can buy, including the following:

- **An audio compressor.** You connect your microphone to an audio compressor and then connect the compressor to your computer. The compressor buffers the audio input between very loud and very quiet sounds so that the changes aren't as dramatic. It also prevents the sound levels from being distorted if they're too loud.

- **A mixer.** Mixers let you use and balance input from more than one mic or audio input simultaneously.

- **A pre-amp.** A pre-amp amplifies a weak signal from the microphone or other audio input so that it can be fed into another device. The best way to think of pre-amps is that they give the input from the microphone a boost so it's easier to work with.

- **Shielded, low-loss microphone cables.** Microphone cables can sometimes allow hum or noise to creep into the audio input and/or can lose some of the signal from the mic. You can buy better cables that have extra shielding and that are designed to lose a minimal amount of the audio input.

- **Mic stands.** You can buy floor and desk stands of all kinds.

The list doesn't stop there, but it's a good idea if you do—at least for now. Don't rush out to buy all the gadgets you can. Work with the basic equipment in the list for a while and see what you may need to add to your collection.

Connecting Your Computer to Your Audio System

One of the biggest complaints about playing podcasts and other MP3 files on the computer is that most generic computer speakers suck. (That's a technical term for speaker quality.) However, instead of spending a lot of money on a great set of computer speakers, you may want to take advantage of good speakers you already own: the ones you're using in your audio system.

Sure, there are some really good options for computer speakers that won't cost you a fortune and give you pretty good sound, but for the best audio, you'll probably want to feed the audio from the computer into your stereo amplifier (that's what it's there for) and play the sound through the good speakers that you have on your stereo. Not only can you save the cost of a set of speakers for your computer, you'll also have the full range of bass, treble, and filtering options your stereo has to enhance the sound of the tracks.

To do this, you'll need a set of stereo cables with a pair of RCA plugs to plug into the line-in jacks of the stereo amplifier and a 1/8-inch 3-conductor (stereo) mini-plug to plug into the line-out or speaker-out jack of your computer's sound card. (This is the same plug that your computer speakers use.) Most electronics stores will have cables like this as a stock item, although you may need to look around for cables long enough to reach from your stereo to your computer.

tip

It's a very good idea to have a small flashlight on hand so you can read the labels on the sound-card jacks and on the back of the amplifier. A small mirror, such as a dentist's mirror, is also handy if you're working in a really tight location. Also, if you think you'll want to record from your audio system as well, buy two sets of cables. Chapter 5 describes the software that lets you connect your audio system to your computer so you can pull tracks off of cassette tapes, records, and even the radio. Chapter 9, "Working with MP3 Players and Peripherals," describes connection hardware that lets you do the same type of thing.

The type of inputs you have on your stereo will vary considerably depending on the make and model, whether you're using individual components or a modular setup, and how many gadgets you have hooked together. In general, though, you'll need to have line inputs free for your cassette deck, your stereo's CD player, and the sound card. If you have only one pair of auxiliary input jacks on your amplifier, or your amplifier's input jacks are all in use, you'll need to get a couple of Y connectors to split the line so you can have input from the sound card and the amplifier's auxiliary input jacks. However, you should *never* send input from the sound card to the amplifier's phono input jacks, as these are enormously more sensitive than the standard line-in jacks. Normal sound-card output can **permanently damage** the phono inputs!

Once the cables are connected, you need to check your volumes and settings on the sound card. Many sound cards have some kind of amplifier built in to drive speakers that has a small physical volume control sticking out near the jacks; others have a soft control that is handled by the sound card's software or by the Windows Volume Control (or the comparable control on a Mac or Linux computer). If you have the sound card send too much signal to the amplifier, it can damage the amp, and the track will certainly sound distorted and fuzzy. Reduce the volume all the way on the operating system's volume control. If your sound card has a volume control knob on the card itself, also turn it down all the way to start with.

Now try a test to set the output levels and to see what it all sounds like:

1. Turn on the stereo and set your amplifier's volume control down almost all the way. (If your initial settings are going to blast the amplifier, it's a good idea not to have the volume turned way up on the amp when you find out!)

2. Open iPodder or an MP3 player and start a few podcasts or MP3 files playing. Playing a music file is better than playing a file of spoken words, because you'll hear any distortion more easily.

3. If you don't hear anything coming through the stereo, turn up the volume a little using both the sound card's volume control and the operating system's volume control. (If you have it running at full blast but the operating system has the sound card output muted, no signal will go out to the audio system. It's a lot like juggling the volume settings on your cable box and the TV; both of them have to be giving you some signal for any sound to come out.)

4. If you don't hear anything coming through the stereo, turn the stereo's volume up slightly.

5. Repeat steps 3 and 4 as necessary. If everything is connected properly, you shouldn't have to do this more than once or twice to hear the music through the stereo. Make sure that the volume on the sound card is set so that the sound coming through the stereo is clear but not distorted. On the other hand, the sound should be loud enough so that you can set the volume about the same as you would for other devices on the stereo, like your cassette deck and CD player.

If you're not hearing anything yet, don't crank the levels too high on the sound card or the amplifier. Turn the volume controls down on the sound card and on the amplifier, then check each of the following items and try running through the steps again. (Be sure that you've turned the various volume controls back down before trying each of these.)

- The 1/8-inch mini-plug is plugged into the wrong hole on the sound card. Make sure that the mini-plug is plugged into the line-out or speaker jack on the sound card, as appropriate.

- The cable isn't plugged into the right input jacks on the amplifier (or might even be plugged into the output jacks).

- The cable is plugged into the right input jacks on the amplifier, but the amplifier is set to the wrong auxiliary channel. (For example, you have an auxiliary switch on the input selector controls, or you have a "source/tape" switch that's set to the wrong setting.)

When you think everything is set up and adjusted correctly, queue up a playlist with a selection of different styles of podcasts and MP3 files and see how they sound. You might want to make a few last adjustments to the volume control. Also experiment with the bass, treble, and filtering options on your amplifier to see what works best.

One final comment on the process of getting hooked up: you'll probably need to do a little tinkering with the cables and the volume controls before you get everything set up and working smoothly. Everybody does. Be careful with your volume levels and you won't damage the amplifier or scare yourself to death while you're doing so.

Software

You don't need a lot of software to create your own podcasts. The hardware may take you a little while to round up, but getting the software is probably just a matter of spending an evening downloading programs from the Internet. Here's what you'll need:

- An MP3 player
- Recording and editing software
- An MP3 encoder

MP3 Player

If you've gotten this far, you've probably already got an MP3 player on your computer. But there's no reason that you can't have several. I have iTunes, Windows Media Player, and Winamp on my desktop computer, although I use iTunes the most. Chapter 6, "Adding Music, Video, and Other Multimedia," describes some of these and other MP3 players in greater detail, and discusses their compatibility with Windows, Mac, and Linux computers. It also describes how most play more than just MP3s.

Recording and Editing Software

You need software that lets you plug your microphone into your computer and record your golden voice, and then edit the results. Your operating system probably comes with something basic along these lines. It's also likely that some audio-editing software came bundled with your computer or your sound card. There are wide variations in the quality and usability of bundled software, but you can be reasonably sure that it works with whatever your sound card is.

One of the best programs for recording and editing audio is Audacity, a free, cross-platform audio editor written by Dominic Mazzoni, Joshua Haberman, Matt Brubeck, and a host of other great people. Like iPodder, Audacity is an open source program that's licensed under the GNU General Public License.

The upcoming chapter on recording and editing podcasts uses Audacity for the examples. It's great software and it's available for Windows, Mac, and Linux computers. That said, there are a lot of other recording and editing programs you can use, such as WavePad, Wave Creator, and Fleximusic for Windows; Amadeus II, Sound Studio, and DSP-Quattro for Macs; and Broadcast 2.1, ardour, and mhWaveEdit for Linux computers. Other recording and editing programs are listed in Appendix A, "Resources."

MP3 Encoder

As you saw earlier in this chapter, MP3 encoders convert digitally recorded information into MP3 files. Some editing programs come with a built-in MP3 encoder, but others don't. Audacity, being a free program, is not allowed to distribute an MP3 encoder with the software because MP3 encoders are licensed technology. However, you can download a copy of the LAME MP3 encoder from http://www.lame.sourceforge.net, and there are other MP3 encoding programs available on the Internet. I cover this process in detail in Chapter 5.

Coming Up Next...

This chapter has covered a lot of ground. It set the stage for you to create your own podcasts. You've learned how analog and digital audio work. You also saw how to identify what kind of podcast you want to do, how to plan your podcasts, and got some tips on rehearsing. The chapter concluded with information about the basic hardware and software necessary to create your podcast. The next chapter shows you how to actually go about the business of recording your show and how to edit the resulting files to produce the best-sounding results.

CHAPTER 5

Configuring, Recording, and Editing Your Podcast

In the last chapter, I showed you how to prepare to create your first podcast. You learned a bit about the theory and concepts behind MP3 digital sound recordings. You also likely noticed that a lot of the hardware and software you would need to create a podcast is already sitting in front of you, and that any needed upgrades won't break the bank. In this chapter, I walk you through the core podcast production process. The main elements of this process are configuring recording software, actually recording a piece, editing what you've captured, and converting it to MP3 or another format. I close by showing you how to tag the podcast with useful information for others to read. Let's start recording!

Configuring Software

In this section, I show you how to configure your recording software, computer settings, and equipment. This is the first stage of the podcast production process.

Configuring Audacity

Because Audacity supports Windows, Mac, and Linux platforms, I'll use it for walk-through purposes. Audacity is very good at doing one of the things it's designed to do: produce podcasts. For your walkthrough, I also use Windows, so the screenshots you see in this chapter will reflect that. If you are a Mac user, don't worry. The setup process is virtually identical and involves the same fundamental recording steps—launching, recording, and basic editing. In this chapter, I go through each of those steps in turn.

GarageBand

Mac users will probably have GarageBand, a great digital recording software package designed only for Macs. It comes pre-loaded on several Macs. GarageBand generally has a few more bells and whistles than its competitors. In addition to podcasts, it handles wild stuff like Apple Loops, creating and editing MIDI tracks for your electric piano, and recording real instruments. If you prefer to use GarageBand (perhaps because you heard rave reviews about it) but have never used it before, by all means use it! You'll find plenty of books about it. Nevertheless, I recommend that you still read this chapter to learn about the general principles of recording audio. Again, the process is the same for Audacity, GarageBand, and similar software: configure, record, edit, and voilá! Only the buttons to be clicked differ. Once recorded, everything created in GarageBand (and most of its competitors) can be put together and exported to iTunes and the web to share with the rest of the planet.

For Windows users, a close competitor to GarageBand is Band-in-a-Box Pro. Other podcast and audio recording software, from the fantastically sophisticated to the really basic, is presented in Appendix A, "Resources."

Okay. Let's start. Power up Audacity to get the screen shown in Figure 5.1.

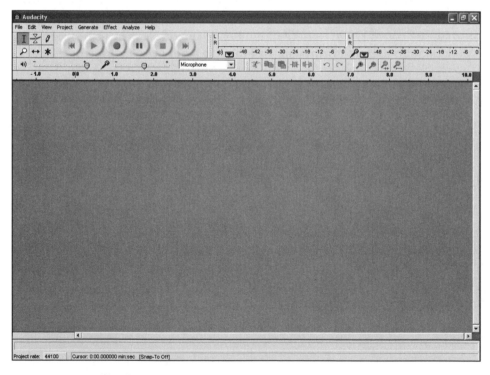

Figure 5.1 Audacity's main operating screen shows many features.

Next, set your preferences. This step is the essence of configuration, in which you define how you like your podcast to sound and what things you want to do with it. The configuration process ensures that audio quality is good, and that everything will work well when you click the Record button! To set your preferences, open the File menu and select—you guessed it—Preferences. This opens the Audacity Preferences window, which features an array of tabs. I clicked the Directories tab, shown in Figure 5.2, to locate the settings that enable me to tell Audacity where on my computer I want to store my podcasts. You can even store podcasts on an external drive to save on storage space.

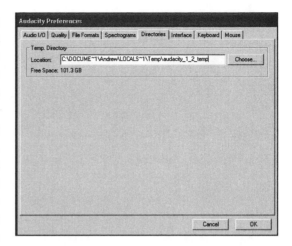

Figure 5.2 Audacity's Directories screen is one of several available preferences.

Take some time to browse through all of Audacity's main tabs to get a feel for some of the settings. I'll revisit some of these tabs shortly.

note

If you're a Mac user running Audacity, you'll notice very little difference between the screens you see in Figures 5.1 and 5.2 and the ones displayed on your monitor. In fact, even GarageBand's interface is a kissing cousin to Audacity's. Linux users, rejoice. You are not alone. The recording software you choose will invariably sport a preference option. If not, download another piece of software that does!

Moving forward, you want to make sure that playback will work. Imagine if you recorded a podcast but couldn't hear it because you forgot about a simple but critical setting! One of those key settings is Windows Volume Control. Yup, it's all about the volume. To adjust this setting, click the Windows Start button and select Control Panel from the menu that appears. In the Control Panel, shown in Figure 5.3, double-click the Sounds and Audio Devices button (the one that looks like a speaker cone). The Sounds and Audio Devices Properties dialog box opens; click the Audio tab, and then click the Volume button in the Audio screen's Sound playback section. The Volume Control screen opens, as shown in Figure 5.4. The key here is to make sure that playback settings are not muted. If anything, err on the side of having volumes a bit higher than needed. You can always reduce volume at the back end of the recording process. Low volumes at the front end, however, are more difficult to edit and correct.

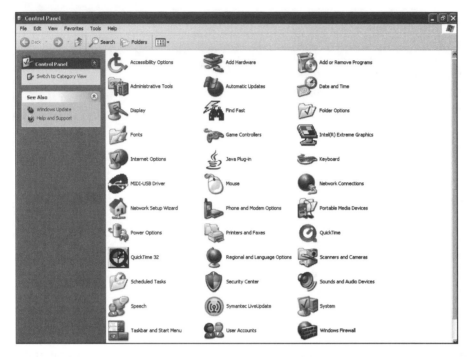

Figure 5.3 The Windows Control Panel.

Figure 5.4 Make sure that audio playback will sound good.

What about the other recording settings? For example, your mic needs to know how much volume to capture, and how the sounds coming into it ought to get processed. To establish this, again open the Sounds and Audio Devices Properties dialog box and click the Audio tab. Then, click the Volume button—but this time in the Audio screen's Sound *recording* section. This launches the Windows Recording Control utility, shown in Figure 5.5. If you set—or find that the preset—recording levels are too high on any of the three sources you selected as an input (for example, a CD player, microphone, or Line In jack), a few things may happen. For one, Windows may pick up the sound of the fly on the wall, the toilet flushing, or your stomach gurgling if you haven't eaten yet. The trick here is balance—not too high and not too low—or worse, muted.

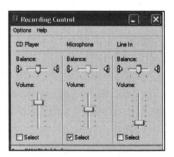

Figure 5.5 Ensure that recording settings are sound.

You're almost ready to record! Before you do, though, you must tell Audacity about your quality-of-sound expectations. To do so, return to the Audacity Preferences window (open the File menu and choose Preferences) and click the Quality tab (see Figure 5.6). Here you can play around with sound quality. Until now, the default settings were probably okay. But for better sound (at the expense of file size and broadband use), I recommend that

you opt for a default sample rate of 64,000 Hz, per the discussion on compression, file size, and sampling rates in Chapter 4, "Getting Ready to Do It Yourself." Go for the gusto if you podcast isn't too long, if your computer is powerful, and if you have a high-speed Internet connection (for uploading your podcasts). Always aim first to maximize quality of sound. On the other hand, if your listeners will get annoyed at a large file size, you'll lose them! Again, as mentioned in Chapter 4, 44,000 hertz and even 22,000 hertz is acceptable. It's all about preference and capacity. Oh, and the Default Sample Format setting, 32-bit float, is more than adequate.

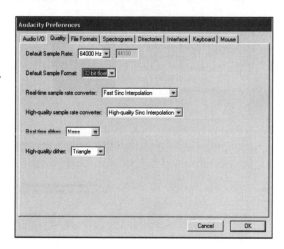

Figure 5.6 Tell Audacity you want high sound quality.

In the Audacity Preferences window's File Formats screen, you'll notice that you can choose to make a copy of your podcast file before editing (see Figure 5.7). Do us all a favor and select that option. After you get the hang of recording, you can revert to the default (and faster) Read directly from the original file setting.

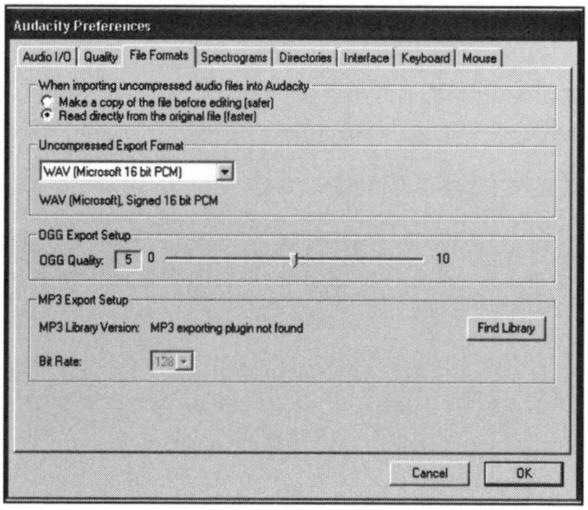

Figure 5.7 To play it safe, tell Audacity you want to work from a copy of your recording.

Giving Your Mix an Extra Stir

The Windows recording volume settings, like those you saw earlier in this chapter, essentially mix your recording. This mix is done at a basic level. If you have a special sound card (like Sound Blaster) to boost your computer's audio performance, great. You can mix sound with even more audio effect settings. At the highest peak of the recording mountain, however, you can buy a dedicated mixer. This is one you can not only see, but also touch and feel. It's not just software, like Windows settings or an Audacity special effect. It's the hardware used in-studio by Creed, Gwen Stephani, and the late Glenn Gould. Okay, I exaggerate. But it's the good stuff!

So what exactly does a mixer do? A mixer powers your mic. It adjusts sound levels, manipulates equalization, creates additional effects, and more. Scores of mixing options exist. Buying a decent mixer won't break the bank, but you want to think twice about how much you really need one. A good mixer will handle multiple sound sources and can easily scale to accept add-ons like musical instruments. Is that what you really need?

A few key factors drive the cost of a mixer: the number of channels, digital functionality, and the quality of the mixer itself. Look for more than 12 channels to allow for future growth at little extra cost. Digital effects such as echoing and fading are entertaining. Look for a selection of functions here, although remember that Audacity has great mixing functionality too. FireWire output (a super-fast connection between your computer and other devices) enhances the quality and efficiency of the mixer because it sends sound from the mixer to your PC or Mac at lightning speed—meaning no hiccups in sound. Quality mixers have less noise and a proven track record. I don't use one myself, but many people I know who are involved in the music world recommend Mackie or Alesis mixers.

Getting Connected

This is the easy—but often overlooked—part of configuration. Sometimes, it's hard to see in back of the computer, and jacks are inserted in the wrong place. The connections you need to worry about are few—the mic, the physical mixer (if you have one), and headphones (when you are ready to record). Ensure that your mic is plugged into the mic input slot at the front, back, or side of your computer or laptop or into the sound card Line-In jack at the back of the computer.

Testing the Mic

Test your mic. This will ease your concerns about whether you are set up properly, and will help you determine whether you are poised to begin recording. To do so, again open the Windows Control Panel and double-click the Sounds and Audio Devices button to launch the Sounds and Audio Devices Properties dialog box. Then click the Voice tab to see the screen shown in Figure 5.8. Click Test Hardware, and you'll see a wizard welcome screen (see Figure 5.9). Follow the wizard's instructions and speak into your mic to test it (see

Figure 5.10). Voilá, success!

Truth be told, it's unlikely that you'll get the sound just right on the first shot. You'll probably have to fiddle around with the settings. But the test wizard is invaluable for

Figure 5.8 Get ready to configure and test the mic.

giving you some assurance that you are really on the right track.

Figure 5.9 The Sound Hardware Test wizard will guide you through the test.

Checking Audacity's Settings

Up to this point, I asked you to check certain settings within your computer, like those that pertained to Windows audio functions. I also showed you how to test your mic to make sure it was capturing the right level of sound. In this section, I'm going to ask you to check

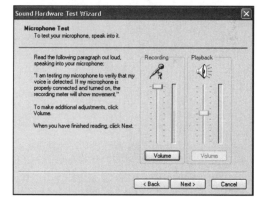

Figure 5.10 Testing, testing.

your recording software—in this case, Audacity. Audacity needs to be able to talk to your computer in a way your computer will understand and accept. The steps I outline here ensure that this will happen. Once your computer, mic, and Audacity software settings are in sync, your podcast can be successfully created and saved on your computer's hard drive, poised for posting on the Internet.

note

Audacity project files (*.aup) cannot be directly opened by other programs. Later, I'll show you how to get around this by using Audacity's Export function in the File menu, which you can use to convert Audacity's AUP files into MP3 files.

As shown in Figure 5.11, I ran a quick sound check to ensure that my microphone was read and recognized by Audacity. To do so, I recorded three tracks. In the first track, I confirmed that my mic was effectively plugged into the mic jack of my computer's sound card. When I tested this in track one, it worked as expected. Then, to show you what happens if you don't pay attention to the drop-down list in the top-middle area of the Audacity interface that shows mic and other input options, I selected Line In there. As a result, when I recorded track two, it did not record my voice even though I was speaking into the mic. The Line In works, but only if that's exactly where your mic is hooked up—the Line In jack. I reset my mic to Microphone in the same drop-down menu, and recorded a third and final track.

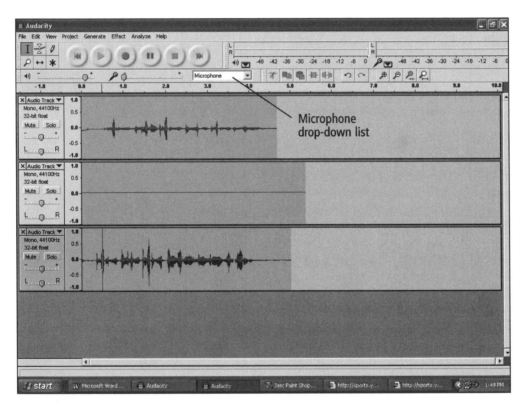

Figure 5.11 Testing the ever-important mic setting in Audacity.

The steps outlined here were overkill; they were merely intended to show you what may go wrong if Audacity does not recognize your mic. To do a sound check of your own, you only have to test one track. Here's how:

1. In Audacity's main window, open the Project menu and choose New Audio Track.

2. Click the red Record button at the top of Audacity's main window.

3. Speaking into the mic, say or sing anything you like.

4. Click the yellow Stop button to stop recording.

5. To see how you sound, click the green Play button and listen to the results.

6. If it worked, pat yourself on the back. That was your first recording!

Exit the sound check without saving any of the test tracks you created. (I show you how to save audio tracks later in this chapter.) To begin recording your podcast in earnest, open the Project menu and select New Audio Track. The result is shown in Figure 5.12. This is the actual track that will contain the beginning of your podcast.

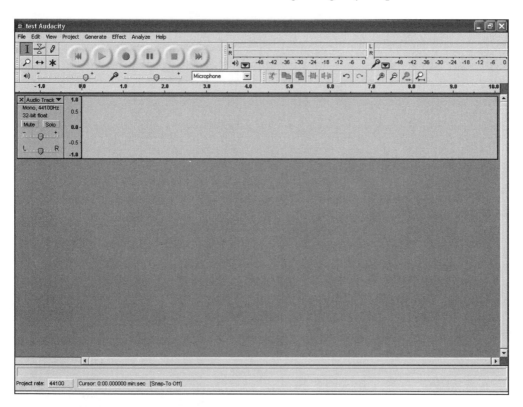

Figure 5.12 Your track is loaded and ready to go.

All you need is one track to record an entire podcast. In practice, however, it's better to have several tracks. You can have one track for your intro segment, another for your main message, and yet another for an interview with someone else, and so on. It is easier to manage multiple tracks when recording as well as editing. It's like Lego pieces—the more blocks you have, the more creative you can be. To create more tracks, again open the Project menu and select New Audio Track. A second track appears. Rinse and repeat until you have all the tracks you need. If you discover you've created more tracks than you needed, you can undo the creation of the most recent track by opening the Edit menu and selecting Undo New Track. Alternatively, you can click the little × at the top-left corner of a track to close it.

tip

If you're not sure how many tracks you'll need, don't worry about creating them up front. If you click Record, and then Stop, and then Record again, a new track will automatically appear.

Just before you actually start recording the first track, open the Audio Track menu, found in the upper-left corner of the new audio track. Select Set Rate, and double-check that Audacity's settings are consistent with your sample rate expectations and with the settings you established earlier. Open the Audio Track menu again and select Set Sample Format to ensure that's also in line with your preferred settings (see Figure 5.13).

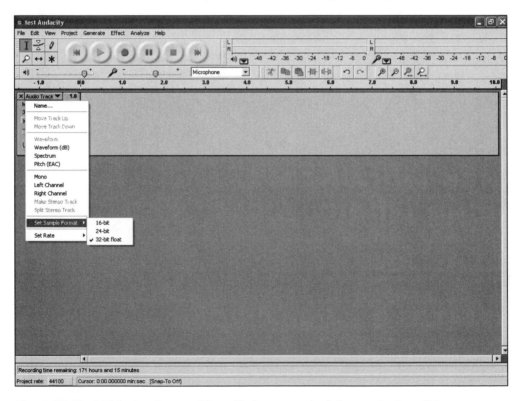

Figure 5.13 32-bit sampling precision will give you tens of thousands of possible recording levels.

Recording Your Podcast with Audacity

To record in Audacity, you guessed it, click the Record button. That's the third button from the left. The round button. The big red one. The one where, if you place your cursor over it, a dynamic icon pops up and says *Record*. (Just having some fun here.)

note

> You've got to be in a good mood and have a positive mindset if you're going to produce a podcast broadcast! Just as TV hosts often get "pumped up" with a team speech to his or her camera staff, producer, and others in the studio, you'll want to prepare yourself. If you're taping a comedy podcast but just opened an unexpected insurance bill, walk away. Podcast another day!

My first bona fide recording in this walkthrough is depicted in Figure 5.14. I started out with the right volume, but then I sneezed, so I selected the offensive and rogue noise (see the highlighted area) and edited it out. I'll discuss editing options in the next section. These functions are the foundation of creating a colorful and effective podcast.

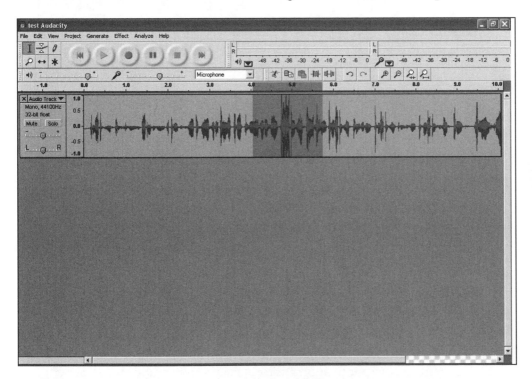

Figure 5.14 You can select areas of a podcast that are too loud and edit them as described in the next section.

To record your podcast, perform the same steps you used when you recorded a test track. In other words, do the following:

1. Open the Project menu and select New Audio Track.
2. Click the Record button at the top of Audacity's main interface.
3. Record your podcast using one or more tracks, clicking the yellow button to stop recording.
4. Click the green Play button to hear how your podcast turned out.

Before beginning the editing process, described next, you'll want to save your project. To do so, open the File menu in Audacity's main window and select Save Project As. The dialog box shown in Figure 5.15 appears; name your podcast file and navigate to the folder where you want it to be stored.

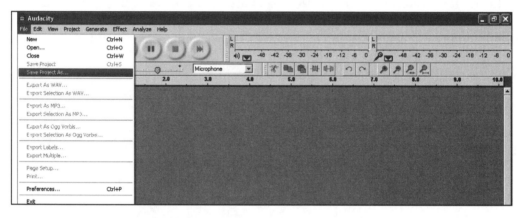

Figure 5.15 Save your recording.

Using Audacity to Edit Your Podcast Recording

Your editing options in Audacity are much like the ones you'd find in Word. For example, you can cut, copy, paste, and so on; the difference is that instead of performing these actions on text, you're performing them on sound.

Audacity's Basic Editing Commands

The basic edit commands are simple to execute. For example, if you wish to move a portion of the audio from one spot to another, select the portion you want to axe by "painting" over the waveform (that's the squiggly line that goes up and down and looks like an electrocardiogram) with your mouse. (In other words, if you make mistakes, don't have a heart attack.) Select only the part you wish to edit, and then open the Edit menu and select

Cut. The selection will disappear, but will be available for further use. If you simply wish to delete a segment of your audio track (as opposed to moving it), drag to select the portion of the waveform that you want to delete. Then, press the Delete key on your keyboard, or open the Edit menu and choose Cut.

To paste the selection elsewhere, move your cursor to the part of the waveform that represents the starting point where you wish to paste your selection. Click the starting point, and then open the Edit menu and select Paste. Figure 5.16 shows you part of this process; the vertical line (and a hand icon that appears on your screen) represents where your pasted content will begin.

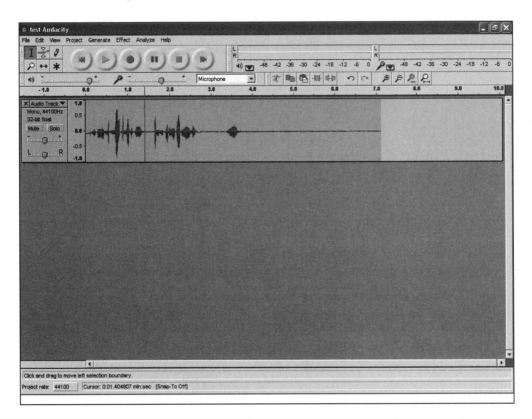

Figure 5.16 You can paste audio content in a new area in the audio file, as depicted by the waveform and vertical line.

Reducing Volume

The sneeze I recorded needs to be eliminated altogether. If, however, there's a loud part of the recording that needs to be retained but reduced in volume, you can do that through Audacity's Amplify function. Before you can apply an effect, however, you must select the portion of audio to be altered. Then, open the Effect menu and select Amplify, as shown in Figure 5.17. This opens the Amplify dialog box, shown in Figure 5.18; here you can reduce volume by entering a negative decibel number in the first box.

note

Audacity automatically controls (for example, amplifies) audio volume, but you can manually override this default setting if you wish. To do this, uncheck the Don't allow clipping check box shown in Figure 5.18.

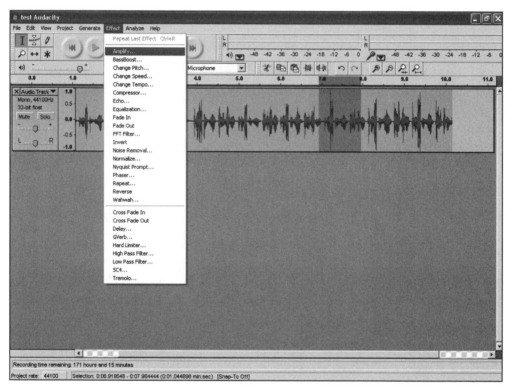

Figure 5.17 As you can see, the Effect menu provides a vast array of editing options. Choose Amplify to change volume levels for the selected audio.

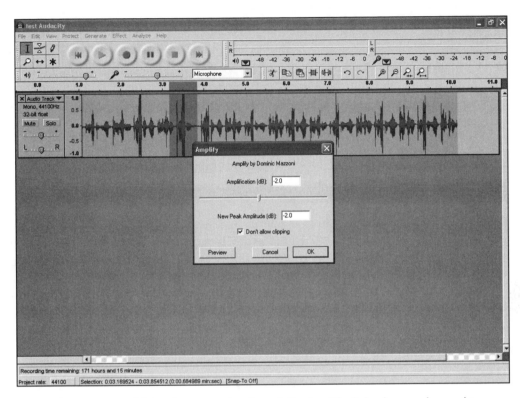

Figure 5.18 Here, a high-volume area is selected; the Amplify dialog box can be used to reduce that volume.

For amplifying sound, Audacity usually does a good job automatically, by default, without any manual intervention. Reducing it, however, is another story. Play around with the Amplify feature to get it just right.

Enhancing Your Podcast

Your podcast recording may be just right with regard to sequence, loudness, and other basic settings. But if you wish to raise the bar a bit further by enhancing the recording, you should explore Audacity's other Effect menu items. These enable you to boost the bass on your podcast to give it a bit more oomph; equalize sound to boost or reduce high, low, and medium frequencies; generate echo effects, which may work well with lighthearted podcasts; and select an audio segment for re-use in the podcast.

note

Of course, there are other effects, but I won't delve into them all because the concept behind all Effect menu items is similar, and you can use the tried-and-true trial-and-error method to teach yourself how to use them.

Converting Podcasts to MP3

You can instruct Audacity to convert your podcast to MP3 format with a simple series of mouse clicks. First, however, you must download special MP3 encoding software. That's because software patents prohibit Audacity from publicly distributing MP3 encoding software within its application. You can, however, easily obtain this software, called LAME, by yourself, as long as it's for individual use. After you have obtained it, free of charge, you can export MP3 files with Audacity and even certain other recording software. It's a must-have application—or no MP3 podcast for you!

Downloading LAME for Windows

To download LAME on your Windows machine, first Google `LAME download PC` to find a download site. (There are many.) Once at the download site, click the appropriate link; for Windows, the link will be named something like "lame-3.96.1." After you download LAME, open it and save the file (usually named "lame_enc.dll" or something along those lines) anywhere on your computer, but preferably in the Program Files folder. (It's easier to stay organized if you keep all programs in one place.) In any case, remember where you saved it. That's important. The first time you use Audacity's Export as MP3 command, Audacity will ask you where you saved the lame_enc.dll file; it helps to remember.

Downloading LAME for Mac OS 9 or OS X

As with Windows, you must first use Google to locate a download site for Macs, this time using the query string `LAME download Mac`; once on the site, click the download link. For Macs, the file will be named something like "LameLib." Save the LameLib file (it will have an .sit extension) on your Mac, preferably in the program directory, and ideally next to where Audacity resides for easy reference. When you first use the Export as MP3 command, Audacity will ask you where you saved LameLib; specify its location.

LAME for Linux

Linux users may find LAME within their distribution package's management system (for example, Portage and Apt-get—stuff that's beyond the scope of this book). If not, never fear. Linux users, by their very nature, are adept at obtaining source code and processing it from there, and the code for LAME is public domain. All this is to say that it's almost certain that someone, somewhere, has figured out how to make the program work with your system. All you have to do is find it.

Running LAME

To run the downloaded LAME program from within Audacity, do the following:

1. Within Audacity, open the File menu and select Preferences.
2. In the Audacity Preferences dialog box, click the File Formats tab.
3. In the section labeled "MP3 Export Setup," click Find Library.
4. Click Yes to locate the LAME encoder.
5. In the dialog box that opens, locate and select the folder where you put the lame_enc.dll file (or the Mac equivalent, LameLib.sit).
6. Click OK.

Converting Files Within Audacity

Now you can begin converting files into MP3s! Here's how:

1. Open the File menu and select the Export as MP3 command.
2. In the Save MP3 File As window, shown in Figure 5.19, choose or create a directory in which to save your podcasts.
3. In the File name field, type a name for the MP3 file.
4. Click the Save button.

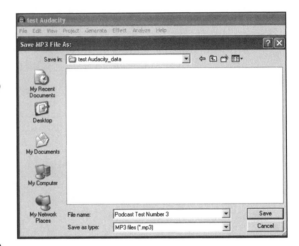

Figure 5.19 In the Save MP3 File As window, you can name your podcast and specify where it should be saved.

Other Saving Options

In addition to enabling you to export your podcast to MP3 format, Audacity also lets you save your podcast recording as an OGG (Ogg Vorbis) file or a WAV file. Although OGG files offer superior sound quality, the format is not widely supported. For this reason, it's best to avoid its use. WAV files are more popular than OGG, but neither format is as widely used as MP3. Because the MP3 format is used by the most listeners, I recommend that you convert your podcast to MP3 only. To save your podcast in these other formats, open the File menu and choose either Export As WAV or Export As Ogg Vorbis.

Do I Really Sound That Bad?

If listening to your podcast makes you wince, don't worry. It's not you, it's me. As *Seinfeld*-ian as that sounds, it may be true. Fade outs, silence, skips, and other *unsoundly* podcast recording problems do happen, and it may be your PC's fault! Okay, it might also be your fault if you didn't follow the configuration instructions to a T. If you're experiencing podcast problems, take a look at these troubleshooting tips:

- Close non-essential programs that may be running before you use Audacity.
- Disable Audacity's Auto-scroll while playing setting to stop the display from drawing waveforms as you record. To find this setting, open the File menu, select Preferences, and click the Interface tab.
- Trim the recording bit depth from the default 32-bit to 16-bit. This will make your computer work less hard and breathe easier. To locate this setting, open the File menu, choose Preferences, and click the Quality tab.
- Defragment your hard drive to improve your computer's performance.

The Red Socket's Connected to the...

Be careful not to use the wrong sockets. Aside from not being able to record podcasts well, or at all, you may damage some of your equipment. In most cases, the red socket is a Mic In socket, which you use to record sounds with a mic. The blue socket is Line Input, also used to input audio signals from audio equipment and filter it into your computer. The green or lime socket is Line Output, used to feed an amplifier and speakers with sound. Note that the headphone sockets located next to your DVD/CD drive are for listening to audio played through DVD or CD only. Programs like Audacity cannot access them, so don't waste your time trying to use them.

note

To download a podcast from any audio recording program (not just Audacity) to an iPod or other MP3 device, open the audio recording program's Preferences window, where you can specify where podcasts should be downloaded. (In iPodder, and on the aggregator side of things, recall that you get there by clicking the Preferences tab as well and by clicking the podcast folder.) To specify in your audio recorder software that you wish to have your MP3 device as the destination, open the Preferences window, then click the tab named "Directory," "Destination," or something similar (in Audacity, it is the Directories tab), and click the folder that holds your MP3 device's content. Your podcast will mix in with any other files that sync to the device. After that, once a podcast is downloaded to your computer, it will automatically sync with your iPod or other device.

Getting Help with Audacity

If you wish to learn about all of Audacity's features, open the Help menu and select Online Help. You'll be directed to a very handy and complete guide on how to use Audacity (see Figure 5.20). Among the Help topics, you'll find information about:

- Using an equalizer
- Generating echoes
- Fading in and out
- Removing noise
- Phase shifting
- Repeating
- Normalizing

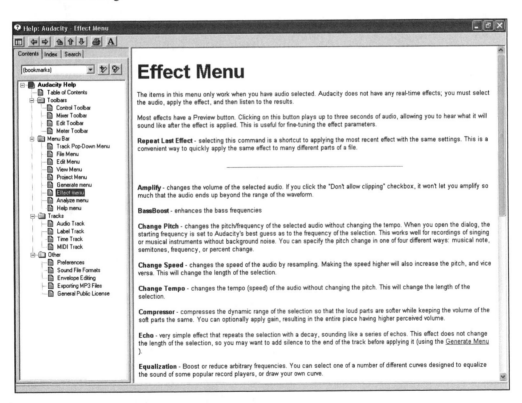

Figure 5.20 Audacity's Online Help is a great reference.

Tagging Your File with ID3

A last but significant step you must take is to add an ID3 tag to your podcast file. An *ID3 tag* is just another computer file that's attached to an audio file. It augments audio content with descriptors, such as the name of the artist (hey, that's you), album, genre, track, duration, and other information. ID3 tags maximize the likelihood that your podcast will be heard because they let listeners easily organize your shows on their computer and other playback devices. Tagging is done in Windows via Windows Media Player; Mac users do their tagging with iTunes.

note

You must convert your podcast file to MP3 format before you can tag it as described in this section.

Tagging with Windows Media Player

To tag your podcast with Windows Media Player, do the following:

1. Launch Windows Media Player.

2. In Windows Media Player, open the Library and locate your podcast file.

3. Right-click the podcast file and choose Advanced Tag Editor.

4. In the Track Info tab, which is displayed by default in the right portion of the Advanced Tag Editor window (see Figure 5.21), enter the requested information. (Make sure that the correct podcast file is selected in the left pane.)

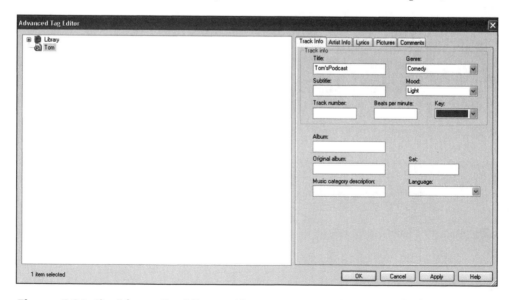

Figure 5.21 The Advance Tag Editor enables you to enter various types of information about your podcast.

5. Click the Artist Info tab.

6. In the Artist Info screen, type your name in the Artist field.

7. Fill out the remaining fields only if you feel these are important; the key is to have completed at least a few of the descriptive fields. That way, when listeners view your podcast file in their media player's window, there will be lots of helpful information beside it.

8. If you want to add a graphic to the MP3 file, click the Pictures tab and follow the onscreen instructions. (Multimedia is discussed in more detail in Chapter 6 "Adding Music, Video, and Other Multimedia.")

9. Click the Comments tab to add your e-mail address, phone number, and other relevant information.

tip

If your podcast involves a raving political commentary, don't tell people where you live! The Men in Black may come to get you.

10. When you're finished, click the OK button to close the Advanced Tag Editor.

Tagging with Apple iTunes

To tag your podcast file using iTunes, right-click your audio file in your directory and select Get Info. You'll see a screen named after your podcast; click the Info tab to access the data input fields. In this field, the iTunes tag editor lets you enter different types of information about your podcast, including the following:

- The name of your podcast
- Your name or another descriptor
- The year of production of the podcast
- Information about the number of tracks

The remaining fields can be completed if you feel they are important; the key is to have completed at least a few of the descriptive fields. If you want to add a graphic to the MP3 file, click the Artwork tab and follow the onscreen instructions. If desired, click the iTunes Comments tab to add your email address, phone number, and other relevant information. After you've entered the appropriate information, click OK, and you're set.

Other Tagging Software

I discuss the tagging capabilities of Windows Media Player and iTunes because chances are you already have one of these applications on your machine. The fact is, scores of other ID3 tag editing applications are available. In fact, Audacity and LAME come with an ID3 tag option box. To find more, check out Tucows (http://www.tucows.com) or run a Web-based keyword search. I like ID3-TagIT (http://www.id3-tagit.de), which edits, adds, and deletes ID3 tags, and supports single- or multi-file editing (a time saver if you're a serious podcaster). Unique features include its ability to read information from the directory structure and tag that information, and its ability to automatically organize podcast files into folders, thus saving editing time.

Coming Up Next...

This chapter presented the podcast-creation process. You learned how to configure the software that actually records your podcast. You then recorded a podcast, edited it, and converted it to MP3 format. You also learned about the importance of the LAME application and the tagging process.

Multimedia (music, video, pictures and more) is catching on fast as a "must-have" podcast feature; if done right, multimedia can enhance your podcast tremendously. If multimedia is mismanaged, however, it can make things messy and confusing. The next chapter shows how to add multimedia to your podcast. It also introduces *moblogging*, which is a way to transmit podcasts (with or without multimedia) by mobile device. Although not multimedia itself, moblogging is closely related to multimedia because camera phones are the device of choice for moblogging pictures and video—both of which *are* multimedia.

CHAPTER 6

Adding Music, Video, and Other Multimedia

Everything up to this chapter was fairly black and white. If you followed the steps as I laid them out, you could listen to or create podcasts. It either worked (because you followed the instructions) or it didn't (because you did not follow instructions, or there was a hiccup in your software or hardware). This chapter starts out black and white, then, things get a bit murky. Don't let this scare you. Things get murky only because I'm going to take you into a few uncharted waters.

This chapter examines how podcasting employs multimedia using existing technology building blocks. You know how you can use the same Legos to build completely different things? That is exactly what is happening in the podosphere. Creative minds are figuring out new ways to package podcasts with multimedia. There is no "right" way—only different ways, each with its own advantages and disadvantages.

As you read this chapter, don't get hung up on the technology or terminology. Is a moblog (audio, video, text, or photo sent to a weblog by mobile phone) a podcast, a weblog, or neither? Does any of this matter? Whether something is technically a weblog or a podcast or video log (vlog) or a moblog is totally beside the point. After reading this chapter, you'll realize that the lines between technologies and methods are blurry at best anyway. What *does* matter is what you want to do. Do you want to be an individual *radio* broadcaster? Fine, podcasting with or without music may suffice. Do you want to be an individual *TV* broadcaster? Then perhaps vlogging (essentially podcasting with video, as I explain in this chapter) is the way to go. Do you just want to be an individual *print* publisher? Fine, weblogging alone will do. Do you want to be a photographer with an online gallery? Can do, with Flickr.

This chapter is about those possibilities. All, especially vlogs, are highly intertwined with podcasting. In other words, you can't have a true TV station without audio, any more than you can have a vlog (like a TV station) without podcasting (audio). Podcasts also complement weblogs and photo sharing. Podcasting is integral to multimedia. So think more about how the technology building blocks can take shape to meet *your* podcasting needs, and less about the technology itself.

Multimedia and Podcasting

There are several ways to present podcasts with flair. You can add a lot of bells and whistles to your audio production to jazz it up. All it takes is a home for your podcast (usually a weblog, a hosting option I fully discuss in Chapter 7, "Hosting and Promoting Your Podcasts") and some cool multimedia software tools to help you along. Put another way, for multimedia to coexist with a podcast, it typically must happen on one's personal weblog page. But a podcast can also reside on a *commercial* online weblog service (again, something I get into in Chapter 7) or a *standard* personal or commercial web site (not a weblog). Again and again, don't get hung up on where a podcast takes up residence. While I present criteria in Chapter 7 to help you reach an important decision about where your podcast should live, this is not really a critical—and certainly not exciting—issue. I only mention it here for context. What *is* exciting is podcasts with multimedia.

As I write, and in the background, some clever software developers are hard at work making multimedia happen directly on your iPod and other MP3 playing device (like iPod Photo). This includes adding images and video to your MP3 device, and not just on your computer. But we're not there yet—at least not with MP3 players. Sure, there are mobile players that can play digital video, but it isn't yet RSS- or XML-based. That is the area under development now. Weblogs themselves are developing into multimedia powerhouses. Names like Flickr, Blogger, LiveJournal, and others will soon become part of your lexicon—if they haven't become part of it already. Odeo is also a recent entry in the podosphere, and can be described as a "podlog." I discuss these and others in this and the following chapter.

note

In the same way that cell phones have morphed into MP3 players, expect MP3 players to morph into video players, and vice versa.

note

iTunes supports more than you think, as does Windows Media player. They simply haven't been hacked or maximized to function at their full potential. I'll discuss their enhanced functionality a bit in this chapter.

RSS, MP3, E-I-E-I-O

You can get a podcast in many ways. One is via an XML aggregator (that is, you add a podcast feed to your RSS aggregator and have the show delivered automatically in MP3 format). Another is to manually go to a weblog or standard web site and download the show in MP3 (or get the RSS feed's URL yourself). Yet another is to subscribe to a podcast directly through iTunes in MP3 format. Had enough? Tough. You can download a podcast production in enhanced AAC format, or download a moblog audio entry that is translated into MP3 or another format. The list of podcast distribution channels continues to grow. The point is, there are many ways to get audio, many different combinations of multimedia, many audio formats, and many different devices and hardware. But there is only one result: a message you create. The media is the message.

A Deeper Look at Multimedia

Multimedia is the sizzle that's added to the steak. In the context of podcasting, it's *adding* visual and more audio elements to the voice aspect of your production. Multimedia includes images, pictures, movies, video, music, and other sight and sound features.

Podcasting and multimedia go hand in hand (that is, it's usually a good idea to add multimedia to podcasts) to help make the podcast appealing, make it stand out, help promote it. But although they go hand in hand, they often (but not always) do so on different platforms. In other words, your podcast aggregators won't catch a feed, and then play *both* multimedia and the podcast at the same time. In other *other* words, you won't *hear* a podcast, and *see* the multimedia on your MP3 player at the same time—yet!

The technology to integrate and morph multimedia into one channel—the XML feed— is still under development. A quick perusal of relevant web sites reveals that a lot is going on, but it's going on in beta! That's okay. It shows that the technological lights are on.

In the meantime, multimedia typically resides on a person's personal weblog page or on a commercial weblog service (a service that hosts your weblogs and runs your software for you). These pages are weblogs first but with podcasts living in them. The good news is that aggregators catch or identify *both* weblog text and podcast audio. It's the playing part that is tricky.

note

Check out the weblog with its array of podcast and other resources at http://www.johnniemoore.com/blog.

Some Popular Multimedia Tools

A quick search of Tucows (http://www.tucows.com) will reveal myriad software tools to enhance your multimedia experience. Some are free and others require you to pay for the privilege. To keep things simple, I'll present some multimedia tools you've likely heard of. They are popular and most importantly, they work.

QuickTime

QuickTime is a multimedia player created by Apple. It supports several formats of digital video and runs on both Windows and Mac platforms. It also plays sound, animation, voice audio, and music. You can even see text scroll across it if you wish to download and stream text data. It also supports immersive images of the type used by real estate companies to enable you to enjoy a 360° virtual tour inside a home. (A company called Ipix developed this technology in the late 1990s in collaboration with Kodak.)

Also of relevance to podcasting is the free QuickTime Broadcaster software. This application lets you produce live events, including audio. QuickTime Pro (about $30) lets you create digital videos to complement your podcast. If your podcast is educational or instructive in nature, you may wish to add slide or video presentations to it; you can then prompt listeners of your podcast to open a QuickTime video on your command.

In summary, QuickTime multimedia tool sets let you create, deliver, and play back multiple formats of multimedia.

Apple and the Land of Oz

Not everything is perfect in Apple's Land of Oz. QuickTime 3.0 and QuickTime 4 do not support true video streaming. In other words, files must partially download before they begin to play, so there may be a bit of a delay. This can be a problem if you try to time podcasts with video presentations. Even during the video's run, a hiccup of several seconds may result during which streaming will freeze the QuickTime screen. Also, QuickTime for Windows does not support MPEG, which is used most often with local (desktop) media playback rather than streaming (online) scenarios. And you thought Apple could do no wrong!

RealPlayer

RealPlayer is the real deal, having more than 50 million registered users. RealNetworks trumpets the fact that "more than 85 percent of all streaming media-enabled Web pages" work on its platform. The Real system comprises two elements: the server and the client. RealNetworks' server—the RealServer (good name)—sits in a lonely building, all by itself

Its role is to upload media to the client—the RealPlayer, which sits in your computer. At least they talk to each other! The most current version supports Windows, Mac, and UNIX platforms.

note

While playback of QuickTime creates potential hiccups, playback with RealPlayer and Windows Media Player (WMP) does not. So what's the deal? RealPlayer and WMP provide continuous playback but at a price—signal quality sometimes suffers.

MovieWorks

MovieWorks Deluxe (http://www.movieworks.com) is a multimedia program that lets you create digital movies, slide shows, and presentations. It has five integrated programs that work in tandem to help you add multimedia to your weblog, including photos, animations, 3D, and MP3 voice. That means you can essentially incorporate a podcast here. However, the podcast may escape the notice of podcast aggregators because this is not a RSS-based approach. Also, making copies of podcasts (one for MovieWorks and one for RSS aggregators) only adds to your storage requirements.

But, if you don't mind the storage overhead, music, narration, text, and titling can make this a good add-on to your podcast productions. Your podcast can prompt listeners to click on button links to synchronize what they hear (your voice) with what they see (a multimedia presentation). For this approach, and for most multimedia applications to work well, your computer processor and broadband connection would both have to be high-speed.

MovieWorks is supported by both Windows and Mac. Productions may be exported as an MPEG, MOV, or AVI video file for web page uploads, and the new 3GP audio file for listening on mobile devices such as PDAs, SmartPhones, and cell phones. MovieWorks allows for multiplexing of dual video and audio file streams in one file. This is critical if you wish to integrate multimedia with your podcasts within *one* media player. Alternatively, you can run a podcast feed separately from the video stream. Storage space, your podcasts's visibility, and duplicated effort are your main considerations with this approach. As you can see, however, converging audio and video is possible.

Other Off-the-Shelf Video Software

Microsoft's Movie Maker for Windows and Apple's iMovie (at http://www.microsoft.com and http://www.apple.com respectively) let you create and edit video productions and add audio and text captions. Both automatically format content to be web-ready. While this is a lot of horse-power, these applications are feature-rich and will save you time because they are very intuitive to use. Also check out Vlog It at http://www.seriousmagic.com. Its strength is its simplification of the video-editing process. I discuss Vlog It and other movie-making software in greater detail in Chapter 10, "The Leading Edge of Podcasting."

Flash

Flash is a multimedia graphics program created by a company called Macromedia. It is geared for use on the web. When a visitor comes to your web site, Flash triggers an inter-active "video" to play on the web (unless you click the Skip icon, or something like it). Graphics can be large, bandwidth-sucking monstrosities, or small video motifs. You don't have to be a programmer to use it, and it's easy to learn.

Flash files or movies typically appear on a web page for viewing with a web browser. They can also be played in a separate Flash Player. You see Flash files most often in ads and ani-mations on web pages. It is yet one more way to enhance your podcast.

That said, be aware that Flash is just that—flash! It's a lot of sizzle. For the purposes of podcasting, use it only to get listeners' attention. It's not really designed for anything deep-er for a number of reasons. First, Flash encourages bad content design because it's more about format and less about content. It also sucks—er, sucks the lifeblood out of your broadband connection. Finally, the "coup de grace" is that it's not conducive to frequent updating, as people typically design a Flash(y) presentation and just leave it there. Podcasting is about updates, change, deltas, and moving ahead. Flash may not be the best tool to communicate your message. But, if you must, use it for your podcast promos. It's great in that regard!

Java

Java is a plug-in technology (and a small island *west* of Krakatoa) developed by Sun Microsystems. I usually get annoyed at the interruption caused when Java loads. Then, when I see the rich features, I'm usually glad the app was there. Java creates a connection between web browsers like Explorer and Firefox and the Java platform. This connection triggers web applets to be run on your browser. Sun Microsystems develops and updates Java on a regular basis, and I'm told that they are working on podcast-specific apps. (If you run a business- or investment-based podcast, it would be pretty cool to have a stock ticker applet run on the stocks you are profiling.)

note

Scratch and sniff—to smell the Java? Isn't smelling multimedia, right up there with sight and sound? Don't laugh too hard. During the heady days of the dot-com bubble, two companies were actually funded to develop this. Where are these companies now, and what about their technology? For answers to this and more, visit the State Bankruptcy Department...

Special Media Players

A *media player* is a computer software application that plays multimedia files. The majority of media players support various media formats in both the audio and video categories. Windows Media Player and RealPlayer are examples. Some media players, however, are one trick ponies and play only one of audio or video—hence the terms "audio player" and "video player." I introduced you to the Audacity audio player in Chapters 4, "Getting Ready to Do It Yourself," and 5, "Configuring, Recording, and Editing Your Podcast"; Winamp is another audio player. Video-only players can be found at Tucows or through a Google search.

Don't dismiss these dedicated options out of hand just because their features are limited to just audio or just video. Instead, consider them in the context of how they fit your needs. If you're leading your listeners by a podcasting hand, and prompting them to open up a video file, it doesn't matter that the video is played with a video-only app! Besides, the video-only player may very likely be better than better-known dual-purpose players because it specializes in that media.

Adding Music to Your Podcast

You can enhance your podcast by adding music. This can occur during the editing phase of the podcast-production process I described in Chapter 5, or later. What matters is that your listeners don't need to visit a weblog or standard web site to hear podcast productions with music built-in. They can sit back and let their aggregator capture your podcast feed. Then, they can listen to the podcast—and hear the music embedded in it—in their iPods and other MP3 players. You can include an entire song, or just part of a song, with fade in and out effects if you choose.

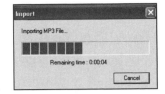

Figure 6.1 Audacity imports your music for further editing and inclusion in your podcast.

In Audacity (and the principle here is similar with other recording software packages), the process is to locate a music file in MP3 format (that is, a file already converted to MP3) and open it within Audacity itself. In other words, click File on the main menu bar, select Open, and you'll see an Import panel showing your music file being opened up. Figure 6.1 shows this process in action.

What you see next is the waveform of the entire song, as shown in Figure 6.2. Pick the parts you want and drag them to the area below the waveform. After the extract is loaded in a new track, you can apply effects to whatever sections of the track you select for editing. (Basic editing functions were described in Chapter 5.) You can adjust volume using the bars on the left. After that, add the new track to the appropriate area of your podcast file (track). After a little practice, you'll get this routine just right.

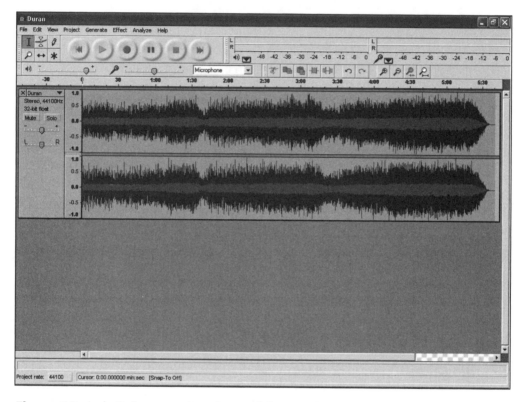

Figure 6.2 Audacity lets you select, drag, and drop songs into new tracks, and edit them for effects.

How Do You Pull Multimedia Together in Podcasts?

Podcasting has evolved beyond word and song. As a result, you may be wondering what the rules are as to when you should podcast with a separate video feed, versus just vlogging, which is a form of multimedia podcast. (Both routes are discussed shortly.) The answer is, there are no rules. To see why, go to vBlog Central and click the Examples icon to get a fantastic idea about what kind of stuff is vlogged. This was done on what is essentially a commercial weblog service. You can also call it a "commercial video log service." See, no black and white!

Now, go to a weblog called Momentshowing hosted on Typepad (a traditional commercial weblog service) at http://www.momentshowing.typepad.com. When you click the video, it plays immediately as a stream without first being downloaded to your computer as an intact file. Most vlogs are efficient like that. Next, check out Susan's Vlog at http://www.kitykity.com/weblog.php/vlog. In this case, you either have to save the video file to your computer's disk or open it and wait a few minutes for it to download. This is a bit time-consuming, but it's okay. With both of these approaches, you can view content with a video-capable media player. Back to Susan. Notice your ability to link to her personal weblog site, and a super-cool link to http://www.vlogmap.org, which is a web site that shows a picture of the world and pinpoints the geographic locations of many existing vlogs! What you wish to do with your weblog is entirely up to you. There are many possibilities.

There are likewise no rules as to how to podcast with multimedia. You can separate your audio and video (and picture) files from your audio file. Or, you can just vlog, which is podcasting *with* multimedia embedded in the digital file. Different buzzwords; similar (if not the same) outcome. Notice also that Susan used her own web site, a weblog with a downloadable video file. On the other hand, Momentshowing was hosted on a commercial weblogging service—Typepad. And the videos on Vblog Central were hosted within that service. Three different platforms (personal weblog, commercial weblog, and commercial vlog); same outcome.

In summary, multimedia podcasts can essentially be delivered in two ways: they can be separated from associated video files and referred to via the podcast, or they can be fully integrated voice/video/picture productions. The following sections discuss when you may wish to use either option. At the end of the day, though, it is up to you and your imagination.

Separating Your Podcast from Video and Picture Files

Think about a six o'clock newscast you watch on TV. Chances are, you watch it on TV not because the video and pictures are the focus of your interest, but rather because you are interested in the news and in what the anchors *say*. That said, you want *some* video and some pictures; they drive home the news anchor's point and convey powerful, frightening, or entertaining images. This multimedia is what sets TV news apart from radio news (that is, with audio and music only). Of course, you can't always bring a TV set to work or put one in your car. That's where audio comes in—podcasting with separate video and picture files. You'll want to consider this option when your podcast show gets most of its points across with audio, and is only *enhanced* by multimedia.

You may wish to podcast about your trips to Europe, and enhance them by referring your listeners to your slideshow or soundless videos that are hosted on your weblog. That way, if listeners wish, they can ignore the pics, and just listen on-the-go with their MP3 player.

Doing so won't ruin the audio (podcast) part of your production. Other podcasts may be educational and instructive, and refer to exhibits. In this case, this "separated" approach would also be great. These are just a few examples. The point is that you'd use this approach if audio is the key medium of the message, and your listeners would be entertained and informed even without the add-on video. If you restrict your show to integrated audio and video (in other words vlogs), you may lose a large chunk of potential audience because most people don't yet have mobile devices that play multimedia on-the-go.

Integrating Your Podcast into a Vlog

You've seen this on CNN. A hurricane is coming and a reporter is streaming news from a camera phone. Or the Toronto International Film Festival is kicking off, and the stars are out in full fashion. These are situations that call for pictures. In fact, they are essential. In these circumstances, a vlog is the only way to go. Voice, video, and pictures are integrated to create a message that tons of people want to hear. One vlog I saw was about a daring rescue, so images were critical. Another vlogger loved her dog, and wanted to both talk about it (like a podcast) and show it off (so videos were included in the weblog). Again—no rules.

Many Multimedia Approaches

You can use Flash to simultaneously play video with audio files. In other words, you can play both audio and video in one app and under one roof—Flash. Aggregators won't likely capture this non-RSS content, however. To mitigate this shortfall, you can also take the approach where you have an XML feed *as well as* a video-only Flash file. Listeners to your podcast can download both the audio (via the aggregator) and Flash files, and when you prompt them to do so in your audio podcast, they open the video-only Flash (or any other suitable app) and follow along. The only time I can see you doing this, however, is to introduce your podcast promo with a bit of flash and pizzazz. Just remember, the name of the game is extending your reach via an aggregator, not creating Flash files no one will see.

Yet another approach is if your weblog or standard web page has an RSS link (to expose it to aggregators) along with a multimedia-free podcast, but you also have a multimedia version running on Flash, MovieWorks, or another (non-RSS) app that resides on your weblog or standard web site. Perhaps you can even charge a fee for the enhanced podcast, and use the regular podcast as a demo and as a way to get people to your site.

note

If your multimedia podcast (say, Flash) resides on your weblog or standard web page, don't put it on your main page, especially if that's the one search engines direct people to. Instead, have your multimedia triggered by another web page so that you first have a chance to warn visitors that an auto-run application lurks in the background. Even if it's a great app that people will enjoy, they may not wish to enjoy it in the here and now. These apps suck bandwidth, waste time, and perturb podcast listeners.

An Example of a Multimedia Tool for Podcasting by Vlog

MediaTuner (http://www.mediatuner.com) is a rich media RSS aggregator and player. It is easy-to-use, and represents the evolution of podcasting into a more multimedia form. It lets you manage both text-based and rich media-filled RSS feeds via your browser. Its MediaTuner Universal Player/Viewer lets you experience podcasts, vlogs, pictures, streaming video, and text weblogs. Look for many similar multimedia RSS tools to crop up in the near future. Click the Demos icon on the home page, sit back, and enjoy the walkthrough. It's really good, and represents a glimpse into podcasting and vlogging's futures. I discuss similar apps in greater detail in Chapter 10.

note

VideoAddon.com has behind-the-scenes software (no downloading) that lets you to incorporate streaming video into your web pages. VideoAddon.com also lets you upload pre-recorded video in several popular formats. These may have been recorded using a webcam or off-the-shelf software packages. Videos will play on Windows, Mac, and Linux.

Is It a Weblog, Podcast, Vlog, or Moblog?

The answer is, as you can now see: It doesn't matter. It's a bit of each. One focuses on print, another on audio, and yet another on video. When they work together, you get multimedia. Usually, weblogs make for excellent landing strips for podcasts and video weblogs. That's because the RSS feeds get noticed by aggregators. As for moblogs, they are merely a *method* or channel by which you ship podcasts, weblogs, or vCasts to a place everyone can access online. That online residence can be run by individuals or by commercial enterprises.

As you read each chapter in this book, just remember that all the resources mentioned are, or can be, joined at the hip. On the other hand, you may have absolutely no need for multimedia. Think about your favorite radio show. Does it need multimedia? Of course not; otherwise, it wouldn't be a favorite of yours!

Always remember that there are many different types of weblogs and web pages in which to park your podcasts. Fundamentally, though, there are personal weblogs ("do-it-yourself" web pages with weblog and perhaps podcast features and content) and commercial weblog services (the specialized providers of weblog platforms that can also host, link, or otherwise refer to your podcasts). The things you can do with personal weblogs have been covered in various sections of this chapter; the possibilities with commercial weblog services, however, are limitless. This is the space where the most creative minds behind weblogging and podcasting technology development live! It's where developments are turning into reality at a very fast pace. I cover some of these developments later in this chapter, in the section called "Multimedia Podcasting with Outside Help: Online Picture and Video Log Services."

note

I have a five-minute homework assignment for you. At this point, I'd like for you to have as clear an understanding as possible regarding key definitions related to podcasting. Flip to this book's glossary and read the entries for *podcasting, weblog, vlog,* and *moblogging.* You'll see how closely all four technologies interrelate.

The Role of Weblogs for Podcasts

There are different ways to weblog and podcast, and a few are covered in this chapter. As you recall from Chapter 1, "Getting Started with Podcasting," a *weblog* is an individual's online repository for posting journal entries. They are also referred to as *blogs,* and can cover any and every topic imaginable. It's the online and personal equivalent of print and commercial journalism. By contrast, *podcasting* is the online and personal equivalent of news and information radio reporting and programming. It too covers nearly every imaginable topic. Both represent freedom for the masses in the truest sense of the word.

Vlogs, Video Blogs, and vCasts Revisited

Welcome again to discussion of this emerging technology. I'd like to go into more detail now. I want to emphasize that vlogging is the bridge that allows audio (podcasts) to integrate and converge with moving pictures. It's the online and personal equivalent of broadcast TV. Again, a vlog broadcast is called a *video weblog.* Right now, vlogs are mostly video without audio because uploads often come from camera phones. Soon, as more robust technology continues to develop, it will be both more often.

Personally, I use for my own purposes what I believe to be a more accurate term to describe video weblogs. Some people, including me, call them vCasts, because these videos are more *broadcast* in nature and less a published log of written entries. vCasts have elements of radio and TV, and both radio and TV stations are *broadcasters* of their signals. A newspaper chain does not broadcast! The fact that vCasts often (but not always) reside on weblogs is secondary to their intrinsic nature—a broadcast.

A Complete Media Triad

So there you have it—the triad of convergence of media forms is nearly complete. Every world citizen has (or could have) access to technology to empower him or her to be radio, TV, and print broadcasters and publishers. This is truly remarkable and nothing short of incredible; and will happen in earnest in 2006.

note

Expect online commercial dating services to prompt the further proliferation of vlogging and vCasting technology. Also expect church, synagogue, and other religious services to maximize the use of this technology. Traditionally, these types of services (not the porn and the defense industries) have been great first-adopters of some of the most exciting online emerging technologies!

The Relationship Between Moblogs and Vlogs

Although I mentioned this before, I'll mention it again. Don't get too hung up on these terms. Moblogging is just a way, method, and path for weblogs, podcasts, and vCasts to be broadcast. It's an "on-the-go" or mobile path. Rather than broadcasting or printing your messages at home or at the office via desktop, you do them on portable devices like BlackBerries, Treos, and basic cell phones.

note

Moblogs are essentially weblogs, podcasts, or vCasts posted usually on a weblog using a cell phone or SmartPhone. It is different from standard weblogging in that a PC or Mac is not used. A mobile camera phone is traditionally used for moblogging—the act of posting content. I'll profile some great sites that house weblogs and other stuff that is transmitted by mobile device later in this chapter. In Chapter 10, I discuss how you can move beyond commercial vlogging services and do it yourself on your own personal weblog.

The end game of moblogging audio is the same as for regular non-mobile podcasting—to convert voice to MP3 and feed it to aggregators in order to get noticed. The end game for moblogging images and video is the same. However, it's not always possible to accomplish. Not all video or even moblogged audio is conducive to RSS and XML feeds. Some moblogged audio runs on non-aggregated technologies like LAME, SoX, Python 2.1, and VoiceXML. They work great at getting your audio posted on a weblog, but not so great at getting noticed by aggregators. Moblogging images can likewise be dependent on technologies other than those used in podcasting. All are beyond the scope of this book.

Audio Posting

A concept that is related to both podcasting and moblogging is *audio posting*. It's audio, so it's related to podcasting. Audio posting is also done remotely and not from your PC or Mac, a characteristic of moblogs. A big difference between podcasting and audio posting, however, is that audio posting does not center around the type of XML/RSS/ATOM-based protocols that podcasting does. Rather, your cell phone or home land line is used to call in and record your entry. Then, behind-the-scenes, at a special moblog commercial site (that houses moblogs), your voice gets converted into an MP3 format—but not with a RSS feed. As a result, audio postings do not always get noticed by aggregators. (I cover some of these providers later in this chapter.) The song remains the same for weblogging, podcasting, vCasting, moblogging, and audio posting—to inspire and compel your listening and viewing audience to respond to and discuss various topics.

Hurricanes Katrina and Rita

Some vloggers did a tremendous job of sending in clips of the devastation that befell New Orleans and its surrounding areas. Texas also took a hit. Some vCasters sent in timely and compelling images, and discussed them with Alan Brown while the images were replayed. Others actually captured images alongside their voice and sent the information to CNN. I am confident that this action by courageous individuals resulted in saved lives. When someone tells you that 123 Any Street is under water, you can bet dollars to doughnuts that that is one of the first places local government emergency teams will go to. Even if they don't, government awareness of the depth of a tragedy is raised, resulting in faster response than otherwise, and lives saved!

Software makers continue to plow ahead to create tools for maintaining vlogs and vCasts. This software may reside in your computer, be online, or be embedded in your smart phone, PDA, or other mobile device.

Multimedia Podcasting with Outside Help: Online Picture and Video Log Services

In this section, I present some new Internet services that cater to vlogs and moblogs. Syndicated XML and other feeds designed to track online digital videos are cropping up on a monthly basis. Google is even developing and enhancing its search platform to include podcasts and vCasts. At the end of the day, all are podcasts with images. Or, all are images with podcasts. A podcast by any other name is still a podcast!

In Chapter 7, I'll introduce you to specific commercial weblog services that take a lot of the hassle out of maintaining personal weblogs and podcasts on your own. With these special hosting services, you lose some flexibility, but may save some time—at least in the short term. The players you'll be introduced to in that chapter include names like Blogger, the Six Apart group, MSN Spaces, Castpost, Blog-City and Odeo. Chapter 7 focuses on these and other hosting options you have. In contrast, the commercial sites profiled in this section are first and foremost visual files—albeit of a "helping hand" nature. The multimedia files in question are pictures, images, graphics, movies, and videos.

Flickr for Pictures

Flickr is the market-leading (based on number of subscribers) online photo management and sharing platform. As to features, Flickr supports Blogger, Movable Type, Wordpress, LiveJournal, TypePad, and other commercial weblog applications. (I discuss most of these in Chapter 7.) That means you can post photos to those leading weblogs and others as well, in addition to just leaving them on Flickr's web site. So if you don't have a web page in the first place, and you like the idea of sharing your photos (and not necessarily sharing photos of the one and only you) with the world, this place is for you.

note

You can use Flickr to add pictures to complement your podcast, whether your podcast resides on a personal or commercial weblog. In other words, you can add Flickr to your personal weblog.

After you post photo entries to Flickr (see Figure 6.3), people can leave comments, even on a photo-by-photo basis if they wish. If you desire privacy, or are apprehensive about what people may post, you have the option of setting privacy levels. This too can be done on a photo-by-photo basis, and you can decide who can see each photo (and who can comment on them). Photos can be of various dimensions—like thumbnail, medium, and large sizes. They can even be manipulated much like you can manipulate photos in software apps like Paint Shop Pro and others.

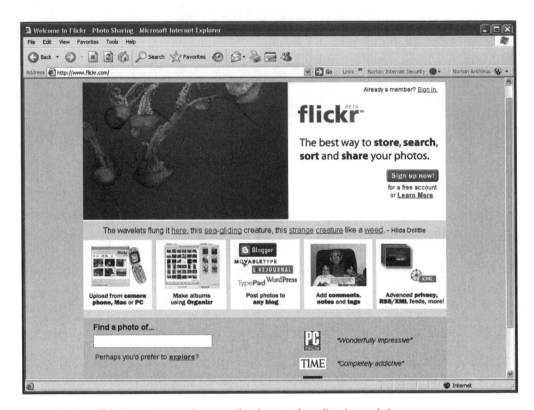

Figure 6.3 Flickr is an extremely versatile photo-only online journal that supports moblogging.

Flickr also supports moblogging in that photos can be posted (uploaded) with email clients like Outlook, or by camera phone or SmartPhone with picture-storage functionality. As for viewing, moblogging is further enabled through a mobile version of Flickr's web site. That means you can view your—and other people's—photographic gems on your mobile and web-enabled cell phone or PDA. You can also use email clients to moblog directly to any blog.

Uploading is straightforward, and Flickr supports transfers of large photo file sizes from both Windows and Mac operating systems. Because Flickr also has full RSS and ATOM functionality, others can subscribe to your photos using specific tags and photo sets that aggregators can reference. You can also simply refer listeners of your podcasts to your photos to help you drive home your points. The key here is that Flickr is XML and RSS-friendly.

TextAmerica Mobile Video and Picture Sharing

TextAmerica (shown in Figure 6.4) is a growing photo- and video-management platform that sorts images into popular categories. You can browse by a general image or video category, by image tags (such as "boat" or "rainbow"), or by community moblogs (also categorized by location or interest). It's a mobility-centric service. It's not surprising that a lot of people use QuickTime apps at this site because it is an app commonly used with camera phones.

Figure 6.4 TextAmerica lets you post pictures and images while on the go.

vBlog Central

vBlog Central is a wonderful service that makes it easy to link multimedia content—podcasts (audio), video, and images—to your existing weblog. It can also host your video and audio (podcast) content. vBlog Central supports many image-rendering formats such as JPEG, MPEG, and more. It also supports Windows Media, Real Player, and QuickTime players. The site, shown in Figure 6.5, works with many major commercial weblog services and certainly with your personal weblog page as well. It costs about $50 annually for several gigabytes of storage space, which is a lot.

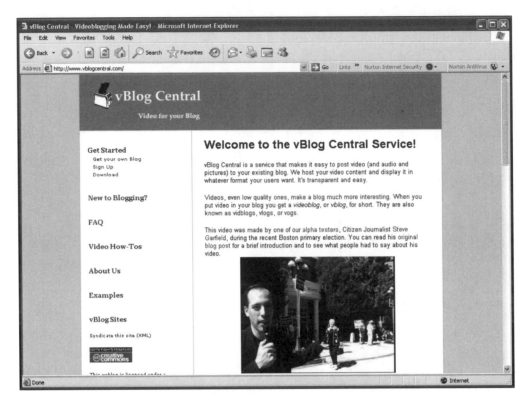

Figure 6.5 vBlog Central handles all multimedia.

Uploads of multimedia to vBlog Central also appear in your existing weblog. You can link to the multimedia by using the standard weblog tools supported by your weblog host. Links will reference a web page containing your multimedia. You cannot yet link directly to the video file itself, however. When vBlog Central incorporates video in blog entries, it has three goals: (1) to function in existing personal weblogs and commercial weblogs like Blogger, TypePad, and Movable Type; (2) to be simple to use by the poster and audience; and (3) to provide multiple rendering formats. Because of these principles, it is not currently feasible to *directly* link the video or other multimedia file. In the future, however, vBlog Central will likely ramp up a parallel service that does in fact support direct linking to video and other multimedia from your weblog site. If it doesn't, competitors almost certainly will. The evolution of podcasting, complete with multimedia functionality, moves on!

note

Moblogging is mostly about pictures and video. It's also about audio. It is less so about text.

Other Picture Sharing and Moblogging Services

The following sites let people transmit photos and movies taken with camera-enabled SmartPhones and cellphones. A lot of these hosted services are free, but most also provide enhanced for-fee packages. Prices are usually driven by storage, feature, and support requirements.

SnapNPost.com

SnapNPost, shown in Figure 6.6, lets you create an online picture album. You can post photos from a camera-enabled SmartPhone or cell phone. Like most commercial and free services, you must subscribe to SnapNPost. The registration form is mercifully short. When subscribing to services such as these, expect and be ready to provide a screen name ("Elvis" is probably taken), password, mobile phone number, mobile phone service provider, and your email address.

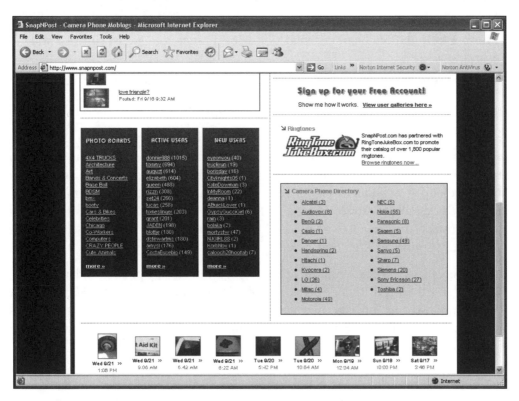

Figure 6.6 SnapNPost has an array of powerful and very podcast-conducive applications.

From your podcast platform, you can include a link to your gallery. It may look something like this:

http://www.snapnpost.com/elvispresley/podcast/Feb82006

Additional SnapNPost gallery management and photo editing features include the following:

- **API access.** A key podcast-empowering feature is the ability to access the webmaster's API (Application Program Interface), which lets you better integrate with other apps to display photos on the web site or weblog on which your podcast resides.
- **Passwords.** Tell only those who listen to your podcast how to unlock photos (with passwords you disclose in audio) as a way to entice them to listen.
- **Advanced privacy controls.** Direct who gets to post in your gallery.
- **Moderate posts.** Curtail irrelevant and inappropriate discussions.
- **Photo manipulation.** Sharpen, rotate, or delete photos, and adjust contrast and brightness.
- **Gallery tools.** Select your entire gallery or individual photos to be shared.

Buzznet.com

Like its peers, this Canadian-based photo-sharing community enables you to share photos within its online community. It is not as feature-rich as SnapNPost, but is strong on the moblogging side and is conducive to podcasts. It's great for when you have to quickly add multimedia to your podcast—say, if your podcasts are geared to news items and you wish to both discuss and illustrate your point. Podcasters who specialize in covering extraordinary, unusual, and irregular events and other developing stories may choose this mobile-friendly option for their podcasts.

Buzznet not only lets you post online via its web page; but also by phone (audio podcast) and via email. Furthering its usefulness as a podcasting partner, it supports RSS feeds; that is, it's a true podcast site. This also means you can post to weblogs, and syndicate photos and other content. In fact, you can link photos to any web page, such as pages where your podcasts reside.

note

VOIP (Voice Over Internet Protocol) and podcasting are likewise converging. Like moblogging, VOIP is another *way* to transmit audio. Again, never let transmission media confuse the issue of what a podcast is—a digital voice file.

SmartPhones and Moblogging

Cell phones with cameras are great. They let you get something online quickly. But it's the SmartPhones that are most powerful when it comes to moblogging, podcasting, and weblogging. That's because SmartPhones, loosely defined, allow for text, audio, and imagery (pictures and audio) due in large part to powerful embedded chips and memory cards that typically reside in the heart of these devices. Because they use programmable logic device technology, they can easily be tweaked by engineers at, say, Motorola to enable them to work with local telecom carriers (on their networks) and "talk to" the technology used by commercial weblog services like those that I'll discuss at length in the next chapter. Hence, they are smart.

Although most SmartPhones don't necessarily *create* RSS feeds—yet—they *do* allow you to get your voice to be heard on a web site or weblog. Today's SmartPhones tend to use MMS (Multimedia Messaging Service), email, or a web browser to transmit multimedia. So moblogging with these is not about RSS, XML, and podcasting per se. Rather, these may come into play only after you have downloaded files via SmartPhone onto a weblog. Once downloaded, though, aggregators will troll the Internet and may identify your weblog files based on weblog-driven tags and headlines.

note

Skype, a growing VOIP player just purchased by eBay, plans to add video chat services to its VOIP software in 2006. Additionally, Skype intends to add its service to SmartPhones and other mobile devices. Look for Skype to appear on more platforms in the future. Definitely look for it to get involved in the world of podcasting. It's all about voice! I discuss Skype again in Chapter 10.

Do-It-Yourself Vlogging

You can create multimedia podcasts, essentially vlogs, all by yourself. In other words, you can put up a weblog site and produce a vlog. The "producing a vlog" part is something I cover in Chapter 10 because vlogging (podcasting with multimedia) is a trend that is just emerging.

Do-it-yourself vCasting is for you if you don't necessarily need the help of a company to get stuff online. It's for you if you don't mind using off-the-shelf software to create web pages, podcasts, and multimedia. It's also for you if you desire an air of permanence for your vCast. It conveys to visitors that you're in control and you know what you're talking about. I just wanted to mention this option here because it is, after all, podcasting with multimedia.

Managing and Storing Multimedia

Videos and other multimedia electronic files take up a lot of space. If you go the commercial weblog route to host your vlogs and podcasts, make sure the host gives you (or you are comfortable paying for) adequate file storage space. For example, LiveJournal lets you buy incremental storage space of 250, 500, or 1,024 megabytes.

Another way to manage the storage space of multimedia files (or just a very large volume of smaller podcasts or vlogs) is to cycle them. Normally, this would be done on a FIFO (first in first out) basis. In other words, the first file in is the first one out after your limit of podcasts (say, 100 megabytes or 50 podcasts) has been reached. That way, your list of 50 podcasts is always the most recent.

What about saving that gem of a podcast you created a year ago and was so well-received? Sure, it's on your computer, but that won't do your online listeners and viewers any good. Consider using (but not abusing) The Internet Archive (http://www.archive.org). The Archive is a non-profit entity with a mandate to build an "Internet library," for the sole purpose of providing a permanent home for text, video, audio, and even old web sites. It is used primarily by researchers and historians to refer to collections of digital information. It is not meant to be a free hosting service!

Putting Your Stamp on Your Shared Works

Creative Commons (http://www.creativecommons.org) provides an array of protections for authors and artists as well as free online search and publishing tools. The multimedia they handle includes podcasts, music, pictures, images, video, and text. They operate on dual tracks in that they follow the intellectual property principle based on the "all rights reserved" traditional copyright, but they also have an optional "*some* rights reserved" copyright. This latter principle is the basis of a lot of shared online works. It's not as protective and proprietary as traditional copyright; but does confer credit (and possibly compensation) where one or both of these are due.

Coming Up Next...

This chapter examined podcasting with multimedia. It reinforced that there is no one way to create a multimedia podcast. You learned not to get worried about underlying podcasting technology or terminology. You saw that you could essentially be an individual radio broadcaster, individual TV broadcaster (via vlogs), or an individual print publisher. This chapter was about innovation and possibility. Podcasting and multimedia work well together. But podcasts—with or without multimedia—need a place to live. Hosting your podcast is the subject of the next chapter. Software options to create RSS feeds quickly and easily are also discussed.

CHAPTER 7

Hosting and Promoting Your Podcasts

The last chapter showed how you can add music, pictures, video, and other multimedia to your podcasts—either by directly embedding multimedia content into the podcast file or by having the multimedia play on your weblog in tandem with your podcast (which could be played either from a computer or mobile MP3 device). You saw that podcasting and multimedia were very much interrelated, and that podcasts are in the throes of convergence with vlogs as well. All of this is great, but your podcasts, however sophisticated, need a home!

You can establish a home for your podcast in one of two ways:

- If you're the Bob Vila type, you can build it yourself. That is, you can create a web site to house your podcasts online, and then find a company to host that site.
- If you most decidedly aren't a member of the "do it yourself" set, you can place your podcasts online using a weblog service.

Of course, regardless of how you go about placing your podcasts online, you'll need to spread the word about your shows. Fortunately, this chapter also covers promoting your podcasts.

Do-It-Yourself Podcast Hosting

If you are adept at web-site design and are comfortable tracking down your own host, then the do-it-yourself route may be for you. For one, it provides a lot of flexibility. In addition, it enables you to really personalize your podcast site.

note

Getting into the ins and outs of building your own web site is well beyond the scope of this book. Fortunately, however, you can find whole shelves of books on that very topic. I recommend *Microsoft Office FrontPage 2003 Fast & Easy* by Brian Proffitt (published by Thomson).

Hosting Options

For the purposes of podcasting, you must choose your host wisely. Failure to do so will result in excessive costs, capacity problems, and worst of all, loss of audience! In this section, I introduce the various types of hosts, and discuss the advantages and disadvantages of each. After you get a feel for the type (category) of host that's right for you, I'll show you some key criteria to apply to choose exactly the right hosting provider. Regardless of which type of host you choose, the key is to get the best value. Look for a triple-E host: one that's *E*conomical, *E*fficient (fast), and *E*ffective.

note

As your podcasts get fancier—chock full of multimedia, yielding a huge following of listeners ready to crash your gates—you may find that the hosting option that worked for you yesterday will not work as well today.

Free Hosting Services

If you browse the Internet, you'll likely come across a few web sites fronting hosting services that offer free or almost-free (less than $3 per month) web hosting. Quite often, pop-up advertisements for this type of web-hosting provider may appear in your browser window. (Ironically, most hosting services come with "pop up blocking" features!) While these may tempt you, it's imperative that you remember the old maxim: "You get what you pay for." Specifically, be aware that low-cost providers tend to be part-time businesses, which means they don't offer the support of their for-pay hosting brethren. And while free web hosts usually involve a full-time business, they typically specialize their services; unless that specialty is podcasting, forget it. They won't be able handle high-bandwidth and high-volume traffic. In addition, free services limit you to using pre-formatted, templated web pages that you cannot customize too much, security is based on a wing and a prayer, and technical support is a message recorded on an outdated telephone answering machine. Next!

note

Later in this chapter, I talk about commercial weblog services. These are actually a great way to get started with your podcasts. These services comprise both free and for-fee hosting options, and are very much dedicated to quality podcasting. For more information about commercial weblog services, see the section "Posting Your Podcasts on Commercial Weblog Sites" later in this chapter.

Shared Hosting Services

Shared hosting means that your web site is hosted on a humongous server alongside about 150 other sites (hence the "shared" aspect). A shared host is like a condo full of web sites. Each condo has its own door number—or, in this case, home page URL or domain. When you opt for a shared host, you typically get an email account (or several), a few web pages (the number may vary, depending on the package you select), web-page editing tools, and decent storage capacity (remember, though, that it's a "condo," not a 3,500 square foot house). Because shared hosts usually rely on good word-of-mouth to grow their subscriber base, technical support is acceptable more often than not. Shared hosts usually support most operating systems—including Windows, Mac, and Linux—and are generally not too costly. Plus, most shared hosts do support weblogs and weblog apps, and more and more are adding support for podcasting standards (RSS and ATOM). Lastly, you'll typically receive at least one FTP account with your account so that you can upload your web page and podcasts.

tip

Check out Godaddy.com (http://www.godaddy.com) for a good sampling of packages, with costs that range from single to double digits. I'm not endorsing the company per se (although I do have accounts with it), but it does have a terrific web presence and offers just about everything you need for podcasting and more.

tip

Of course, you'll want to hear from your fans via email, but don't use that as an excuse to give out your primary personal email address—you know, the one your mom uses to email you. Instead, provide fans with the address of the email account that resides on your shared host's server. That way, when the fan mail comes pouring in, it won't clog up the works on your personal account.

On the down side, the corridors of this "condominium" will be somewhat crowded when everyone goes to work at once. As a result, these hosts typically limit volume, which may include the number of podcasts. (More on this later.) And although shared hosts have decent storage capacity, you may find yourself outgrowing it. There's nothing wrong with condos, but there *is* something wrong if yours doesn't meet your space requirements! If you want to podcast with a shared host, seek one that offers bandwidth of more than 120 gigabytes, and storage capacity of at least 5 gigabytes—about the size of three high-end iPods or two new PCs. Other essentials include SQL databases and web site plug-ins to help you add multimedia and other effects.

note

Security is important, but it's not like you're guarding the secret of the Caramilk Bar on your site. The whole purpose of podcasting is to share content! Nevertheless, you don't want some techno-geek erasing your rock music–related podcast and replacing it with classic Mozart—or vice versa. So although security is important, it is less so in the context of podcasts on shared hosts than in other cases.

Dedicated Hosting Services

A dedicated hosting service is no condo—it's a house! This type of host, which is often used to support businesses, boards your site on a server that is dedicated to you and only you. Dedicated hosts typically provide multiple URLs, and will very likely support podcasting, vlogs, and everything in between. Most dedicated hosts have more than enough bandwidth and storage capacity. Moreover, reliability is one of the two key aspects that these companies try to ensure (the other being privacy, or security); as such, they are as reliable as hosting service providers get. The "rent" for a dedicated host will set you back accordingly, with prices ranging from about $50 to $250 per month depending on what package you select. In addition, working with a dedicated host requires a bit more technical knowledge than do the other options discussed thus far.

note

If the popularity of your podcast soars, you may find you need the added capacity typically offered by dedicated hosts. You may also decide you want the additional security that dedicated hosts provide, simply because your reputation and other content on the server are at stake.

Collocation

Collocation is almost the exact same thing as a dedicated server. The only real difference is that the server is actually *owned* by you. The main reason you would opt for this route is if you expect the demands on your server to be very high. In other words, you don't want to be restricted by a hosting company's bandwidth or storage capacity limits. By owning your own server, you can easily scale it to meet your needs.

As with dedicated servers, your collocated server resides at the physical location of a hosting service provider. Why not just purchase or lease a computer for your own building or home? Simple. Keeping it off-site provides for remote backup, enables quick data recovery, and because the hosting location is well-designed for physical and data security, allows for peace of mind. Unless your podcast achieves superstar status, however, this option is not for you. It's for heavyweights. It's also an expensive and high-maintenance proposition, requiring training and programming skills.

Specialized Podcast Hosting Services

Specialized podcast hosting services are relatively new. Recognizing the special needs of podcasts, such as the need for greater bandwidth, these services are geared accordingly. Here are two examples of specialized podcast hosting services:

- **Liberated Syndication (http://www.libsyn.com).** Libsyn.com, which hosts many popular podcasts, offers various plans that range in price from single digits up to $30 per month. The cost depends on the storage capacity purchased; at the entry level, you get 100 megabytes. Regardless of what plan you choose, however, bandwidth is unlimited, which means you avoid overage charges. You can use Libsyn.com to upload podcasts, write relevant weblog journal entries, and automatically create RSS feeds so that your audience can find your shows. As an added bonus, Libsyn.com functions with the Apple iTunes podcast list, extending your podcast's reach to even more listeners.

- **Audioblog.com (http://www.audioblog.com).** Audioblog.com offers many nice features: a simple window for adding related weblog entries, podcasts, and vlogs; an integrated weblog recorder that enables you to create podcasts with ease online instead of through your desktop; and support for a Flash MP3 player that can be appended to your podcast on your weblog page, allowing listeners to play your podcast immediately without a long download. (I discussed Flash multimedia in Chapter 6, "Adding Music, Video, and Other Multimedia.") Even better, Audioblog.com's basic service is under $5 per month. With this service, you can create podcasts on your existing or new weblog. One of its best features, however, is that it lets you easily create iTunes-ready podcasts. After a few steps, which Audioblog walks you through, just copy and paste your podcast URL (which they provide you with) into iTunes and you are published. This is significant because iTunes is building one of the largest podcast directories on the Internet—you definitely want to be a member! If you're looking for a bit more than basic, you can opt to pay Audioblog.com's annual fee, which licenses you to upload even more podcasts, although each podcast is restricted in length to a maximum of one hour and the bandwidth is limited to 5 gigabytes monthly. (An overage charge of $1 per additional gigabyte may apply.)

Finding a Host

After you've determine what *type* of host you want to use—free, shared, dedicated, or specialized—it's time to pinpoint a hosting service of that type that meets your precise needs. A great way to find a host is to visit a host directory such as TopHosts.com (http://www.tophosts.com) or WebsiteHostDirectory.com (http://www.websitehostdirectory.com). These directories are reasonably objective; other directories may be less so in that they tend to feature hosts that double as site sponsors. If you fail to find the right host using these directories, try performing a Google search using the keyword string `web hosts`.

Assessing Hosts

When it comes time to assess and evaluate various hosting sites to determine which one is right for you, you'll want to consider the following:

- **Initial size and projected growth of your audience.** If you are just starting out, chances are you can safely opt for the basic, entry-level package. Before you do, however, make sure the host offers adequate scalability (see the next bullet).

- **Scalability.** As your needs grow, you'll want to be able to upgrade without hassles and without penalty. For this reason, you should gain an understanding of the costs associated with upgrading up front. Of course, if you do expand, you should expect to pay for a more expensive package; obscene penalties, however, are another matter.

- **Features.** Look for behind-the-scenes (and non-desktop) interfaces that make it easy to manage your web site, email accounts, databases of podcasts, and so on. The more applications that can help with podcasts (audio RSS feed and weblog management capabilities are obvious examples), the better.

- **Your own address.** If you're going to podcast, your springboard web site should look and feel professional. The first and quickest way to do that is to have a web site you can call your own—literally. Don't go the Geocities route, where your web site address must include the Geocities tag line. Also, make sure that URL registration is included in the hosting fee.

- **Capacity and capability.** Know what storage, bandwidth, and speed you are getting, and at what cost. Again, avoid plans that levy excessive financial penalties if you exceed what's in your plan. You can really get dinged with high fees for things you may not even be aware are happening. It's great if your audience is skyrocketing, but it's bad if it's costing you a fortune in extra fees. See if the host you're considering offers enhanced storage services (for a fee, of course). Also, be aware of plans that terminate your feeds if you exceed storage, bandwidth, or other limits. If they do terminate, make sure you will be automatically and quickly notified so that you can take appropriate next steps.

- **Customer service.** Know the hours of available customer service and support. 24/7 is best but not essential unless you're a vampire. Be sure that in addition to email support, you can also obtain live support.

- **Feedback.** A confident host will have public discussion forums for new members and veterans. An unscrupulous one may also have a forum, but will delete the more unflattering posts. Use your good judgment, and review potential hosts on a case-by-case basis to determine whether the forum is bona fide. Then see if the forum is sending you any messages about service.

- **Warranty.** As with many legal contracts, look for guarantees that the product or service will be delivered—and for acceptable remedies if it is not. These include rebates, fee waivers, or free time.

BitTorrent

Some aggregators and hosting service providers offer support for BitTorrent, a peer-to-peer method for distributing MP3 files (a.k.a. file sharing), at a relatively low cost. Although *file sharing* has become a four-letter word for many, especially in the music industry, BitTorrent can be useful as an alternative method for distributing podcasts (as long as the podcasts themselves are legal). In a nutshell, BitTorrent enables listeners to obtain bits of a single podcast from multiple sources. Because the file is distributed by a multitude of computers, the request does not clog the bandwidth at any one source. If your podcast has a large audience (i.e., thousands of listeners) or is bandwidth heavy (due to multimedia or what have you), but you don't have the resources to fund a big server and host, BitTorrent technology might help. Be aware, however, that in order for BitTorrent to work effectively, your podcast files must be shared by many people. If no one participates, your files can't be easily downloaded. Then again, because BitTorrent typically is used only for very successful podcasts, participation will likely not be a problem.

Using FTP to Upload Your Podcast to a Host

Once you've chosen a host and performed the necessary tasks to sign up, you'll need to upload your web page, including your podcast files, to the host's server via File Transfer Protocol (FTP). This can be done either with your browser or with an FTP client—although I don't recommend the browser route because they are not as robust as FTP clients and tend to crash. As for FTP clients, you have many to choose from. I recommend WS_FTP Pro for Windows (http://www.ipswitch.com), which runs about $45, and Captain FTP for Mac OS X (http://www.captainftp.com), which costs in the $30 range. (Although they're available for a fee only, these programs are packed with features, such as wizards, which may come in handy if you are just starting out with podcast downloads.) Others FTP clients, including free ones for Linux, can be found at Tucows (http://www.tucows.com).

After you acquire an FTP program, it's time to define the web address where you want the web page, including your podcasts, to be uploaded. You'll also need the user name and password needed to access your host's server. (All good hosts will provide detailed instructions to guide you through this process.) Then, execute the following general steps, which apply to most FTP clients:

1. When your FTP client has connected with your host's server, you will see two windows, both showing a set of files. The window on the left shows the folders and files residing on your computer. Move through the folders until you have located the web pages and podcast files to be uploaded; then select those files.

2. The window on the right displays files that reside on your host's web server. On your initial upload, this area will likely be empty. Drag your selected files in the left window and drop them in the right window. The files will upload, and their names will appear in the right window.

To check the upload, direct your browser to the page containing your podcast. Your web site should appear, with the podcast available from it. Then, test the podcast with iPodder or another client. You are set.

Building RSS Feeds

Before others can subscribe to your podcast, you need to build an RSS feed for it. Before you start, though, humor me by launching your browser, opening the View menu, and selecting Source (or its equivalent if you're using something other than Internet Explorer). What you see is HTML code. If you're like me, you probably think it looks pretty scary. Unfortunately, RSS code looks just as horrifying. Fortunately, though, just as there are software tools to help you create web pages without having to memorize a gajillion different code tags, there are tools for easily creating RSS feeds. Indeed, few people code HTML manually anymore, and the same ought to be true of RSS. So I'll pass GO here and get right to two software programs that can help you generate RSS feeds (and even help you produce podcasts).

note

As with HTML, RSS coding happened mostly in the early days. When RSS was invented, there was no software to make coding easy. Indeed, to build your own RSS code, you had to be a bit of a techno-geek! RSS coding has typically been the domain of software developers who wish to "hack" or tailor their code to suit their specific needs. One need may be to create code to inform aggregators that special enclosures (such as video) are part of the podcast, but because software is now available to do this, there is no compelling reason to self-code.

FeedForAll 2.0

With FeedForAll, new RSS feeds can be quickly and easily created. Wizards that come with it hold your hand throughout the process. The software also lets you download feeds from the web for your own reference and re-use (with permission, of course). It has an intuitive three-tab interface for editing overall feed settings, and for editing individual files. After you upload your podcast show to your web hosts's server, you can create a link to the show within FeedForAll. At the time of this writing, an upcoming release was expected to produce improved HTML tag editing, support for many languages, and improved FTP logging. In addition to its core support for Windows, its latest version (2.0) also supports Mac OS X 10.3.9 and the new Apple iTunes RSS extension. FeedForAll costs about $40, and is available at http://www.feedforall.com.

note

FTP is used to load web pages—and in this case, RSS feeds—to a hosted server. In addition to FTP, Secure FTP (*SFTP* for short) is also employed for this purpose, although FeedForAll does not support its use. This should not be a problem with most podcasts, however, because they are open by nature.

Feeder 1.1

If you use a Mac, you might prefer to use Feeder 1.1, which is primarily an RSS feed creator program. It offers drag-and-drop functionality, enabling you to drag podcast files from your music directory in your desktop or laptop directly to the Feeder 1.1 editing window. Feeder's dual-window interface enables you to itemize your RSS feeds on the left, and shows you previews of individual items on the right. You can also customize the look and feel of your podcast web page with templates, using wizards to help you along. Feeder 1.1 then uploads the podcast along with the file that contains the links and other data (the HTML-looking stuff) that is the foundation of the feed. Frequently used server addresses are memorized and re-used, saving you the trouble of manually entering them every time you upload a podcast. It's like the "Remember My Password" feature on many secure web sites. Feeder 1.1 allows for secure FTP transfers as well as unsecured transfers. At just $30, Feeder 1.1, available at http://www.reinventedsoftware.com/feeder, is well worth the money. Just remember: It's only for Macs.

Posting Your Podcasts on Commercial Weblog Sites

A year or two ago, commercial weblog services were barely on the radar. Pioneering podcasters placed their podcasts on their own personal standard web pages, according to instructions provided by the hosting service's online manual. The few fledgling commercial weblog services that did exist were nothing more than bit players with low storage capacity and only the most basic features.

Today, all that has changed. Commercial weblog services now provide compelling business cases for podcast enthusiasts to post their productions on these sites. For one, commercial weblog services make the practice of weblogging very low maintenance. No complex configuration is required; just log in and build your own personal weblog using wizards that guide you through the entire process. These sites provide a measure of hosting services, and most importantly, they are typically very conducive to podcasts. Another key benefit of choosing the commercial weblog service route over the regular personal web site route is that most commercial weblogs have communities and powerful interoperability with other weblog services, as well as with XML and RSS aggregators. This enhances the exposure of your podcast, which is, of course, one of the main end games of podcasting.

Best of all, these services are now offered at about the same price point as regular, do-it-yourself, personal web sites—or less. Indeed, many podcasters currently pay more for standard personal web pages but get less in the way of helpful features than podcasters who use commercial weblog services. Even the cheapest commercial weblog services offer good quality weblog, podcast, and other features. Of course, the lower the cost, the smaller the number of audio files permitted, and the less megabytes and bandwidth supported. Pay extra, and you'll receive much more in the way of bells and whistles, storage space, and bandwidth. For information about some of the more popular commercial weblog sites, read on.

note

If you're a beginner or intermediate podcaster whose show is still in the growth stage, just about any commercial weblog service will do. As you build your podcast program, consider an enhanced commercial weblog service package—one that offers more storage and bandwidth.

Six Apart

Six Apart (http://www.sixapart.com) operates, and is a dominant player in, the Blogosphere. Specifically, it integrates three related tool sets—LiveJournal, MovableType, and TypePad—the collection of which is dubbed The Six Apart Group. I discuss each of these tool sets in turn.

LiveJournal

LiveJournal is a simple weblogging tool that enables users to post journal entries, store and edit photos, and add multimedia content such as music and—you guessed it—podcasts. In addition to being easy to customize, LiveJournal has many features that let you do more things than more generic competitors or freeware—in part because it is open source software. LiveJournal's basic package is free, but users can pay a fee to get additional functionality, including 100 megabytes of image hosting and the ability to moblog.

But the key feature is LiveJournal's interoperability. The RSS feed of every journal entry enables others to aggregate your content. Podcast aggregators and special search tools currently under development by Google and like-minded search sites will also find your podcast if it resides here.

Here are a few other pertinent features of LiveJournal, shown in Figure 7.1. (Note that some are available only with the for-pay version.)

- LiveJournal comes with a built-in aggregator for weblogs as well as syndication protocols (RSS) that let you read news sources, including podcasts.

- Using LiveJournal, you can track statistics such as number of visitors and votes, and restrict journal entries to certain groups such as yourself and your friends.

- Discussion threads like those you find on Yahoo! message boards are supported.

- LiveJournal's profiling functionality enables you to advertise yourself and your podcasts by including a bio or resume, a mission statement that explains why your podcast matters, and a communication link to a proprietary text message gateway (which keeps your cell phone number private).

- LiveJournal enables you to interact with a community of close to four million people, making it a great platform for publicizing your podcast.

- You can use wizards and templates to alter the look and feel of your LiveJournal weblog.

- As your podcast grows and you decide to jump to a dedicated or shared host, you can embed your LiveJournal weblog into your own web page.

- LiveJournal is supported by Windows, Macs, and Linux.

- You don't have to open a web browser to post a LiveJournal entry.

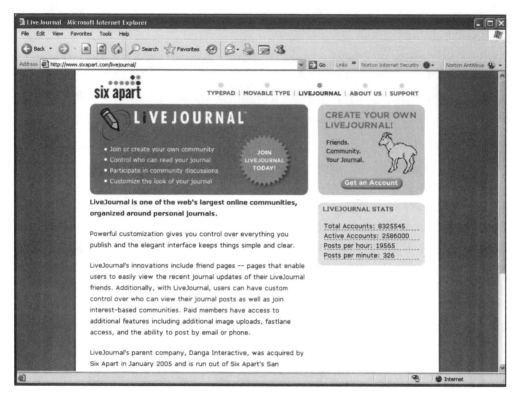

Figure 7.1 LiveJournal is a simple program that's easy to use.

MoveableType

MovableType—which provides a professional-grade weblogging platform that is also simple, flexible, and extensible—is for very serious webloggers. Because of its many features, MovableType (shown in Figure 7.2) is a heavyweight in the industry. These features include the following:

- MoveableType enables you to post a virtually unlimited number of weblogs. That means there can be a separate web page for every podcast you post on a weblog page.

- Each podcast can have its own profile, which gives your site an even greater professional appeal.

- MoveableType's weblog-management tools and interface are intuitive and easy to learn.

- If you wish, you can customize the MoveableType interface to make it more consistent with your weblogging and podcasting needs.

- Another way to customize the app is to add any of a vast array of free or low-cost MoveableType plug-ins from developers around the world.

- MoveableType supports most major operating systems including Windows, Mac, and Linux.
- MoveableType supports remote and secure online system access.
- To help you run your weblog more effectively, MovableType allows you to select between static (immovable type) page generation or dynamic (movable type) pages.

note

The folks at MovableType recommend that you optimize your weblog performance on a per-template basis, using static page generation for high-traffic pages that house RSS feeds, and dynamic pages for any archives. It's beyond the scope of this book to get into these technicalities, but the bottom line is that if you appreciate high-performance web sites, you'll appreciate this product feature. It's also highly beneficial for podcasting sites, which have structures that lend themselves to both static (i.e., podcasts with RSS feeds) and dynamic (i.e., older web pages) page generation.

- MovableType's design makes it easy for people to access your weblog, and each other.
- You can maximize your podcasts' exposure on MoveableType via the comments or TrackBacks features, which are discussion form tools that rival Yahoo!'s forums. Good word-of-mouth can be like a virus, spreading quickly across the Blogosphere.
- On MoveableType, readers can reply to your journal entries, and you can manage the traffic flow of the discussion board.
- You can subscribe to MovableType or look for it as a feature offered by a commercial weblog service or standard web page hosting service provider.
- MoveableType offers you the critical ability to publish feeds automatically—including podcast feeds.
- At the time of this writing, MovableType continues to build on syndication functionality. (In other words, it is going to support more multimedia and other bells and whistles in the future.) In the meantime, its templates currently support all common data syndication formats including XML formats like RSS and ATOM.

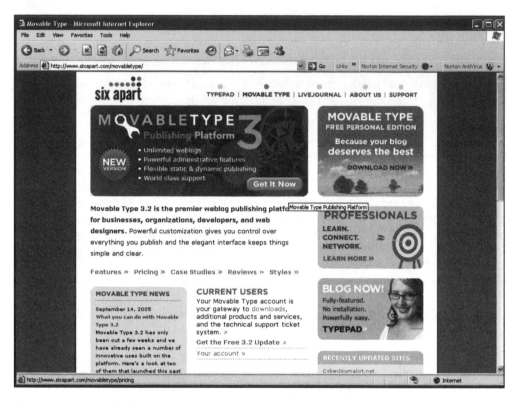

Figure 7.2 MovableType has a dynamic page generation option and a powerful interface.

TypePad

TypePad is yet another easy-to-use Six Apart tool that you can use to design your weblog and add podcasts, music, pictures, video, and more. If you already have a personal weblog, you can apply the TypePad template to it or apply the template to an altogether new weblog. TypePad also has community features much like those offered by MovableType. TypePad is geared to the everyday individual weblog and podcast publisher. Its services are much like those offered by Blog-City and other commercial services that I profile next. In contrast, MovableType is geared more toward corporate and professional use, or to those who take weblogging and podcasting *really* seriously! It comes with more features that are not found in most generic apps.

Blog-City

Blog-City (http://www.blogcity.com), another commercial weblog service, has a bit of a scrapbook feel to it because people use it to post their personal diaries, photos with comments, other multimedia, and of course podcasts. You can use Blog-City (see Figure 7.3) free of charge or upgrade to an enhanced account—the current monthly rate is $3.50—for more features. (For podcasts, the latter offers significantly better support.) It's easy to use, customizable, and compatible with most major computer operating systems. The site's community feature ensures that your podcast gets better exposure.

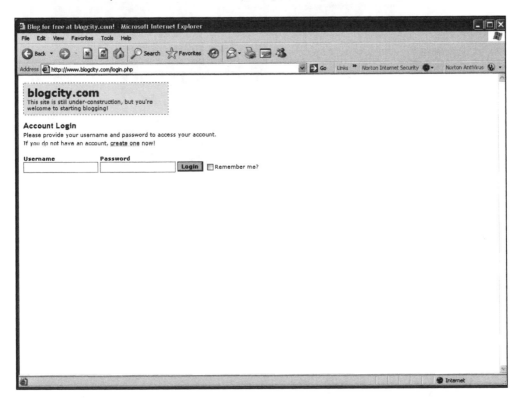

Figure 7.3 Blog-City supports the use of multimedia to enhance your podcast platform.

MSN Spaces

Microsoft is everywhere, and the world of weblogs and podcasting is no exception. MSN Spaces (http://www.msnspaces.comwww.msnspaces.com), shown in Figure 7.4, does all the basics: weblog creation, photo sharing, and moblogging (essentially, MSN Spaces enables you to use your mobile device to include photos to your weblog). I could go on, but frankly, with more than $300 billion sitting in the bank, I figure Microsoft can afford to run their own ads.

Figure 7.4 MSN Spaces supports moblogging and is easy to use.

Blogger.com

Although Blogger.com (http://www.blogger.com) is not as user-friendly as some other commercial weblog sites, that's in part because it's loaded with features (see Figure 7.5). These include:

- Blogger.com offers free image hosting of up to 300 megabytes, and allows for the posting of podcasts.

- Those who read your weblog or listen to your podcast can enter feedback about it. You can manage these comments on a post-by-post basis, deleting offensive material if you wish.

- If your podcast and weblog are group activities, you'll enjoy using Blogger.com's Watercooler Weblogs feature, which enables many users to post to a single weblog; with this feature, your group has its own space in which to share thoughts.

- You can use Blogger.com's Blogger Profiles feature to find weblogs of like-minded people. By the same token, you can employ Blogger.com's privacy features if you choose not to be found.

- Using a feature called AudioBlogger, you can call Blogger.com from any phone (not just a SmartPhone) and leave a message; Blogger.com will then convert your message to an MP3 audio file and post it on your weblog.

- The Blogger.com interface makes uploading a photo from your computer—or from the Web—as easy as a mouse click. Alternatively, you can attach photos to an email message you send to your own mail-to-blogger address.

- Blogger.com offers free moblogging with its BloggerMobile feature, which enables you to send images to your weblog while you're away from home or office. In addition, by using a mobile phone to send a message to go@blogger.com, you can automatically create a new weblog entry; to post a photo along with your text, simply attach a photo to the message as you would with an email message. If you wish, you can even use a phone to lay claim to any photos on your weblog by using a claim code that Blogger.com sends to you via phone.

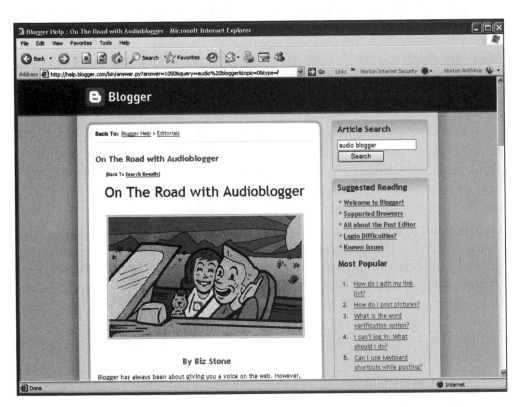

Figure 7.5 Blogger.com's AudioBlogger feature lets you post a message from any phone.

Odeo

Not a weblog service per se, Odeo is a hybrid of many of the types of sites I've discussed so far. It's a podcast directory, but it also lets you *create* podcasts, and even offers a specialized podcast hosting service. At the same time, Odeo, which is free for now (but likely to add fee-based features soon) has the look and feel of a commercial weblog service. And because Odeo is a community, allowing for comments and rankings of podcasts, you can enhance the exposure of your podcast just as you can with a weblog service.

So what does Odeo, shown in Figure 7.6, enable you to do?

- **Listen to podcasts on your computer.** Odeo acts as a podcast directory, providing featured channels, Top 10 lists, and a directory of new shows.

note

If you're looking for a quick introduction to listening to podcasts, using Odeo or any other directory is no easier than following the instruction in Part I of this book. In fact, going this route may indeed limit your reach because the only podcasts you'll find will be ones within the Odeo community and its partners. The only real benefit that Odeo offers over iPodder for listening to podcasts is the fact that you can get your feet wet online without having to download as many tools. But although you save time up front, you lose out big time by not using the many other time-saving features provided by traditional podcast aggregators.

- **Sync.** Most Odeo shows can be played through your browser, iTunes, and other desktop media channels. If you like an Odeo channel, a few clicks of the mouse let you subscribe. The shows go to your online queue, where you can manage your subscriptions. Then, you download the shows to your computer, and ultimately to your iPod or other MP3 player.

- **Create podcast productions.** At the time of this writing, this option was in testing mode. When this feature is up and running you'll be able to use a browser-based tool to record and create podcasts. You'll also be able to moblog by leaving voice-mail messages for others to hear. Although this may not be RSS-based, it may work to complement your podcast. You'll also be able to upload any MP3 audio to Odeo and have Odeo convert it to a podcast.

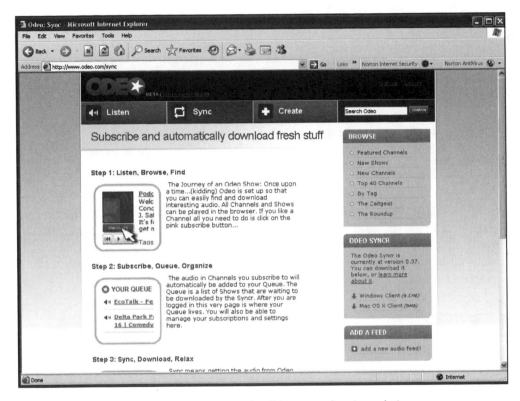

Figure 7.6 Odeo is soon to become a simple all-in-one podcasting solution.

Sure, other sites let you perform these tasks, but only a few let you do all three in one place. As I mentioned, however, Odeo isn't yet entirely operational. Because I want to get you up and running on your timeline—not Odeo's—I suggest you employ the more traditional approaches to listening to and creating podcasts as described throughout this book. That said, it won't hurt you to try the site out. It's so easy to use, taking a look at it won't lose you much time.

note

I predict that Odeo's features will remain quite basic for the next few years, but will evolve in time to include elements such as multimedia. In the meantime, you may find that Odeo is unable to keep up with your needs; proceed with caution if you are thinking of creating podcasts using this tool only! That said, this is a great site for beginners.

Castpost

Castpost isn't so much a commercial weblog service as a tool that's designed to *enhance* such a service. Specifically, Castpost, which works on both PCs and Macs, enables you to view your TV show or video clip, or listen to your podcast, from either an online and offline environment. In other words, you can access and enjoy content from your commercial weblog from your Castpost account or from an MP3 player like a Sony Network Walkman. That's because your Castpost account comes with an RSS feed that can be captured by most podcast aggregators. You can also send your video and audio clips to Castpost using avenues such as the web, your mobile phone, or even email.

You can use Castpost, shown in Figure 7.7, in conjunction with several different commercial weblog services, including Blogger, TypePad, MoveableType, and more. Because Castpost interfaces directly with your weblog service, there's no need to cut or paste HTML code. Castpost is currently in the testing phase, so it's free for now, and currently comes with unlimited bandwidth—which is especially useful if your podcasts include multimedia.

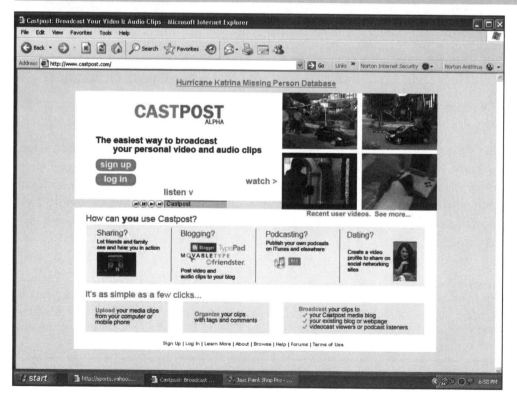

Figure 7.7 Castpost is geared to support commercial weblogs with rich multimedia.

Assessing Commercial Weblog Services

The criteria and principles that apply when evaluating shared and dedicated hosts are also relevant when assessing commercial weblog services that support podcasts. In other words, these commercial services ought to have scalability, lots of relevant features, the capability to let you use your own web address, strong customer service, feedback forums, and a suitable warranty. With commercial weblog services, however, you need to look for a few more specialized features that directly or indirectly relate to podcasts:

- A commercial weblog service should be simple to customize, easy to use, and application-rich.

- It's not a bad thing if the commercial weblog service is free, as long as it also offers enhanced "for-fee" packages. The free features will get you up and running; as you get better at podcasting, you'll be ready for more capacity and functionality without having to jump the commercial weblog service ship.

- Look for image hosting capacity (at least 50 megabytes) if you want to include multimedia with your podcasts.

- Commercial weblog services should support a wide variety of operating systems, including but not limited to Windows, Mac, and Linux. This signals that the service takes its business seriously; any business worth its salt will want to maximize its customer base.

caution

Because podcasting and open source go hand in hand, you should be especially suspicious of services that don't support Linux.

- Commercial weblog services should support all common data syndication formats like XML, including XML-based formats like RSS and ATOM.

- The weblog service's interface—that is, its main window and other screens where key functions reside—should be intuitive, well-designed, and interoperable with other weblog and podcast-related sites like Flickr (discussed in Chapter 6).

- The RSS feed, weblog-management tools, and multimedia management tools should likewise be intuitive.

- Good commercial weblog services will provide remote access and moblogging capabilities, dynamic pages, and a weblog community.

Weblog Managers

To manage your weblogs (whether they live on a shared or dedicated host or on a commercial weblog service), you'll need a special web or desktop application called, you guessed it, a *weblog manager*. Specifically, these apps let you edit the weblogs and podcasts you *create*; this is in contrast to aggregators, which obtain podcast feeds for you to *listen* to, and which are profiled in Chapter 8, "Podcasting Software," and Appendix A, "Resources."

Weblog managers come in two forms:

- **Web-based weblog managers.** Web-based weblog managers live on a web site—usually a commercial weblog service provider's site—instead of on your hard drive. You can use these apps to post a journal entry via a web browser or with online software applications designed specifically for weblogs; either way, the action occurs online. The advantage of web-based weblog managers is that they enable you to update your weblogs and podcasts remotely, either from a remote desktop or via moblogging with a SmartPhone; keep this advantage in mind when evaluating weblog-management apps and the hosts that provide them.

- **Desktop-based weblog managers.** Desktop-based weblog applications operate on your desktop, where they must be loaded and sometimes configured. You can use a desktop-based weblog manager offline to edit your weblog and podcasts (for example, add new podcasts); you can use the application to upload your new materials, preferences, and settings to the host web site or weblog when you go online. The host site interprets the instructions from the desktop-based weblog manager and updates your weblog and podcast feed information accordingly. With desktop-based weblog managers, one computer does all the work. If your computer crashes or is attacked by a virus, you may lose the data and settings that enable you to upload your next podcast (but it won't affect your existing and already-uploaded podcasts).

Uploading Your Podcast with a Weblog Manager

One example of a weblog manager is Radio Userland (http://www.userland.com). This desktop-based program is easy to use because it is intuitive and well designed. Moreover, Radio Userland recognizes that providing support for podcasting is essential to its success. For a fee, it also provides a hosting service, podcast-management capabilities, and reasonable storage space and podcast upload capacity. If you do opt to use Radio Userland's hosting service, you can upload your podcast to it by doing the following:

note

The instructions in this section focus on Radio Userland, but the principles behind them apply to other services.

note

Radio Userland hosts MP3 files that are smaller than 1 megabyte only. To determine whether your podcast is of a sufficiently small size, browse the MP3 file's properties. If your file is too large, you'll need to find a home for it on another host. (Follow the instructions supplied by your hosting service provider is to upload your podcast; the exact process will vary by host.)

1. After you've created, edited, tagged, and converted your podcast to MP3 format, open the Radio Userland application folder on your computer.

2. Locate the WWW subfolder and open it.

3. Inside the WWW subfolder, locate and open the CATEGORIES folder.

4. Launch Radio Userland.

5. In the main Radio Userland window or in your weblog workspace, open the PREFS menu, select News Aggregator, and choose RSS Enclosures.

6. In the dialog box that appears, mark the check box labeled "Check this box if you want to be able to add enclosures to your own output channels."

7. Click the SUBMIT button.

8. Still in the PREFS dialog box, click the RSS configuration option and mark any relevant check boxes. When you're finished, click the SUBMIT.

9. To place your podcast on Radio Userland's server, click the MP3 file and drag it to the GEMS folder on your hard drive. When your MP3 file is in the GEMS folder, it will automatically be uploaded to Radio Userland's server when you run Radio.

10. Ensure that the file has been uploaded by opening your weblog work page and viewing the FOLDERS menu. You'll see your folders, including the GEMS folder, listed; see if your MP3 podcast file is there.

11. Now that your MP3 file resides in the GEMS folder, you need to put its link in the RSS enclosure field. This field—which is blank except for the text http://—is located on your weblog home page, just below the field where you enter your weblog text. Suppose for the sake of example that the file you placed in the GEMS folder is named "MY.mp3"; in that case, you'd type `http://radio.weblogs.com/your-site#/gems/MY.mp3`, where `yoursite#` is your site's number.

12. Radio Userland doesn't accept blank weblogs, so you must type something meaningful in the blog field.

13. Click the Post to Weblog button. Your weblog should appear with a tiny speaker icon to the right. You can click the speaker to play your podcast!

14. To test your feed, open iPodder or another aggregator, add your feed, and see whether you can retrieve the podcast.

note

To find out how to download, rather than upload, MP3 files, see your software's user manual; each client is different.

Publicizing Your Podcasts

The whole point of podcasting is to get your message out. Sure, once your XML and RSS feed is posted online, some aggregators will pick up your show, but relying on that is like flying on a wing and a prayer. You have to be proactive, or all the time you spent creating, editing, and distributing your podcasts on expensive hosts will be for nothing!

There are a few different ways to publicize your podcast. One way is to use directories; another is to associate your podcast with a well-known commercial weblog service or specialized podcast hosting site. (Lots of aggregators and podcast search tools rank weblogs and podcasts that live on commercial weblog services and specialized podcasting hosts higher than their counterparts on "home-made" sites.) If your podcast resides on a web site that you built yourself, you'll need to adopt a more aggressive approach; at the very least, you'll need a written face (that is, a weblog) to accompany your podcast.

Publicizing Podcasts in Directories

Getting listed in the large and popular podcasting directories is key. These directories include but are not limited to the following:

- iPodder.org (http://ipodder.org)
- iPodderX.com (http://ipodderx.com)
- Podcast.net (http://podcast.net)
- Podcastalley.com (http://podcastalley.com)
- Podcastbunker.com (http://podcastbunker.com)
- Podcastcentral.com (http://podcastcentral.com)
- Podcastingnews.com (http://podcastingnews.com)
- Yahoo! Podcasts (http://podcasts.yahoo.com)
- Podnova.com (http://podnova.com)

tip

Find other podcast directories using search tools on Wikipedia (http://www.wikipedia.com) or Google. A search string such as `podcast directory` will generate many useful results. There are tons of them out there, and the number continues to grow.

To add your podcast to one of these directories, follow the online instructions. (Just be sure that you tested your XML and RSS feed first!) Make it a point to post regularly and include links back to your podcast. This will likely get noticed by the directory's manager, and may result in a feature of your podcast.

Publicizing Podcasts on Commercial Weblog Services or Specialized Podcast Hosts

The most obvious way to promote a podcast is to utilize the XML and RSS syndication functions available on most weblog, podcast, and related software (as well as online apps that are part of a commercial weblog service offering). That way, podcast listeners and weblog readers can subscribe to your productions and postings, and be alerted via email when a new podcast is posted. Whenever possible, try to add a link to your site on other weblogs in your weblog service's or podcast host's online community. This community-driven approach may result in viral marketing—the online version of word-of-mouth.

Publicizing Podcasts on Standard Web Sites

If you've opted for the do-it-yourself approach to podcast hosting, you'll need to take some additional steps to publicize your podcast. In particular, you can implement the traditional tools for generating publicity as well as online marketing.

Traditional Publicity

To get your name out, contact local and national newspaper and magazine editors and offer to write some informative articles related to your podcast topic. (Many newspaper editors are very receptive to new ideas and trends.) Then, in the article, refer readers to your web site. That alone can get you thousands of new listeners. In addition to the printed word, use word-of-mouth to generate interest in your podcast. Include your web address on special business cards, and distribute them at conventions, association meetings, trade and hobby shows, and any other locales where you're likely to find individuals who may share your interests.

Online Marketing

Here are some tips for getting your standard web site—including podcasts—noticed online:

- **Submit your web site to search engines.** Search engines are what most people use to find stuff online. Because most people read only the first page of results, and seldom click more than a handful of links on that page, getting a good ranking on search engines such as Google, Ask Jeeves, and others (including ones that specialize in your field of interest, which, ironically, can be located via a Google search) is imperative. To make sure a search engine returns your site in its results, you must first submit your site to that search engine. (Just follow the on-site instructions.) When you do, you'll be asked to supply some keywords that describe your site. If someone conducting a search enters one or more of your keywords, your site will appear in the search results—and the more keywords that match, the higher your site's ranking will be.

Google

Google is the king of search engines. It uses "spiders," which troll web sites looking for keywords, index content, track links, and rank results. Google and other search engines consider many factors during the ranking process, including number of web site hits, web page titles, the nature of the web site (e-commerce or personal), and a host of other factors. You can submit your site to Google free of charge, but if you want Google to feature your site as a premium listing, you'll need to pay up. Because new sites may emerge that supersede yours, you should make it a point to submit your site for inclusion on a regular basis.

- **Submit your web site to directories.** Earlier, I listed with some podcast-specific directories and related resources. You should absolutely add your site to these directories. In addition to those, there are also mega directories, like Yahoo!'s, which list just about everything under the sun. Research suggests that almost half of all web-site visits stem from Yahoo! searches and directory listings. Unfortunately, Yahoo! charges a fee to list sites; unless you are a serious podcaster, this option probably isn't for you. If, however, your web site's primary purpose is commercial in nature, and your podcast is an add-on rather than the focal point, then this option may be great.
- **Use a for-fee service to submit your site to multiple search engines.** For example, Google AdSense charges a fee to get a good ranking within its own search results, while SearchLeads.com asserts that, for a fee, it will place your web site near the top of search return pages of the most popular search engines. This shotgun approach may not work well if your podcast is very specialized in nature. If, however, it covers a more general topic, you may find it worth your while to use one of these services.

- **Use meta tags to attract spiders.** *Meta tags* are coded keywords that do not appear on a browser, but are caught by spiders. Adding meta tags to your site improves the chances of a search engine spider noticing it in a search.

caution

Be cautious when developing meta tags because the text in these tags is often what people see in search results. Don't insert cheesy or second-rate tags just to get better hits. Sure, adding a Paris Hilton tag will boost your hits, but if your podcast is about snow-plowing techniques, your motives will be transparent and highly unappreciated.

- **Be an active participant in newsgroups that relate to your specialty to make a name for yourself.** That said, don't spam (an unabashed attempt to promote or sell yourself or your product or service). Be subtle and professional. Adding contact information will help bring visitors to your site, and boost the odds of them listening to your podcast!

- **Participate in discussions on related weblogs.** If your podcast is about fly-fishing, then fellow fly-fishing enthusiasts who read your forum posting may find their way to *your* weblog and podcast.

- **Make regular updates to your journal.** Doing so draws attention from search engines. It also trains your visitors to check back often for new entries and new podcasts.

- **Make and use custom podcast logos on your web site.** One way to do this is to use graphic tools such as those found at FeedForAll. This custom logo will make it clear to your visitors just where the feed is located.

- **Pay attention to your podcast page's design.** Add strong visuals, well-structured show notes, and a brief but informative description of your podcasts.

- **Create a podcast promo.** This is similar to a TV commercial in nature and length. Then, see about exchanging promos with others—that is, offering to add their promo on your site if they'll place yours on theirs. Bartering this way is a no-cost way of generating publicity.

note

Podcastpromos.com (http://www.podcastpromos.com) is a repository of links to podcast promos, and offers a great way to circulate and exchange promos.

Coming Up Next...

This chapter outlined the various hosting options available to you, including some of the top players in the podcasting field. It also presented criteria for assessing which hosting solution is for you. In addition, you saw how podcasts could be uploaded, and discovered strategies for promoting your podcasts. The next chapter returns to the topic of finding and listening to podcasts by profiling in detail some of the podosphere's most powerful and useful podcast aggregators and other tools.

PART THREE

PODCAST SOFTWARE, HARDWARE, AND VIDEO WEBLOGGING

CHAPTER 8

PODCASTING SOFTWARE

This chapter explores the growing world of podcasting software, which includes aggregators, RSS readers, podcatchers, feed readers, hybrid aggregators, and other programs with *Star Trek*–type names. (Don't get hung up on the terminology here, or you'll get dizzy. If your head starts to spin, don't panic. Just look up the offending term in the glossary at the back of the book.) Because one of the key purposes of this book is to get you up and running now (hence the title, Podcasting Now!), I'll focus on the more common software available today for all computers and MP3 devices. Whether you're a Mac addict, a Linux geek, or a Windows fanatic, I'll fill you in on the relevant software and all the bells and whistles that come with it. I'll also outline the key criteria for determining which software is for you.

note

> The driving force behind the growth of aggregators and other podcasting software is the fact that much of it is based on open source code. *Open source* means that the code used in the software is out in the open, for all to see. (This stands in contrast to *proprietary software*, which software companies tend to want to keep secret. Microsoft Word is a good example of a type of proprietary software.) Some podcasting programs improve upon existing open source code, while others simply build a brand new mousetrap based on the principles and ideas behind the open source code.

Aggregators Explained

Aggregators are pieces of software that tell your computer and MP3 devices what to do. They are the boss. The premise behind aggregators is that they collect *syndicated* content, such as RSS and other XML feeds. Like a syndicated TV show, reruns of podcasts are available to all who know how to find them. These podcasts can be anywhere—on a commercial weblog site, mainstream media sites, college sites, Internet radio, satellite radio, and more. The RSS, ATOM, and other feed code functions like a channel number, accessible with your aggregator, which acts like a remote control.

Aggregators are important because they trim the time you'd otherwise spend searching for podcasts of interest. Here's how it works: Aggregators subscribe to a feed, much like you subscribe to a pay TV channel. The software then trolls for new content at intervals you define. It retrieves that content and manages how it is organized and sized. That is, your desired podcast is "pulled" to you. Aggregators do the legwork required to get updates of your favorite podcasts for you, even as you do something else. They also make it easy to unsubscribe from an RSS feed.

note

> You can plug aggregator functions into other client software such as Firefox, Explorer, Outlook, blog-creation programs, or MP3 media player programs. Likewise, many mobile phones and video recorders that aggregate TV programs likely utilize XML and other special aggregators. At the end of the day, though, content processed by aggregator software will usually be in a syndicated feed format like XML.

Just as there are many different types of cars—some run on diesel and have few extras, while others run on high-octane gas and are fully loaded—there are several makes and models of podcast aggregators, each meeting a different need. One such model is the iPodder aggregator, which you read about in Chapter 2, "Listening to Podcasts." Other podcast aggregators fill different needs. For example, some are bare-bone programs that are supported only by Windows while others can be used on all types of computers and are chock full of functionality and features. Indeed, some of the more powerful aggregators enable you to subscribe not just to audio, but also to video, text, documents, newscasts, satellite radio, images, and more!

note

> A lot of information about specific software features—as well as user discussion forums—can be found on the web site or weblog where you download a particular podcast aggregator. These resources go into detail that is beyond the scope of this book.

While there are many makes and models of aggregators, all fall into two main categories:

- **Desktop-based aggregators.** As you probably guessed, desktop-based aggregators reside on your desktop. Examples of desktop aggregators include BottomFeeder, Sage, and NewsMonster. The downside of using desktop-based aggregators is that they tend to involve a bit more of a learning curve than their web-based counterparts. On the other hand, most desktop-based aggregators display content in a user-friendly and visually appealing way. Many look like email programs, except that they handle podcasts; others look like web browsers, except that they operate on your local computer and you have lots of control over the commands. Regardless of their appearance, desktop-based aggregators obtain syndicated content for you, manage your subscriptions, and help you sync with your MP3 device. Some desktop aggregators possess aggregator functionality in addition to their main purpose, which can be web browsing, email, blog editing, or media playing.

- **Web-based aggregators.** Like with desktop aggregators, web-based aggregators routinely troll RSS and other feeds for updates. Examples of web-based aggregators include Kinja, MyYahoo!, and iNews Torrent. These aggregators, which are typically hosted on ISP servers, mega-portals like Yahoo!, or podcast Goliaths like iTunes, offer full functionality. They do all the work; you just sit back, point, and click. Even better, because they live on the Internet, you can access them from anywhere. That said, using a web-based aggregator means you lose some degree of control. Things are done their way or no way at all. Worse, choice of content may be limited; directories they associate with may be restricted to paying podcast-posting customers. In addition, service reliability could be at risk.

Aggregator Software for Windows

In this section, I'll discuss podcast aggregator software that's geared toward the Windows operating system for PCs. As I present this mainstream software, I'll do so wearing the twin lenses of *support requirements* and *notable features*. That means I'll mostly limit my discussion to new or dominant features that are not found in the majority of competing aggregator products. I'll also throw in my opinion, especially in those cases where I've had a chance to kick the software's tires.

note

Some of this software (also referred to as *clients*) in this section may also be cross-platform, meaning it also works on Mac and/or Linux operating systems.

iPodder (http://ipodder.sourceforge.net)

I know, I know, you already read about iPodder in Chapter 1, "Getting Started with Podcasting," and Chapter 2, "Listening to Podcasts." Why again? Fair enough. But some extra features merit attention:

- Of course, iPodder has the generic ability to download selections of shows and music to play on iPods, other portable digital media players, or computers. It supports RSS protocols like ATOM and others.

- In addition to being cross-platform compatible, which not too many other podcast clients can boast, iPodder supports BitTorrent downloads. In fact, iPodder ships with BitTorrent functionality included. (Read: You don't have to hunt down software add-ons in Tucows.) If BitTorrent is in fact needed, iPodder will trigger its functionality. After it does, you'll be able to get faster BitTorrent downloads. This will come in especially handy as podcasts become more sophisticated in the future (including stuff like video, images, and documents).

- With iPodder, importing and exporting OPML files is possible, extending the power of iPodder to do more.

- One reason I use iPodder is because it automatically downloads my files to my iTunes desktop media player. I can then manage things myself from there. (More on iTunes later in this chapter.)

- The folks behind iPodder are hard at work with development projects. One project under development at the time of this writing was the construction of a super database to track broadcast feeds based on keywords. It'll be sort of like when you type a search term (instead of a URL) right into the address field of your web browser and receive list of web sites or are immediately directed to the most relevant one.

Doppler (http://dopplerradio.net)

Yup, Doppler is an aggregator. It's for Windows, but it supports imports to both Windows Media Player and Apple's iTunes. In fact, you *could* use both players at the same time by tweaking the file extensions that specify the media player to which files are added. Synchronizing multiple MP3 devices with one client is also possible with Doppler. Like iPodder, it will load files automatically into your desired MP3 media player. Here are a few other key features of Doppler:

- Using Doppler, you can locate podcasts yourself (for example, by cutting and pasting the URL of the web site's RSS or XML feed) or browse directories of podcasts.

- Doppler's built-in feed parser lets you review a podcast show's outline notes within its GUI.

- Doppler is open source. That means the client's source programming instructions are publicly and readily available—which means some techno-geek may take it on to build a better mousetrap.

- Doppler's OPML import function lets you add several RSS sites at a time. You can also create and tailor playlists within your media player to stay organized.

- If you are short on time, Doppler lets you download only the most recent episode of a podcast. This is especially useful if the program is time-sensitive, as is often the case with news feeds (after all, news becomes "old" after only a few days). In other words, you don't want your aggregator sucking up bandwidth to pick up old news stories. Additionally, if you're low on bandwidth, you can set the client to place a limit on the file-download size.

- When it comes to cleanup, Doppler does a better job than most aggregators. It removes files that are older than a pre-determined date of your choice. You can also reduce podcast overload in Doppler by setting the maximum number of downloads that can occur at the same time.

Microsoft .NET Framework

Some Windows podcast clients, like Doppler, require you to download and run the Microsoft .NET Framework (see Figures 8.1–8.3 to grasp the Doppler download process). According to Microsoft, the .NET Framework provides improved scalability and performance, support for mobile device development, support for Internet Protocol Version 6 (a next-generation web structure), better online communication, and robust connectivity to information databases. In short, it sets the stage for podcast clients to become greater in power, reach, and excitement. The .NET Framework's Version 1.1 Redistributable Package includes everything you need to run applications developed using the .NET Framework. To get it, visit http://www.microsoft.com, click the Downloads icon, and use the search tool with the keyword string .NET Framework Version 1.1.

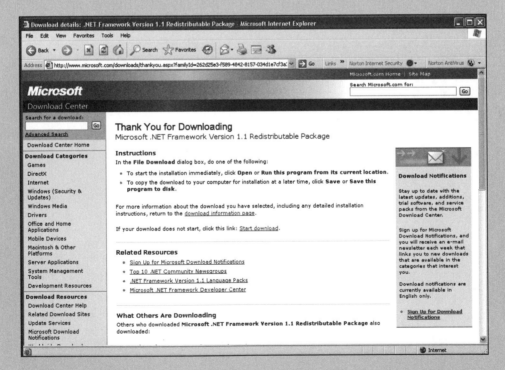

Figure 8.1 Doppler asks you to go to Microsoft's web site to download the Microsoft .NET Framework.

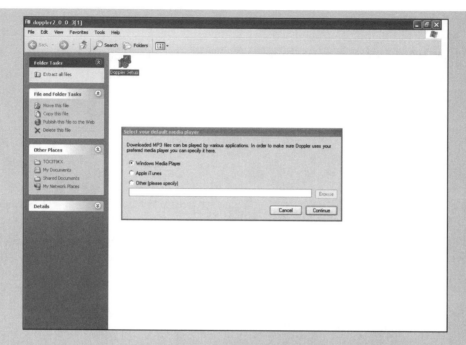

Figure 8.2 You can tell Doppler where you want it to load your podcasts.

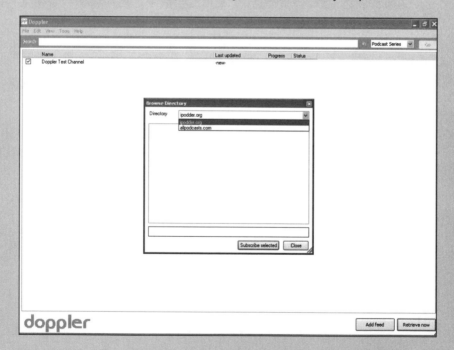

Figure 8.3 Voilá! Simple but powerful. Once Doppler is loaded, you'll see this window.

jPodder (http://jpodder.com)

Like Doppler, jPodder for Windows is an open source podcast aggregator, supporting both Windows Media Player and Apple iTunes. The jPodder interface is appealing to the eye, and its built-in directory is reasonably complete (it uses the searchable iPodderX directory, which you can also find at http://www.ipodderx.com/directory). Using jPodder, you can listen to and create podcasts via its Personal Feeds and Podcast Production tabs, respectively. Figure 8.4 shows the jPodder web site, providing a glimpse of the many features that jPodder offers.

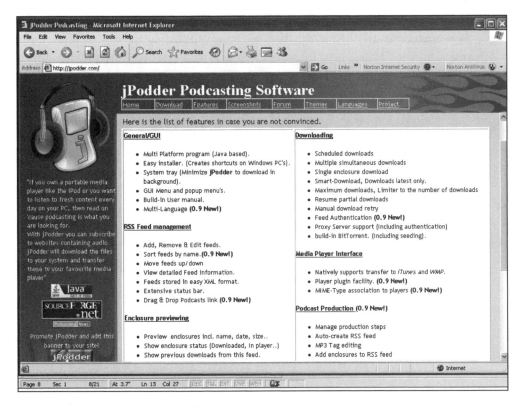

Figure 8.4 jPodder is all about features.

jPodder has many features that are similar to those found with other aggregators. For example, like most other clients, jPodder lets you cut and paste the URLs of RSS feeds that you select. And like Doppler, jPodder enables you to set the maximum number of downloads that can occur at the same time, as well as synchronize multiple MP3 devices. But while other aggregators have similar features, jPodder stands out with extras such as a Java engine. Java provides podcast client developers with access to even more tools, resulting in more feature-rich podcasting clients. But as with many Java-linked applications, you need a powerful computer to enjoy the benefits Java provides. Don't run jPodder if you use an older operating system such as Windows 98 or Mac OS 9; otherwise, you may experience an occasional computer crash.

One limitation of jPodder is that BitTorrent capability is not built-in. You must download BitTorrent (http://www.bittorrent.com) before using jPodder so that when jPodder calls it, it already resides on your computer.

Nimiq (http://nimiq.nl)

Nimiq runs on Windows and supports both Windows Media Player and Apple iTunes. It's very simple to use and has good functionality, including OPML readiness, as shown in Figures 8.5 and 8.6. The OPML feed browser is linked to an active podcast directory. (Although when I tried to access the directory, it was a hit or miss proposition; sometimes the server worked, and sometimes it didn't.)

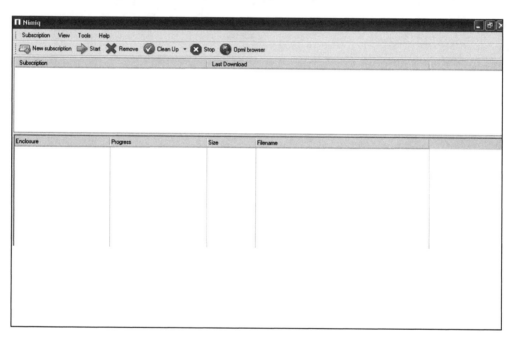

Figure 8.5 Nimiq's main window.

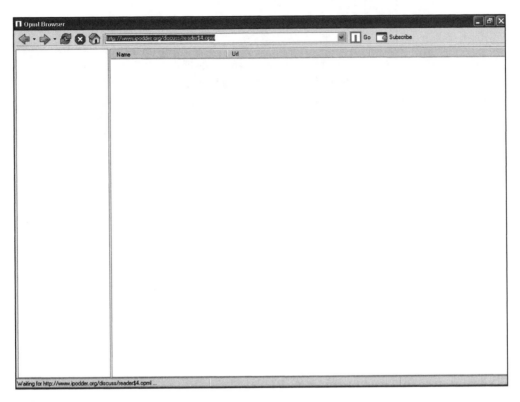

Figure 8.6 Nimiq's OPML window.

Like almost all aggregators, Nimiq enables you to subscribe to podcasts. But unlike all podcast clients, Nimiq has a scheduling function that lets you determine when and how often Nimiq trolls for new podcasts—and you can restrict the number of downloads performed at the scheduled time. This feature helps reduce the volume of information and time spent on podcasts.

OPML Sesame

Extensible Markup Language (XML) denotes many different kinds of data. Its role is to ensure the smooth sharing of data across different connected computer systems. OPML (Outline Processor Markup Language) is an XML format created by the folks who developed Radio Userland (discussed in Chapter 7, "Hosting and Promoting Your Podcasts"). OPML is a base file format for an outliner program. (An *outliner program* is a text-editing tool that permits the grouping of text in sections that are organized in a hierarchy, or tree structure. Outliner programs have several uses, including the exchange of lists of RSS feeds between RSS clients.) The OPML standard or protocol defines an outline as a hierarchical and organized list of data. The specification is open, making it useful for organizing many types of list data such as playlists and directories. As fascinating as all this is, you may be wondering, "So what?" OPML is becoming a standard format for podcasting directories. OPML means better file access, feature-rich podcasting clients, better multimedia support, and organized data. Also, although RSS retrieves tons of news, not everything is newsworthy. Things that don't change, like the letters of the alphabet; or things that change slowly, like the offensive roster of the Indianapolis Colts, should not be caught as news. OPML editors excel at capturing *change*. Enough said.

HappyFish (http://thirstycrow.net/happyfish)

HappyFish runs on Windows machines under the Microsoft .NET Framework (Version 1.1). It manages and can support virtually every type of information enclosure—podcasts, MP3 music files, videos, special applications, images, news headlines, documents, and more. Moreover, it can operate behind the scenes while you do something else on, or are away from, your computer. That's because HappyFish can automatically check your podcast downloads for new enclosures based on a minute, hour, or day interval that you choose. Alternatively, you can be more precise and ask it to update, say, every Friday at 2:55 AM.

HappyFish includes the capability to sync content to most USB-based external storage devices (such as the SD-Card or CF-Card) or MP3 devices (such as an iPod or Rio). You determine the criteria that suit your needs. If your player has loads of memory, sync the whole library. If it has limited memory, you can pick and choose files based on file size and preference. HappyFish also supports the download of podcasts to multiple devices.

Like with a Palm PDA, HappyFish lets you automatically sync your device as soon as you attach it to your computer or laptop. And as with some other clients, you can first screen the enclosures (content) before you download them. This enables you to pick and choose, thereby saving time and saving space on your storage media and devices. As an added bonus, the included Web browser lets you get RSS feeds without having to open up another browser.

iPodder.NET (http://ipodder.net)

iPodder.NET runs on Windows. Like HappyFish, iPodder.NET requires the Microsoft .NET Framework Version 1.1. It supports iTunes and can automatically transfer podcasts into iTune's library—and ultimately to your MP3 device. It has a lot of the classic iPodder functions, so I won't go into information overload here. The key point is that it's free and can do just a little bit more than iPodder's vanilla version due to .NET functionality.

Now Playing
(http://brandon.fuller.name/archives/hacks/nowplaying)

Like many of the aggregators discussed so far, Now Playing runs on Windows and supports iTunes or Windows Media Player. What is different about Now Playing is that it is not a discrete program. Rather, it's a plug-in for a version of Windows Media Player or iTunes that resides on a Windows machine. *Plug-ins* integrate added features or functions into a web browser, web site, or various computer programs.

Now Playing is geared toward downloading music podcasts more than anything else (although it does download voice-only podcasts as well). This is reflected in its special features. For example, its Amazon tab lets you connect to an area on Amazon.com where you can access all sorts of electronic and podcast-friendly data, including e-books and music. Now Playing also creates an XML file with song information that you can read in iTunes, and lets you retrieve, if available, the album image cover art from Amazon.com. In addition, you'll find a link to the Amazon.com page that relate to the CD that features the song in which you are interested, and a link to the Apple iTunes Music Store product page with the song highlighted.

You can also plug Now Playing into your own web site for your visitors to use. In other words, when someone visits your web page or weblog, Now Playing can display the song currently launched and playing, as well as recently played tracks. Users can in turn take advantage of the aforementioned features.

Special News Aggregators

Some aggregators specialize in delivering news. One such service is NewsGator (http://www.newsgator.com), which is less a program and more a full-service company that also happens to provide a great news aggregator. NewsGator is for serious podcasters! It provides an integrated and synchronized reading and viewing experience across multiple media including the Web, mobile phones, and email clients. One thing that makes NewsGator special is that it works within Microsoft Outlook. That is, you can access and read news attachments via email. (Although NewsGator's web-based aggregator is free, the company's Mobile Edition services, which enable you to read your news feeds on your phone or PDA, and special Email Edition services cost money—about $50 annually for the Platinum plan.) Here are a few of NewsGator's key features, which are offered free of charge:

- Using NewsGator, you can read your news, a key focal area of the client, using Windows Media Center.

- Automatic news feed subscription is as easy as clicking a NewsGator button.

- NewsGator offers a powerful feed keyword search capability, enabling you to search more 10,000,000 weblogs, as well as news, information, entertainment, and sports feeds.

- You can browse for feeds using the app's browsing section.

- NewsGator can recommend content based on your pre-set preferences.

- NewsGator's BlogRolls feature enables you to automatically display any news feeds you read on your own weblog.

If you opt for one of NewsGator's fee-based plans (these are geared more toward corporate clients, but others can use them too), you'll have access to a special feature called FeedDemon, which is a leading desktop RSS reader for Windows that integrates with Feedster, Flickr, and Bloglines—three very popular RSS-based services. This feature-rich news aggregator supports automatic updates to both Windows Media Player and iTunes. FeedDemon's easy-to-read newspaper display gets you informed in a visually appealing way, and the program makes it easy to download audio to your iPod or other MP3 player. In addition, alert features are available, and news bins store your selected feeds for future reference.

NewsGator isn't the only news aggregator around; another is Newstex (http://www.newstex.com), which provides content on demand. This includes tailored, real-time news and commentary from thousands of branded newswires, newspapers, magazines, business sources, government feeds, and weblogs. It captures full-text news feeds, standardizes the way content is presented, and quickly delivers the result as easy-to-integrate XML or RSS newsfeeds.

Podcast Aggregators for Macs

Why is it that so many of the greatest software applications seem to get their start on an Apple computer? Is it because the best and brightest of the tech world also happen to be Mac-heads, refusing to assimilate into the more structured world of Microsoft? No one knows for sure. One thing we *do* know, however, is that once the folks at Microsoft get wind of a tech trend, they build it into their own operating system. True, they usually improve on a product—but only after parroting the concept. The only real platform that both Apple and Microsoft can run on is the fact that podcasting aggregators for both systems are essentially the same. In this section, I discuss some of the oft-used aggregators that are geared to Macs. Some are outright Apple software products, while others are cross-platform programs with the brains to operate a PC, but a heart that's loyal only to a Mac! Following are some of the Mac world's rising stars of podcasting.

iTunes 4.9 (http://itunes.com)

Not long ago, Apple pulled an arrow across the bow of the podcasting world and announced what was inevitable—iTunes media player now has podcast aggregator functionality. Although this was another Apple masterstroke, it was not one that took anyone by surprise. Why? Because even though Apple's market share of MP3 devices has been diluted by new entrants such as Sandisk, its iPods *still* represent almost 50 percent of the MP3 player market; in other words, Apple continues to have a stranglehold on the podcasting device market. At the same time, Apple's iTunes is a leader in podcasting's software space. In fact, with Apple's recent introduction of iPod Video, the stage is set for RSS-based video weblog (vlog) feeds to be played on portable devices. This would represent a very big but highly likely technological leap. I discuss the exciting and evolving world of vlogging in Chapter 10, "The Leading Edge of Podcasting." Indeed, iTunes has functions that Windows Media Player simply cannot touch. The natural thing for Apple was to build a bridge to podcasts that runs through the heart of iTunes. These days, one of the simplest ways to get a podcast *now* is to use iTunes (http://www.itunes.com); it does everything for you with a few clicks of the mouse. Let's take a very important test drive.

To access the iTunes podcast directory and to download podcasts quickly, first click the Podcasts icon directly below the Library icon in the iTunes main window. When you see the main podcast window, click the Podcast Directory link in the bottom-left part of the window (you may need to scroll down to see it), shown in Figure 8.7. What you see next is a list of popular podcasts as depicted in Figure 8.8 (you may have to wait a few seconds for stuff to appear, so don't panic if it doesn't pop up right away); I selected a series of movie reviews, as shown in Figure 8.9.

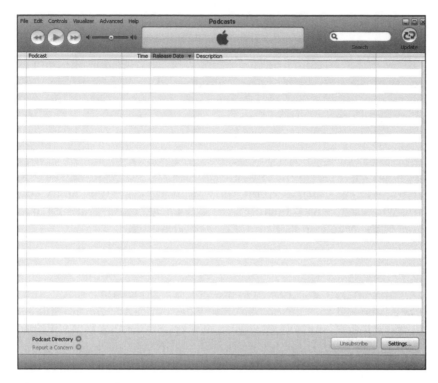

Figure 8.7 iTune's main podcast window is waiting for your selections.

Figure 8.8 iTune's colorful and full directory helps you choose your podcast.

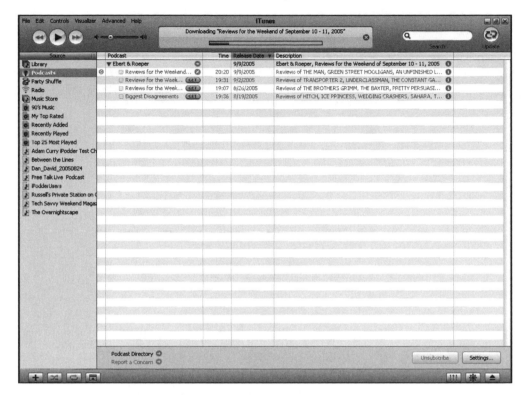

Figure 8.9 Ebert and Roeper weigh in on some movies.

iTunes 4.9 lets you set preferences such as the frequency, timing, and extent of podcast downloads, as shown in Figure 8.10. To get there, open the Edit menu on the iTunes Podcast screen (refer to Figure 8.7) and select Preferences. It also lets you direct what gets placed on your iPod and boasts important parental control options. You can access podcasts outside iTune's Podcast Directory by opening the Advanced menu and choosing Subscribe to Podcast, resulting in the URL input dialog box shown in Figure 8.11.

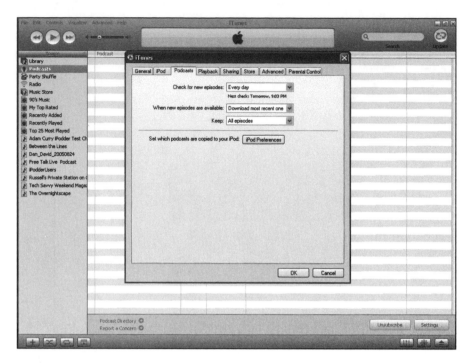

Figure 8.10 Podcast now, or later.

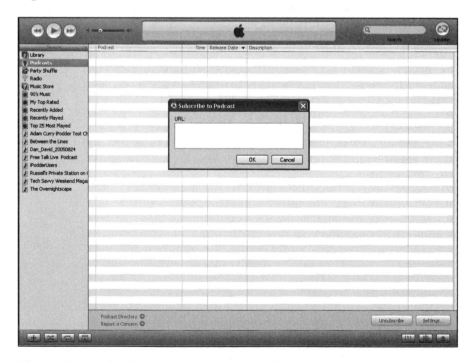

Figure 8.11 Using iTunes, you can grab any podcast you like, even one that is located outside the huge iTunes Podcast Directory.

In summary, using iTunes, you can browse, search, sample, and subscribe to thousands of podcasts featured in the iTunes directory (which has about 10,000 free podcasts, ranging from ABC News to John Q. Public's first foray into the podcast arena) as well as podcasts found elsewhere. Once you subscribe to a podcast, iTunes automatically does the behind-the-scenes stuff, trolling for updates and downloading new podcast episodes to your Mac or PC. With iTunes, you can also automatically organize and update your podcast library. It's easy to sync your podcasts to your MP3 device, enabling you to listen to them any time and any place. iTunes even lets you publish your own podcasts in its burgeoning directory. This directory is a critical stopping point for any podcaster—whether he or she listens to or creates podcasts! It's big, easy-to-use, and represents a great way to get your own podcast noticed.

iPodderX (http://ipodderx.com)

Unlike many of the aggregators I've discussed so far, iPodderX for Macs comes at a price: $19.95. So what do you get for the price of eight Big Macs? In truth, what the iPodderX offers is not so different from the features included with other aggregators. For example, Apple iTunes support is a given. In addition, iPodderX has a search function. That said, it does do a few things *really* well:

- iPodderX picks up a wide range of information, including podcasts, news, video, images, documents, or anything else that can be wrapped into an RSS feed.

- iPodderX employs RSS and ATOM newsfeeds to automatically provide up-to-date content to your desktop. It's like having a newspaper.

- iPodderX's NewsCaster function translates any text-based news into an audio podcast—in other words, it "reads" the news—or any other text-based feed—to you. That means you can listen to the news on the way to work on your iPod or other mobile MP3 device. It's also a great way to follow news about World Cup soccer games, especially when they're being played across the globe in Europe!

- Using iPodderX's space-saving utility, you can prevent your hard drive from filling up with outdated podcasts. Simply set the amount of space you would like to dedicate to your podcasts, and old files will be eliminated.

- A playlist builder feature lets you quickly create iTunes playlists or iPhoto albums with your downloaded podcasts and images. Select the podcast data you want to import, click Create, and your album or playlist is generated.

- Using iPodderX's full-screen video provides for an enhanced podcasting experience.

Watch for this app to soon support RSS vlog feeds for the new iPod Video device.

PoddumFeeder (http://www.macupdate.com/info.php/id/16546)

Although PoddumFeeder will set you back $4.95, it does have many great features:

- PoddumFeeder includes full and complete information about feeds to which you are subscribed.

- Using PoddumFeeder, you can convert MP3 files into AAC, making it easy to index segments of podcasts with placemarkers.

AAC

When you download music from the iTunes Store and other commercial music sites, it's likely to be in Advanced Audio Coding (AAC) format, which is supported by iTunes media player. The AAC format provides better compression and sound quality than does MP3, but like MP3, it is a form of lossy compression. That means certain frequencies of sound are eliminated during the encoding process (hence the "lossy"). AAC encoding is considered to produce very good sound.

- PoddumFeeder enables you to email a podcast. Just click the Email a Podcast URL button to forward a podcast feed URL to others without having to open Outlook or another email application.

- You can use the Download Fewer Podcasts and Download More Podcasts sliders to calibrate the number of podcasts to download on a feed-by-feed basis.

PlayPod (http://iggsoftware.com/playpod)

Although you can use PlayPod free for a trial period, it costs $16.99 after that. That said, PlayPod, which is built for the powerful Mac OS X platform and is simple to run, offers a bit of everything. One particularly notable feature is its built-in tutorial, which makes it easy to get up and running—especially if you are new to podcasting. Other special features include the following:

- PlayPod has a picture-in-picture three-window format, with a window for a directory, a window for directory files, and a window for the media player. It's visually appealing.

- PlayPod's media player window works not only to play files, but also as an information repository that describes the nature of files that are about to be downloaded. That means that you can check out a podcast prior to actually downloading it.

- PlayPod enables integration with iTunes. For example, after you've downloaded a podcast, you can instruct PlayPod to automatically transfer the podcast files to iTunes. You can also set genres and playlists, and convert your podcasts to AAC-bookmarkable files that can later be edited.

- PlayPod has a built-in text-to-speech feature, which converts weblogs or news headlines into audio files; you can then ship these audio files to your iPod and listen to news.

- A built-in directory makes it easy to find podcasts of interest.

- Style and Apple go hand in hand, so it's no surprise that a good Mac aggregator like PlayPod would let you customize how podcasts and news items are previewed. You can select from some built-in styles.

- With PlayPod, you can schedule downloads, back up and restore your RSS feeds, and browse news items and podcasts before downloading.

iPodder for Mac

The iPodder aggregator on your Mac has the same look, feel, and functionality as the one for Windows, which I described in Chapter 2 and other parts of the book. It is very user-friendly and has many features; I won't waste your time by repeating those features here.

Podcasting Software for Linux

Some aggregators are designed to support open source operating systems, the biggest being Linux. Linux can be run on most PCs and on certain versions of the Mac. (You need to check the specifications of your Mac to see if Linux can be installed; in general, however, newer Macs support Linux operating systems.) This section reviews a few podcast clients for Linux.

CastGrab (http://developer.berlios.de/forum/forum.php?forum_id=11481)

CastGrab, best used in a desktop environment, is written in Practical Extraction and Report Language (Perl), which is freely available for Unix, Macintosh, OS/2, and other operating systems. Perl has very good text-manipulation and code recognition functionality, making it great for grabbing a more complete set of newscasts and other RSS feeds. Perl is both glue and gateway between systems, databases, and users, so it's great for podcasting. In other words, it promotes interconnectivity. At the time of this writing, CastGrab was in its fifth beta testing; keep your eyes open for increased functionality in the months to come. One additional pending function is recognition of RSS feeds for vlogs, which are discussed more fully in Chapter 10.

BashPodder (http://linc.homeunix.org:8080/scripts/bashpodder)

BashPodder is designed to run primarily on Macs (but can also run in Windows, Solaris, Net Open, and FreeBSD). It is a very basic open source aggregator, and was designed to be fast and simple to use. Because it is open source, all are welcome to add and remove stuff from the code in order to modify and improve it. Notable features include a directory, a search feature, and the ability to schedule downloads of subscribed podcasts. In addition, BashPodder supports BitTorrent, which enables it to handle large multimedia files very well. Best of all, BashPodder comes with great instructions for installing and using the program, which is handy in the sometimes complex world of Linux.

In order to use BashPodder, you must attach three files (for specific instructions, see the BashPodder web site):

- **bashpodder.shell.** This is the main program.
- **parse_enclosure.xsl.** This is an XSL style sheet for grabbing enclosure info.
- **bp.conf.** This podcast config list contains the application's preferences and other settings.

One drawback of BashPodder is that downloading podcasts into your mobile MP3 device is tricky at first because it requires a few more steps and mouse clicks than other aggregators. Once you set your preferences and get the hang of it, however, it's easy to transfer files from that point on.

jPodder Linux (http://jpodder.com)

jPodder Linux is as feature-rich as the Windows version, except that it does not support Windows Media Player. (To get around that, you can use another Linux-friendly player, many of which are available on Tucows.) In addition to acting as an aggregator, you can use jPodder to listen to podcasts (via the Personal Feeds tab) as well as create them (via the Podcast Production tab). jPodder Linux makes it easy to edit downloaded or created podcasts, auto-create an RSS feed, edit MP3 tags, add enclosures to RSS feeds, launch a recorder, execute FTP file transfers, and even test RSS feeds.

Notable interface features include Java, popup menus, multi-lingual support, feed editing, and drag-and-drop functionality. Enclosure previewing—that is, the ability to see code elements and other items that are normally invisible—can be done for podcast elements like names, date, size, previous downloads from a given feed, and scheduled download settings. Memory control features enable you to opt to download only the latest podcast of a subscription, specify maximum downloads, and perform other management functions. Feed authentication is a recent feature, and BitTorrent is built-in. In the near future, jPodder Linux is expected to support transfers to iTunes and Windows Media Player.

Podcast Aggregators for the Mobile Internet

The mobile Internet is big, real, and has finally arrived. A big part of the mobile Internet is the devices that make it happen—SmartPhones, PDAs, BlackBerries, Treos, cell phones with MP3, and so on. In addition to making it possible for us to connect to the Internet, these devices also enable us to listen to recorded podcasts on the go. Whether you walk, lounge, run, ride, boat, or fly, your podcasts can come with you. This section describes the special aggregator software that makes it possible to download podcasts to these mobile devices.

Aggregators for Pocket PC

A *Pocket PC* is a hand-held computing device (also known as a *pen computer*) that runs Windows CE (compact edition), which is a special version of the Windows operating system. You can use your Pocket PC to store and retrieve emails, contacts, and appointments; play multimedia files and games; exchange text messages with MSN Messenger; browse the web, and more. In addition, Pocket PCs can boast many add-ons like GPS receivers, cameras, and of course the capacity to play MP3s and podcasts! In fact, if your Pocket PC has wireless connectivity, you can download podcasts on the go from anywhere.

note

Some Pocket PC devices may run on Windows Mobile Phone Edition (i.e., they run on cell phones) and include mobile phone features.

The capacity to play podcasts on your Pocket PC is made possible with aggregator software applications built specifically for Pocket PC. In addition to supporting mobile downloads of podcasts, this software also makes it easy to synchronize your Pocket PC with your computer, in reverse of the typical order. You can also use many of the regular aggregators already discussed in this chapter to download podcasts to your Pocket PC by connecting the Pocket PC to your main computer and selecting it as the device on which downloaded podcasts should be saved. In addition, Pocket PC synchronization programs like ActiveSync allow files that reside in a specific folder to be downloaded to your Pocket PC.

caution

Podcasts can be memory and broadband hogs. Before you subscribe to a podcast for use on your Pocket PC, verify that the podcast is available as a low-bandwidth file. Otherwise, you may get a hefty bill from your mobile connectivity service provider, and you'll have cobwebs on your device by the time downloading is complete!

FeederReader (http://www.feederreader.com)

If you want to test drive some specialized Pocket PC podcast applications, try FeederReader. It's a mobile RSS aggregator that runs on Windows CE, and it's designed for downloading podcast feeds on a Pocket PC without the help of a host desktop or laptop computer. Using FeederReader, you update podcast feeds while your Pocket PC is connected to the Internet—perhaps through a cell phone or local area network. You then listen to them offline.

note

Like Doppler, FeederReader requires the Microsoft .NET Framework Version 1.1.

It has many features—most notably its file- and feed-management capabilities. FeederReader is focused on what counts: reading and sorting podcast feeds behind the scenes. It can be told when and how to capture RSS feeds, and how much information should be downloaded. Feeds can be stored for future listening directly on a flash memory card. In addition, FeederReader has detailed error messaging, keeps tabs and statistics on all downloaded files, allows for the viewing of all feed elements, and supports OPML import and export. The aggregator is not memory-hungry because the installed file is under 1.6MB, and it's open source, which means you can build on it, tailor it to your needs, or even re-brand it for your own use.

FeederReader supports all major RSS syndication formats, including Dublin core and Slashback extensions (these are beyond the scope of this book). In addition, it comes with scores of built-in quality feeds from leading syndicators such as NewsIsFree. If you like a feed, FeederReader permits one-click subscription to popular news-geared services such as Radio Userland and AmphetaDesk. If you seek a deeper mobile podcasting experience, you can use FeederReader's search tool and enjoy its multi-language support.

Other Aggregators for Pocket PC

Other Pocket PC aggregators include Skookum (for SmartPhones) and Playlist Sync (which works with iTunes). For a more comprehensive list of Pocket PC podcast applications, check out indiepodder.org at www.ipodder.org/directory/4/ipodderSoftware/ pocketPc (see Figure 8.12). In addition, many applications for the Pocket PC—of both the free and for-fee variety—can be downloaded from Tucows (http://www.tucows.com).

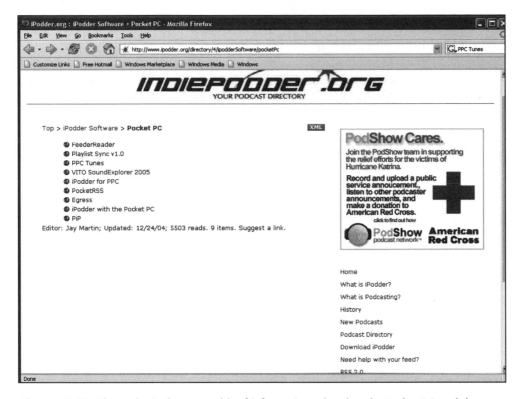

Figure 8.12 This web site has a wealth of information related to the Pocket PC and the mobile Internet.

Pod2Go for iPod (http://www.kainjow.com/pod2go)

Pod2Go, which is designed for all iPods that feature screens (including iPod Photo), enables you do more than just listen to vanilla podcasts. It represents the fun stuff you can do on the mobile Internet, all centered around podcasting technology! This includes the following:

- **News.** Pod2Go has a big collection of news sources, with about 1,000 built-in feeds. You can add your own RSS or ATOM feeds too.

- **Weather.** Pod2Go's weather feature lets you see weather forecasts and current (as current as your last sync) conditions for most cities around the world. Just enter a city, and it will do the rest.

- **Movies.** You can access and view movie titles, ratings, and times (in the U.S. and Canada).

- **Stocks.** Stock quotes are provided as you sync. Details include the classic data fields—last price, opening price, change, and so on.

- **Text.** You can bring your text documents with you on your iPod! This includes web pages as plain text, or RTF, Word, or simple plain-text files. You can also create text notes directly within the client.
- **Directions.** The Directions feature helps you find your way. You can download directions for the U.S. and for most places in Canada and Europe.

note

Pod2Go is a shareware utility that offers a free trail period of 15 days. After the trial period, you must purchase the software to continue using it.

In essence, Pod2Go enables you to convert your iPod into a PDA, synchronizing your contact list, calendars, email messages, and notes to your iPod. If you require a PDA but only need to view your data (that is, you don't need to enter data), using Pod2Go with your iPod may be the way to go. Be aware, though, that Pod2Go runs on Mac OS X only.

Evaluating Podcast Aggregators

There are certain things you should consider when evaluating podcast aggregator software. To help you cure your analysis paralysis, I've compiled some key criteria for assessing which aggregator is best for you:

- **Operating system.** The operating system you use is the most important "support" criterion you need to consider. Do you have a Windows, Mac, or Linux operating system? The answer to this question is a key driver of your selection of podcast aggregator. There's no point in downloading a Mac-only aggregator if you use a PC!
- **Overall ease of use.** Are tons of extra software add-ons required? Is the aggregator a plug-in that requires a bit of technology savvy? Are there too many functions to track? Is downloading easy and smooth? The answers to these questions affect the quality of your podcasting experience.
- **Dynamic queries of multiple directories.** The best aggregators will troll many directories, not just those that are canned with the program. The entire raison d'étre of podcasting is to slither away from the cookie-cutter broadcasts dictated by Big Radio!

note

One of these few exceptions to the rule in the preceding bullet is iTunes. True, iTunes controls its directory, but it offers a critical mass that has something for everyone. In general, however, don't put up with a biased directory.

- **Integrated support for Windows Media Player and iTunes.** Many aggregators support Windows Media Player or iTunes—and some aggregators support both. Look out for software that makes you work too hard to upload to your media player and MP3 device. On the other hand, some software gets ahead of itself. It may do too much, like automatically uploading stuff to iTunes or Windows Media Player that you don't want it to upload! My advice? Find a balanced product.

- **BitTorrent support.** BitTorrent is a standard for peer-to-peer (P2P) file distribution. As I noted in Chapter 7, BitTorrent enables you to obtain bits of a single podcast from multiple sources. Because the file is distributed by a multitude of computers, the request does not clog the bandwidth at any one source. Without BitTorrent, you can't do a lot of the fun stuff with podcasting—at least not efficiently.

- **OPML support.** A detailed discussion of OPML import and export support is beyond the scope of this book; suffice to say that if you see this feature, it's a good thing. OPML support enables you to do a lot more with the aggregator, including multimedia.

- **Level of overall functionality.** Does the software do a lot of stuff? Does it manage your files according to your preferences? Make sure the software you choose does everything you want it to do, without overdoing it.

note

Whether an aggregator is web-based or desktop-based is not a show-stopping criterion. The more important criteria are those outlined in the preceding list. They are the ones that deal with what *really* makes an impact on your podcasting experience.

note

Overall level of support is an important criterion; it indicates how well the app works with various media players, BitTorrent, OPML and other electronic tools not mentioned in the preceding list. It speaks to how well the app gets along with other apps with which it may have to communicate.

Table 8.1 lines up the competition based on some of these criteria.

Table 8.1 Key Criteria for Assessing Podcast Aggregators

Aggregator	Operating System Player	Integrated Media	Ease of Use	Level of Program Support	Level of Overall Functionality
BashPodder	Mac OS X, Linux	No	Medium	Medium	Medium
CastGrab	Linux	No	High	Medium	Medium
Doppler	Windows	Yes	Medium	High	High
FeederReader	Windows CE	No	Medium	High	High
HappyFish	Windows	Yes	High	High	High
iPodder	Windows, Mac, Linux	Yes	High	High	High
iPodder X	Mac	Yes	High	Medium	High
iPodder.NET	Windows	Yes	Medium	Medium	High
iTunes	Mac OS X, Windows	Yes	High	High	High
jPodder	Windows, Linux	Yes	Medium	Medium	High
Nimiq	Windows	No	High	Medium	Medium
Now Playing	Windows	No	Low	Medium	Low
PlayPod	Mac OS X	Yes	High	Medium	High
Pod2GO	Mac	Yes	High	Medium	Medium
PoddumFeeder	Mac	Yes	Medium	High	High

Coming Up Next...

In this chapter, I covered podcast aggregators for Windows, Mac, and Linux; the mobile Internet as it relates to podcasting; and key criteria for assessing aggregators. The next chapter covers hardware used to play podcasts.

CHAPTER 9

WORKING WITH MP3 PLAYERS AND PERIPHERALS

In Chapter 4, I introduced you to the equipment required to create podcasts. This included a computer, a sound card, headphones, and a microphone. I also introduced you to the software needed to actually record, edit, encode, tag, and upload your production. Discussion ranged from stuff you could get for free all the way to very expensive and high-end hardware and software options.

In this chapter, I'll ask you to wear the hat of podcast listener. I'll introduce you to some MP3 players and the accessories that can go along with them. Once again, discussion will range from the relatively inexpensive all the way to the pricier stuff. Most bases are covered, including discussion of some key specifications behind the MP3 players, earphones, headphones, and speakers covered in this chapter.

MP3 Players

The market for handheld MP3 players is flooded with hundreds of models from dozens of manufacturers—too many to list here. At this time, two main types of players dominate the market:

- **Hard drive MP3 players.** These use a traditional drive format; hard drive players historically have provided more storage capacity than flash players, but that is changing.

- **Flash memory players.** Flash memory makes miniaturization possible. These players do not use a spinning drive, but still store data in a way that will not lose content when power (such as the battery) is removed. Flash players tend to be lighter and smaller—sometimes less than two ounces—and have begun to challenge hard drive players in storage capacity per unit of space taken in a device. They also require less battery power because they typically contain no moving parts.

note

The Rolling Stones recently introduced an entire album in flash memory format.

The big player in the portable MP3 player market is Apple; its main line of iPods (iPod, iPod nano, and iPod shuffle) has cornered just under 50 percent market share. Some iPods use hard drives; others, like the iPod nano, employ flash drive technology.

PDAs, BlackBerries, and SmartPhones

The other way to listen to podcasts or any other MP3 production on-the-go is through a PDA or mobile phone with MP3 functionality. This includes a lot of new cell phones introduced in 2006. It also includes BlackBerries, SmartPhones like the Treo, Palm handhelds, Palm LifeDrive, iPAQ pocket PC, and more. A full discussion of these devices is beyond the scope of this book; just be aware that they represent yet another way to listen to podcasts, and are big reasons why moblogging podcasts and other digital files is possible.

Hard Drive Players

The following MP3 players use a traditional drive format similar to the one found in your PC or Mac, only smaller.

Palm LifeDrive Mobile Manager Handheld Computer

The Palm LifeDrive mobile manager—which ships with a 4-gigabyte hard drive and supports SD, SDIO, and MultiMediaCard expansion cards (sold separately)—is one of only a few handheld computers that work with both Windows and Mac systems to handle email, text messages, calendar organization, spreadsheets, documents, and music. You can use Palm LifeDrive, which retails for $499, as you would a standard MP3 unit to download audio from the Internet via your desktop or notebook computer. Alternatively, if you have a Bluetooth-capable phone, you can download MP3s directly. These devices can also record and play back voice memos, and are multimedia-, vlog-, and moglog-friendly. With a weight of just 6.8 ounces outside the protective case, the unit fits comfortably in your hand.

The Palm LifeDrive comes with Pocket Tunes software and offers simple step-by-step instructions to quickly get music off the web and in your ears. It works with certain podcast aggregators to enable you to automatically direct podcasts to its internal memory. Although the LifeDrive does not have a camera to capture video, you can organize and view full-length movies or downloaded vlogs (I discuss vlogs in Chapter 6, "Adding Music, Video, and Other Multimedia," and further in Chapter 10, "The Leading Edge of Podcasting.") on the 320×480-pixel high-resolution screen.

Cowon iAUDIO X5

The iAUDIO X5, which retails for $299, is one of the first of a new breed of players that plays MPEG4 videos and can hold a photo library. This sets the stage for listening to podcasts with built-in multimedia—a technology expected to take shape near the end of 2006. From Cowon, this player has 20 gigabytes of space—about 5,000 songs, if stored as MP3 files—and comes with its own software, called JetAudio and JetCast, for downloading, editing, and setting up your own podcasting files. (A second offering from Cowon, the iAUDIO X5L, which retails for $379, boasts a whopping 30 gigabytes.) To help you locate and download podcasts, the iAUDIO X5 works with certain podcast aggregators. This unit is also vlog-friendly. In addition, the iAUDIO X5 features an internal microphone that you can use to record voice input from meetings, for interviews, or for audio commentary on the fly—and you can use it to listen to and record FM radio. A line-in encoder allows for recording from an external source.

As for file formats, the X5 audio works with MP3, OGG, WMA, and WAV, as well as FLAC. The video player software can convert and play a 15-frame-per-second video on the 160×128 dot screen (about $1^1/_2 \times 1^1/_4$ inches)—and the converted file can be played on the X5. The viewer also allows for text and image viewing. The X5 allows you to import pictures from a digital camera with the USB host input, or to import text documents and to read them on the viewer. (I describe the import process in detail in Chapter 10, which covers vlogs.) Figure 9.1 shows the Cowon iAUDIO X5.

Figure 9.1 The Cowon iAUDIO X5.

iRiver H10

iRiver offers several versions of this player, ranging in storage space from 5 gigabytes, which retails for $249, to a jumbo 20 gigabytes, which goes for $299. The 20GB version, shown in Figure 9.2, plays up to 600 hours of digital music at 64Kbps. In addition, it features an intuitive interface with a convenient touch strip, displays digital photos, uses a rechargeable battery, boasts an FM recorder (this may have some podcast applications), includes an integrated voice recorder (again, more podcast possibilities), and supports ultra-fast USB 2.0 transfers. File formats supported include MP3, WMA, JPEG, and TXT; you can subscribe to RSS feeds of text documents and save them on this device for later viewing.

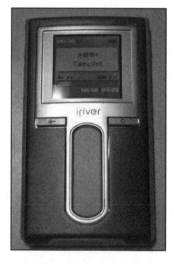

Figure 9.2 The iRiver H10.

Sony NW-HD5

In the NW-HD5, Sony has introduced a 10-gigabyte competitor to the iPod. This unit, which retails for $299, is smaller and has a simple interface, with a bi-directional display, and a rechargeable battery with a life of as much as 40 hours. (It charges directly via USB or with the AC adapter supplied.) The NW-HD5 supports MP3, ATRAC3, and ATRAC3plus audio formats.

Flash Players

The MP3 players featured in this section use flash memory, similar to flash memory you have in your digital camera. Flash memory may be built in (embedded) or removable. Embedded flash has certain advantages over hard drives due to its decreasing cost-per-megabyte and increasing capacity. Solid-state flash memory is high-performance, has increased durability (that means no skipping), and is small in both size and weight. (*Solid state* just means that if you eliminate the power supply, the flash device does not lose information.)

iPod nano

Apple's iPod nano is an ultra-portable, light-weight, feature-packed iPod that can hold either 1,000 songs or 25,000 photos (which you view using the unit's color screen). Speaking of the color screen, you can use it to view album art while playing music or to view photo slideshows, setting the stage for viewing multimedia podcasts on mobile devices. When you plug the nano into a Mac or Windows computer using a USB 2.0 cable, the unit integrates with the iTunes digital music player and uses Auto-Sync technology to automatically download your digital music collection, podcasts, or photos. Full operation of all functions is enabled by a click wheel. iPod nano's 4-gigabyte model weighs in at $249, and the 2-gigabyte model runs $199.

n o t e

iPod nano features the same 30-pin dock connector as the iPod and iPod mini, allowing it to work with a lot of other accessories already developed for iPod.

SanDisk Sansa

The SanDisk Sansa supports Windows Media Player 10 and a wide range of popular music formats such as MP3 and Windows Media Audio (WMA) in both unprotected and pro-tected form (like the WMA files you buy from music download sites). The Sansa m200 series is 512-megabytes in capacity, the highest capacity at the time of this writing. In addition, 1-, 2-, and 4-gigabyte devices are also available. Other features include a voice recorder with built-in mic, a high-speed USB 2.0 interface and cable, and an easy-to-read LCD display. The 4-gigabyte model has an MSRP of $200, and the 1-gigabyte model runs $80.

Cowon iAudio U2

Weighing in at a mere 1.2 ounces, this model, shown in Figure 9.3, won an Editors' Choice award from CNET.com in November of 2004. It features high-speed USB transfers, a wide graphic LCD display, up to 20 hours of rechargeable-battery life, and text display. High-quality sound is supported via multi-codec (it supports MP3, WMA, ASF, and WAV formats). The MSRP is $99 for a 256-megabyte unit or $279 for a 2-gigabyte unit.

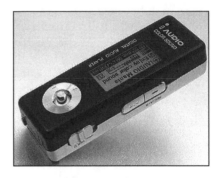

Figure 9.3 The Cowon iAudio U2.

iRiver T10

iRiver's T10, shown in Figure 9.4, comes in three fruity colors and comes with a curved design that fits in the palm of your hand. It has lots of features, including a 65,000 color LCD. This model plays up to 53 hours with a AA-size battery; supports MP3, WMA, ASF, and OGG Q10; has an FM radio and FM and voice recording; and has an image viewer (BMP only). Its ultra-fast data transfer supports Windows and Mac OS, and has the PlaysForSure logo (for U.S. and E.U. only, with WMP10). PlaysForSure is a certification conveyed on a device that helps you feel secure that the digital music and video you purchase online will play back on the device every time. Although PlaysForSure is nice to have, all MP3 players discussed in this book are reliable when it comes to playing music downloads. The MSRP for the 512-megabyte iRiver T10 is $149; the 1-gigabyte version runs $199.

Figure 9.4 The iRiver T10.

Sony NW-E505

The Sony NW Series of MP3 players includes nine new flash-media Network Walkmans with several very cool designs. All models sport a leading-edge organic light-emitting display and long battery life (up to 50 hours). Network Walkmans play back both MP3 and ATRAC3/3plus music files, the latter being proprietary to Sony. They also support WMA and WAV formats, making them more flexible. SonicStage software helps you manage and transfer music collections, although rumor has it that SonicStage will be replaced by another version of software soon.

The Integration of MP3 with Home and Car Entertainment Systems

Some of the more powerful MP3 players can serve as the center point of your home or vehicle entertainment system. For example, you can hook up powered speakers to the headphone jack of your MP3 player. With many MP3 players, you can also connect an FM transmitter to the headphone jack of your portable device and broadcast your podcast over FM. In other words, you can tune into your podcast or music through the FM tuner of your car or through your home entertainment system.

You can also use special cables to connect your MP3 player to output audio over your boom box, or to receive audio from a turntable as I show you at the end of this chapter. The bottom line is that you can amplify MP3 player sound, establish a wireless connection between your MP3 player and your stereo system, and more. Many companies that sell MP3 players offer these peripherals and show you how to hook them up; you can also get appropriate add-ons at most big-box electronic retailers.

You should note that some MP3 players have codecs (*coders* and *decoders*) that allow for conversion of non-MP3 audio to MP3 and other digital audio formats from an audio feed. In other words, you can connect your CD player to your MP3 player via a USB connection, without requiring the use of a computer to do the MP3 conversion for you. You can also download music from online music stores directly into the MP3 player. The sky is the limit as to what you can do. That is why MP3 players are the platform of choice for listening to podcasts, music, and sometimes even video on the go.

Earphones and Earbuds

The ear pieces typically sold with players are of minimal quality. Indeed, some audiophiles say that the first thing you should do when buying a portable player is stomp on the headgear and buy a better set. The earbuds presented in this section received high rankings at credible web sites, and demonstrate that you can have high quality within a wide range of prices.

Etymotic ER4P

According to Etymotic's assessment of these earbuds as compared to their other products, these earbuds, shown in Figure 9.5, rank highly. These buds, which retail for $330, are lightweight and portable, have high accuracy and noise isolation, and provide enhanced bass response and higher sound output. They also have a custom ear mold option.

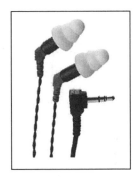

Figure 9.5 The Etymotic ER4P earbuds.

Shure E4c

The Shure E4c earphones, which retail for $299, follow in the tradition of Shure's quality products, optimizing the listening experience with a new high-definition driver, featuring tuned-port technology to enhance bass response. The E4c's sound-isolating sleeves contour to the inner ear, sealing out more background noise than do noise-canceling alternatives (see Figure 9.6).

Shure E2c

The most affordable of Shure's earphones, the E2c, feature a single high-energy micro-speaker in a unique comet-shaped enclosure that optimizes the acoustic environment in your ear for the best possible sound. These headphones, which are shown in Figure 9.6, retail for $99.

Figure 9.6 Shure E4c sound-isolating earphones

Sony MDREX81LP/W

Sony's MDREX81LP/W are described by Sony as their premier lateral in-the-ear headphones, designed to deliver deep bass and clear treble sounds. Eliminating the headband, these buds, which retail for $50, feature small 9mm drivers and soft silicon earbuds. Two sizes of earbuds are included.

Wireless Headphones

Logitech is great at computer peripherals. Indeed, you most likely have a mouse, keyboard, or computer speakers made by Logitech. The company also make wireless headphones, giving new meaning to mobility and allowing you to leave your player on the counter or in a backpack. Integrated controls enable you to adjust the volume from afar.

One of three headset designs recently released by Logitech, the Logitech Wireless Headphones for MP3 work with any MP3 or CD player. You can connect them instantly by plugging the adapter into the standard 3.5mm headphone jack on the music player. They feature 40mm full-range neodymium drivers that deliver rich audio and enhanced bass performance. The headphones, which retail for $129.99, use rechargeable batteries, which can play up to eight hours of music per charge. In addition, the headphones have a behind-the-head design for comfort and are made of lightweight, durable material.

Wireline Headphones

Traditional wireline headphones and earpieces use, you guessed it, wires. This section outlines some of your options in this category.

AKG K 28 NC Headphones

Unlike most headphones—which are bulky, over-the-ear models—AKG's K 28 NC headphones weigh only 2.6 ounces and feature a closed back. These headphones, shown in Figure 9.7, significantly reduce ambient noise in a few ways. First, subminiature microphones integrated in the earphone shells pick up low-frequency ambient noise. Then, the noise reduction filter reverses the polarity of the noise signal to generate its exact mirror image, which coincides with the original noise at the ear. As a result, ambient noise is almost completely cancelled out, while the music signal remains practically unchanged. The unit, which retails for about $120, comes with carrying bag, airplane adapter, and mini to $\frac{1}{4}$-inch stereo adapter jack.

Figure 9.7 The AKG K 28 NC headphones.

Logitech Identity Headphones for MP3

The Logitech Identity Headphones for MP3 work with any MP3 player or iPod and feature powerful audio in a small and lightweight form—all for the low price of $40. The headphones feature folding loops to help keep them on, and the behind-the-head fit is designed for extended-wear comfort. In addition, the look of the headphones, which come with four color plates, can be customized.

Portable Speakers

Portable speakers have been around for some time, but the quality has taken a while to become anything near acceptable for the audiophile. With the advent of handheld MP3 players, more attention has been directed toward producing products that sound great.

Altec Lansing iM4

The Altec Lansing iM4, which runs $100, is a one-piece system with two small, lightweight speakers on either side of a 4.5×5-inch no-skid rubberized platform that holds a music player of any size firmly in place. The speakers stand nearly vertical when the system is in use, and fold down to platform level to form a flat surface slightly larger than 5×10 inches for easy storage or travel. A retractable connector eliminates cable clutter, and an auxiliary input jack allows a second audio device connection from another MP3 or CD player or even a PC to create a two-in-one speaker system. The 4-watt digital amplifier powers four micro drivers for clear reproduction over the entire frequency range and an audio advantage over two-driver products.

Logitech mm28

Just 1.25 inches wide, with an input cable that fits into a recessed area, the Logitech mm28 portable speakers, which retail for $80, offer a thin-profile, one-piece solution for MP3 portability. These speakers, which can last up to 45 hours on a single set of batteries, can be used with any MP3 or CD player that has a standard 3.5mm audio jack.

Logitech mm22

The Logitech mm22 portable speakers complement the design of the much-celebrated iPod—but also work with any portable music player or notebook PC that has a 3.5 mm jack. The system, which retails for $60, includes four neodymium micro drivers—two on each side—designed to produce a rich, smooth sound with depth. The speakers fold into a traveling case that's about the size of a hard-cover book, and work with batteries or an international (100-249V) AC power adapter. The set comes with a 10-inch cable for connecting the speakers to the audio player, and a 24-inch cable to connect the speakers to a notebook. The case is also roomy enough to store most portable music players.

Additional Peripherals

The Griffin iMic universal audio adapter, shown in Figure 9.8, functions as an external sound card. This USB device adds stereo input and output to your Mac or PC. It is better than an internal sound card because it processes sound outside the somewhat noisy computer case. It uses USB for the audio signal, resulting in higher quality sound when you record and when you play back to external speakers.

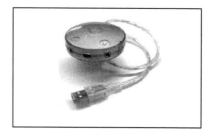

The iMic, which retails for $40, connects to just about any mic or sound-input device to your iBook, PowerBook, PowerMac, or other Mac or PC with a USB port, as well as headphones. The iMic supports both mic-level and line-level input, and also supports line-level output for connecting speakers or an external recording device.

Figure 9.8 The Griffin iMic, showing the off/on switch, as well as mic and speaker connections.

Griffin Technologies also offers the Turntable Connection Cable, shown in Figure 9.9. This is a must have for anyone who is interested in hooking up a turntable to convert old record collections into MP3 form. The cable, which costs $13, serves as the connection from the two RCA jacks on your turntable to the stereo mini-jack input, and also provides a connection for your turntable's grounding wire.

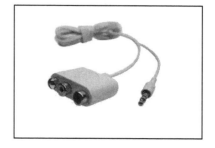

Figure 9.9 Griffin Technologies' Turntable Connection Cable.

note

Some people find a buzz or hum on their recordings, often resulting from a little gremlin called "ground loop hum." The simple way to eliminate the noise—and record the true sound of the album—is to connect the ground wire to the Turntable Grounding Cable.

Coming Up Next...

This chapter shows only a representative sample of the available MP3 and related equipment. Some of the MP3 players profiled here are powerful enough to run some of the rich multimedia applications discussed in Chapters 6 and 10. Other devices are more basic and will simply play what you need them to play—podcasts. In the next chapter, I take you to the leading edge of podcasting, showing you how you can create and listen to vlogs—essentially podcasts with video.

CHAPTER 10

THE LEADING EDGE OF PODCASTING

If you appreciate the fruits of technology, it can be very exciting to observe, in a front-row seat, how a technology like podcasting emerge. It's even more exciting to be a pioneer in the field! This chapter pushes you over the leading edge of podcasting by discussing some of the emerging technologies in the podcasting arena. A key focus of this chapter is vlogging, which I introduced in Chapter 6. Vlogging is essentially podcasting, but with video added. As you'll discover, there are a couple ways to create vlogs. One way is to do-it-yourself, and the other is to utilize a web-based service that specializes in vlogs.

In this chapter, I also introduce you to some exciting developments in the realm of RSS aggregators and other software for video. In that section, you'll see what technology can be tapped to place you in the role of vlog listener or producer. I show you that not only can you subscribe to videos the RSS way, you can also use the new-fashioned way: via a Google or Yahoo! search for podcasts, weblogs, and vlogs. I also introduce you to the groundbreaking video iPod recently introduced by Apple, and discuss its exciting implications.

I close out the chapter by discussing the role of voice over Internet protocol (VOIP) in the context of moblogging and podcasting. I also outline some interesting business models that may help you make money from your podcasts.

Vlogs

Vlogs, which are essentially the multimedia version of podcasts, began in earnest when indie filmmakers and movie fans began posting weblog entries of video publishing tips. These days, vlogs are gaining big-time traction on the Internet. Of course, video posts had been around for years; what makes vlogs different from regular video posts on the Internet is that they tended to be housed on weblogs where the video supported the story, not the other way around. For vlogs, the story is the primary medium of the message. Another difference between vlogging and regular video posts is that vlogs are posted mostly by individuals, whereas most videos are traditionally posted by commercial enterprises.

In the last few years, vlogs have grown virally thanks to word-of-mouth, and because everyone with weblogs, podcasts, and vlogs are linking to each other. That has been possible in part because of better distribution technology, and because of the emergence of RSS aggregators for vlogs. (I discuss vlog aggregators later in this chapter.)

Another key aspect of the proliferation vlogs, which are broadband-hungry, is that broadband now services almost 45 percent of U.S. households with Internet access. In other words, about 35,000,000 people can now view video online without too much grief. Some vlogging business models have also cropped up, which means that vlogs are being further promoted and publicized as a new broadcasting medium for individuals. Indeed, there are now on-demand video services, like an indie version of TiVo that's online. One final but colossal development is that iTunes, used by millions, already supports vlogging! These shots in the arm will almost certainly ensure that vlogging will take off—just as podcasting in raw form has.

note

One difference between vlogs and podcasts is that the audio portion of vlogs may not be in MP3 format. The implications of this are discussed later in this chapter.

Vlog Video Formats

Just as it's important to understand audio formats for podcasting, it is important to understand video/audio formats for video files. The formats you can embed in or link to your weblog or standard web site are as follows:

- **Moving Picture Experts Group (MPEG).** MPEG encodes and compresses movies, video, and audio (voice and music) into a format that results in a smaller file than most other video formats. The good thing about MPEG is that quality is not degraded in any significant way. It is conducive to a range of compression options, making it a flexible file format.

- **Windows Video Files/Windows Media Video (AVI/WMV).** These audio and video files are compatible with Windows Media Player; they have very good compression technology that reduces loss of data during compression.

- **Windows Media Files (ASF).** This is a streaming file format utilized with Windows Media Player. Streaming sounds and images are played in near real time as they are downloaded instead of first being cached (stored) in your computer and then played. Streamed content may include audio, scripts, ActiveX controls, and HTML documents. In other words, they support rich multimedia podcasts.

- **RealAudio Files (RM/RA).** This streaming-file format is used with RealNetworks RealAudio Player. Although it is proprietary, it boasts millions of users. It is often used to watch live sporting events because of its streaming nature.

- **Apple QuickTime (MOV/QT).** QuickTime, which I introduced in Chapter 6, is used by most Mac apps that include any sort of video. In addition, provided that QuickTime is installed, a Windows PC can run QuickTime apps.

Do It Yourself Vlogs

So you want to vlog—that is, post a podcast on the web that includes multimedia—and you want to do it yourself. This is where I show you how. There is nothing groundbreaking here; just the essential processes you need to be familiar with in order to vlog. These include the following:

- Selecting your video camera and movie-making software

- Connecting to your computer, transferring video to it, and editing the video into a vlog

- Uploading your production to your weblog

Selecting Your Video Camera

In this digital age, you can use a digital video (DV) camera, a webcam, or a digital snapshot camera with some video functionality to film for your blog. This section covers each of these options in turn.

note

The additional hardware required to transfer vlog videos to your computer depends on the nature of your video camera. With a DV camera, either a FireWire card (IEEE 1394) or an analog video capture card will suffice, although FireWire is recommended for faster and better quality results. If you have an analog video camcorder, analog webcam, or another analog format, an analog video capture card is required. A computer store can help you identify the right one for your needs.

Using a Digital Video Camera

In general, most video cameras today can be segregated into two categories: analog or digital. Analog cameras record video in a non-digital format (that is, it uses no 1s and 0s) that computers do not understand. Digital cameras, on the other hand, record video in a digital format (that is, it uses *many* 1s and 0s), thus making it easier for your computer to talk to your video files. As a result, transferring digital video footage to PC file format is relatively easy. Because of this and other advantages, like longer life and smaller size, digital video cameras are more commonly used today than their analog counterparts.

note
***

If your camera is of the analog variety, don't despair. Later in this chapter, I'll show you how you can transfer such videos to your computer.

***

Digital video cameras can vary widely in digital tape format and in functionality, like image stabilization, zoom, and on-the-spot effects editing. As a result, the cost of digital video cameras also varies. If you shop carefully, you can purchase a great digital video camera for about $500.

tip
***

A discussion of the various makes and models of digital video cameras is beyond the scope of this book. If you're in the market for one, check out *Consumer Reports*; it often profiles and rates them.

***

Many digital video cameras have a digital video (DV-out or DV-in and out) socket. These let you hook up your video camera to your PC using high-speed connection protocols like FireWire (also known as IEEE 1394); most newer computers sport these connections as standard fare. If they don't, consider purchasing a FireWire card. They retail for about $40.

note
***

During the 2005 Toronto International Film Festival, Motorola doled out about 20 of its video-capable mobile phones to producers of indie film, provided they agreed to vlog some of their pieces to the web. The company also distributed phones to students at a few U.S. colleges, challenging them to use their phones to film the best 30-second spot about "not using cell phones while driving." Obviously, the technology to moblog vlogs exists—and the adoption of that technology is being encouraged.

***

Using a Webcam

Chances are, you probably already have a webcam. If you don't, they run about $40. Webcams feature a charge coupling device, which is a photo sensor conducive to digital imaging. Webcams are typically used for videoconferencing on the web in real time, but they can also be used to record your vlogs. Be aware of the fact that webcams are low in resolution, so it may not meet your video-creation needs in those situations where a good picture is important.

On the down side, webcams are geared to create small web clips. Also, webcams are often tethered by a USB cable, so your venue is limited. Even wireless webcams have distance restrictions. To mitigate this, you can get a more expensive webcam with decent image quality, a built in mic, and editing apps that enable you to record in multiple file formats.

Using a Digital Snapshot Camera

Digital snapshot cameras have soared in popularity in the last few years as their resolution, capacity, portability, and functionality have greatly improved. Indeed, high-end digital snapshot cameras provide great resolution, audio, length of video clip, and choice of file formats, making them eligible for vlogging. For the purposes of podcasting and vlogging, a digital snapshot camera may make sense if your podcasts and vlogs are very brief but need pictures and video to enhance their message. Digital snapshot cameras are also conducive to moblogging pictures or vlogs.

Selecting Your Movie-Making Software

Although web video has been around for some time, recent technology apps make vlogs easier to create, share, and find. One such app is Windows Movie Maker 2.1, which can be found on any XP-based PC, free of charge. Using Movie Maker 2.1, you can create, edit, and share your videos, and can edit and produce vlogs with drag-and-drop functionality. When you're finished, you can upload your movie via the web or email. Using third-party apps, you can even turn your vlogs into DVDs, or port your vlog back to your video camera (assuming it has storage space) for playback on a TV screen or on the camera's LCD screen.

note

If you use a Mac, chances are you'll have a similar embedded app on your machine. If you use Linux, look into downloading freeware that performs the same tasks as Movie Maker. Rather than exploring these various apps, I've opted to stick with Movie Maker because I want to convey the principles and processes used in these programs, not the exact commands.

To use Movie Maker 2.1 (and most other movie-making software), your computer must have the following:

- SP2 for Windows XP Home Edition or Windows XP Professional
- A 600 megahertz processor, such as an Intel Pentium III, Advanced Micro Devices (AMD) Athlon, or equivalent processor, and at least 256 megabytes of RAM
- 2 gigabytes of available hard disk-space (videos are real byte hogs)
- Audio and DV or analog video capture devices (specifically, a good video camera, as discussed previously, and good connections, as described later)
- An Internet connection, preferably broadband

note

> For more information about Movie Maker, visit its pages on the Microsoft web site (http://www.microsoft.com/windowsxp/downloads/updates/moviemaker2.mspx).

To play vlogs created with Movie Maker, you'll need Microsoft Windows Media Player (WMP) 7.0 or later. For best playback, Microsoft recommends WMP 9 Series.

Serious Magic

Serious Magic produces Vlog It, special video-creation software focused on vlogs. Although it essentially does what Windows Movie Maker can do, it has a few extra features geared just for vlogging. For example, the app provides you with an on-screen teleprompter just like newscasters use. You can then type your notes into the program for display while you perform, click Record, and read all the while staring into the camera. You can also drag and drop pictures, video, and audio clips from your snapshot camera, DV recorder, or SmartPhone to the app. Just place the image or audio clip alongside relevant text in your teleprompter notes. Then, as you speak during the recording process, the clips you added are automatically displayed onscreen at the appropriate time. It is a very professional effect.

The app records, compresses, and formats the video. It also automatically arranges creative overlays and transitions that you pre-selected. When complete, you can output the vlog into Windows Media Player or RealPlayer format and upload it to your weblog. No special web host is required; you can simply upload your vlog to a regular web server and post a link to the vlog on a standard web page or weblog page. This is a great example of what others are doing to make vlog creation easy.

The software was still in beta testing at the time of this writing, but is expected to cost about $49.95, and will be available at Serious Magic's web site (http://www.seriousmagic.com).

Connecting Your Camera to Your Computer

- **Connecting a digital video camera to a FireWire card.** To get the best quality from your digital video (DV) or mini–DV camera, you should have an IEEE 1394 capture card installed on your computer. An IEEE 1394 card is a piece of hardware that passes the information from the DV camera to your computer. Because the data is already in digital form, it can be read and transferred directly to your computer without any processing or conversion. That means you'll enjoy the highest quality video possible with a consumer video camera.

- **Connecting a DV camera to an analog video capture card.** If you do not have a FireWire (IEEE 1394) card in your computer, but do have a DV camera, you can still transfer video to your computer if you have another type of video capture card on your computer called an *analog video capture card*. Be warned, though, that when you transfer video this way, you will experience some degradation in resolution. There are two types of input with this approach: S-video and composite video. If you have the corresponding connector cables and your computer accepts one or the other, opt for S-video because it provides better quality picture and superior sound. On the other hand, composite video is better when a home entertainment system comes into play.

- **Connecting a webcam to a USB or analog video capture card.** How you connect a webcam to your PC or Mac depends on the type of camera you have. Although some webcams can connect to any video capture card, others stipulate that a certain capture card be used. Refer to your webcam's user manual to determine what kind of card you need. Also, some webcams have a built-in mic. If yours doesn't, you'll require a separate mic to capture sound.

- **Connecting a VCR to an analog video capture card.** As more and more people use their computer monitor to watch television, TV tuner and related video cards are becoming standard features on many computers. If your computer is so configured, all you need to do to connect a VCR to it is attach a coaxial cable to your VCR, and then attach the video and audio connections from the VCR to your computer. The video out connects to the video in jack on your computer, and may be labeled as composite. The audio out connects to the line in jack.

caution

Using video and TV excerpts can really add a lot to your vlog. However, if you do use video captured from TV networks or VHS tapes, be wary of copyright issues and seriously consider getting permissions. Make sure you are not breaking the law!

Transferring Video from Your Camera to Your Computer

Now that you're all hooked up, let's proceed with Windows Movie Maker. In the following sections, you'll learn how to transmit video files to your computer's hard disk. Before you begin, however, you'll need to launch Movie Maker; to do so, click the Windows Start button, select Programs, choose Accessories, and then select Movie Maker.

note

Remember, I've opted to stick with Movie Maker because I want to convey the principles and processes used in these programs. If you use a different program for this purpose, I urge you to read along anyway so you'll understand the various considerations.

Capturing Video from a Tape in a DV Camera

To transfer video from a tape in a DV camera to your computer, do the following:

note

This section assumes you are FireWire-ready and have connected your DV camera (with digital tape and not flash memory) to your computer.

1. Set your camera to play mode to run the recorded video.

2. If you haven't already, start Windows Movie Maker as outlined earlier. You'll see the program's main window, as shown in Figure 10.1.

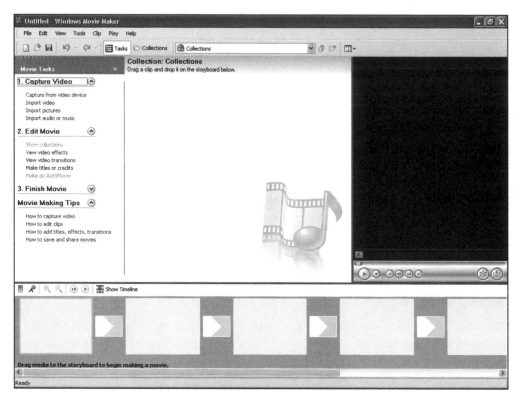

Figure 10.1 Windows Movie Maker has an easy-to-use guide to help you capture and edit a vlog.

3. Open the File menu and select click Capture Video. This launches the Video Capture wizard. Alternatively, click the link labeled "Capture from video device" under Capture Video in the Movie Tasks pane. This also launches the Video Capture wizard.

4. On the Video Capture Device screen, under Available devices, click DV camera. (Although I'm assuming you're using this is the type of camera, other types are available.)

5. In the text box labeled "Enter a file name for your captured video," type a name for the video.

6. Where prompted to choose a place to save your captured video, specify the folder in which you want to save your vlog (click Browse to locate the folder if you're not sure of the exact path).

7. On the Video Setting screen, select the desired video setting for capturing video and audio.

8. On the Capture Method screen, select the "Capture the entire tape automatically" option. The tape in the DV camera will automatically rewind to the beginning.

9. Go make some tea while Movie Maker captures the video.

note

If you realize that don't want to capture an entire tape after all, you can click Stop Capture (in mid-stream) and then click Yes in the dialog box to save the video that has been captured so far. In other words, you don't have to wait for the whole thing to capture. However, you lose out on the tea. At this point, you can also separate the resulting video into smaller clips by selecting the "Create clips when wizard finishes" check box.

10. To close the Video Capture wizard, yep, you guessed it, click Finish. You have recorded a vlog!

note

For more information about using Windows Movie Maker, click any of the links under Movie Making Tips in the Movie Tasks pane.

Capturing Live Video from Your DV Camera

You don't *have* to save a video to a tape. With Windows Movie Maker, you can store video shot with your DV camera directly on your hard drive. To do so, connect your DV camera to your computer as required. Then do the following:

1. Set your camera to camera mode to capture live video and audio.

2. If you haven't already, start Windows Movie Maker as outlined earlier.

3. Open the File menu and select click Capture Video. Alternatively, click the link labeled "Capture from video device" under Capture Video in the Movie Tasks pane. This launches the Video Capture wizard.

4. On the Video Capture Device screen, under Available devices, click DV camera.

5. In the text box labeled "Enter a file name for your captured video," type a name for the video.

6. Where prompted to choose a place to save your captured video, specify the folder in which you want to save your vlog (click Browse to locate the folder if you're not sure of the exact path).

7. On the Video Setting screen, select the desired setting for capturing video and audio.

8. To avoid having audio echo over your speakers while you capture live video, mark the Mute speakers check box.

9. To begin recording, click Start Capture. To stop recording, click Stop Capture.

10. Repeat step 9 to capture another segment of live video.

11. To separate the video into smaller clips after video is captured, mark the "Create clips when wizard finishes" check box.

12. Click Finish to close the Video Capture wizard.

Creating and Editing Your Vlog

To get a feel for editing options, check out the Movie Tasks pane on the left side of Movie Maker's main window. Play around with some of the features in the Edit Movie section to get a quick idea of what Movie Maker enables you to do in terms of editing and adding effects to your vlog. You can also find step-by-step instructions for working with audio, choosing a video host, uploading to the web, building a storyboard (a series of panels arranged to indicate the flow of your vlog), and more—some of which is covered in this section.

Using Storyboards

The *storyboard* is a platform where you put your production together. To build a storyboard, click the Import video link under Capture Video in the Movie Tasks pane. From your video device, this command imports the video—which Movie Maker automatically segments—to your computer, displaying the clips in Collection view. Movie Maker also automatically draws your video from your video device into your computer's memory, so there's little effort on your part. To pre-screen a clip, double-click it. When you've decided which clips are keepers, drag and drop the clips to the storyboard in whatever order you prefer for the final cut of the vlog. If you change your mind, just rearrange your clips on the storyboard using drag and drop.

Editing Your Clips

Using Movie Maker, you can "clip" your clips. Here's how:

1. In the Timeline view, click the clip you'd like to cut down to size. (Odds are you're already in Timeline view; if you are, you'll see timeline bars in the lower half of the main window. If you are not in Timeline view, open the View menu, select Storyboard, and choose View.)

2. In the Timeline view's Preview window, drag the scroll bar slowly and watch as the video progresses. Stop at the point where you want to trim the clip.

3. Open the Clip menu and choose Set Start Trim Point.

4. Drag the progress indicator until you reach the desired end point of your clip.

5. Open the Clip menu and choose Set End Trim Point. The result is a smaller trimmed clip.

Adding Music Effects

Music is a great way to introduce and end your production. To add music to your vlog, import your favorite music and drag and drop it into the timeline as follows:

1. Click the Import audio or music link under Capture Video in the Movie Tasks pane.

2. Locate and select the song you wish to add to your vlog.

3. Click Import. The music track will appear in your Collection view, as shown in the top half of Figure 10.2.

4. Click the Show Timeline button in the Storyboard section of your screen, as shown in the lower half of Figure 10.2.

5. Drag your music track to the Audio/Music level of the timeline and place it in the appropriate spot.

6. Click the Play button to test the music and its placement, as in Figure 10.2.

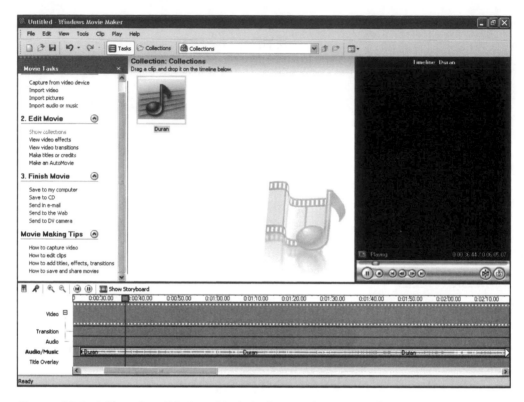

Figure 10.2 Add music to Windows Movie Maker to enhance your vlog.

Managing File Size

One hour of digital video can consume about 10 gigabytes of hard drive space. Obviously, if you're producing a vlog, that won't cut the mustard. You'll need to reduce the size of the file to a few hundred kilobytes to make it manageable for you and your vlog's viewers. You can accomplish this by using Windows Movie Maker or a similar video app to tinker with the file's resolution and/or download method.

Tinkering with Resolution

Many cameras shoot video to completely fill the screen at a high frame-per-second rate, making for a very byte-heavy file. Fortunately, most video apps make it easy to reduce the size of source video files by reducing the amount of footage and its duration, by reducing the size of the frame (for example, shrinking it from 640×480 to 120×90), or by altering the bit rate. You can also play around with compression ratios and frame rates by increasing the former and reducing the latter. Be aware, though, that all these actions affect the resolution (quality) of your vlog. If resolution is poor, you'll lose your audience very quickly. Then again, if you produce an epic, they'll likewise exit stage left. You need to strike a balance.

Streaming

Normally, when you download video, your computer downloads the file entirely before giving you the option to play it. With streaming media, however, you can play the video as it downloads. (In actual fact, you must download part of the video file to create a buffer; after sufficient buffer has downloaded, the file plays as it continues to download behind the scenes.) Consider configuring your vlogs to stream rather than requiring users to download them in toto before viewing. Be warned, though, that streaming media vlogs and other types of digital video may rapidly use up the bandwidth allotted to you by your host; the files are often very big.

note

Most streaming media requires a stream-friendly server. Unfortunately, a discussion of stream-friendly servers is beyond the scope of this book.

Saving and Sharing Your Vlog

The last step is to upload your vlog to a weblog or web page host. Assuming you have a host, you can embed a video in a weblog or web page using a web authoring tool like FrontPage. (Hosting options were discussed at length in Chapter 7. If you don't have a host, Movie Maker will walk you through the signup process for a couple of providers that currently offer free trial accounts.) The general principle of uploading is to first open an offline preview of the web page you are authoring, which will include the link to your video. Next, you will likely select a design function—in this case, the function that lets you add a video. You would then position the insertion point of your video or vlog before opening the Insert menu, selecting Picture or Image (depending on your software), and then selecting Video or Movie (again, depending on your software). Finally, you would locate and select the video file you wish to add and then click Open. With most web-authoring apps, you can preset the number of loop repeats or change the loop delay value to set the amount of time between repeats. You can also determine when the video will commence. Options include when viewers click a button or when they mouse over an icon. Finally, almost all apps let you see whether you were successful via a web page preview feature. Variations on this theme exist; my point is that it's really simple to add a vlog to your weblog.

note

At the time of this writing, there wasn't much in the way of video RSS aggregators for do-it-yourselfers. That said, when they do come out in full force—and they will—the fact that you opted for the do-it-yourself route will set the stage for more flexibility.

Commercial Vlog Services

Just as commercial weblog and podcasting services have emerged, commercial vlogging services are emerging as well. These sites, some still in beta mode, include or specialize in RSS video syndication, making it easier for people to distribute and view vlogs in a timely way. The services profiled in this section are pioneers in commercial vlogging.

Ourmedia.org

The people on the cutting edge of podcasting, vlogging, and weblogging tend to take full advantage of multimedia, integrating print, video, and voice to create compelling content that ranges from political rants to indie music videos and quality films. The problem is, because aggregators don't yet offer much in the way of support when it comes to locating vlogs online, many of these great productions are hiding somewhere on the web, buried in the memory chips of thousands of computers, portable digital media players, and laptops. That's where Ourmedia comes in. Ourmedia is a video-focused online archive supported by the Internet Archive. It hosts at no charge any video, audio, image, or text file that does not violate copyrights and does not include pornography or other objectionable content. Those who use Ourmedia—and as of this writing, the site boasted 60,000 members—realize that it is no cheesy free hosting service; rather, it is meant to promote creativity and to provide a home for creative works. Indeed, proponents of this archive recognize that we are in the midst of a creativity boom, fueled by the fact that the media tools once available to only a few specialized professionals can now be mastered by laypersons. In other words, technology is allowing individuals to become radio announcers, online print journalists, and now TV broadcasters. Big Radio, Big News, and Big TV now have some company.

According to its web site, Ourmedia has some exciting plans in the works for 2006, including the following:

- Enhanced search functionality, including the ability to search by multimedia element such as video, audio, photos, and text, as well as being able to organize by characteristics like image resolution or audio format

- Ratings for each post incorporated into the site search

- Thumbnail images for faster browsing

- A new-generation social-networking system, or "PeopleAggregator," which uses open standards and network interconnectivity as catalysts to bring social networking to the mainstream

- Online tutorials on video and audio production, and tips on the creation of a storyboard and other best practices

- The ability for members to create a new forum topic

- The ability to browse by subject, utilize smarter metadata display, and access better-organized content categories
- A single point of registration (instead of the current system, which requires you to register on both Ourmedia and the Internet Archive)
- Enhancements to the Ourmedia Publisher tool, which lets members drag and drop files into Ourmedia
- BitTorrent support
- The creation of a Remix area that lists productions in the public domain or with a Creative Commons license, enabling others to remix or build upon a work
- The ability to search for an RSS or ATOM feed by artist
- The ability to notify family or friends by email whenever you upload content to the site
- A new license permitting commercial use of productions with compensation paid and with appropriate consent

Yahoo!

In early 2005, Yahoo!—in conjunction with Ourmedia and an independent film site called AtomFilms—launched an online search service that utilizes RSS. The interesting aspect of Yahoo!'s RSS feeds is that they include syndication functionality. This means that aggregators designed to identify and subscribe to vlogs can capture feeds residing on Yahoo!— or more specifically, on My Yahoo!.

My Yahoo! is in the process of morphing into a news aggregator by pulling in current headlines and displaying them on a single page you create or define. It works a lot like the traditional My Yahoo! service, which pushes Yahoo! content to your special My Yahoo! page, except that with its RSS Headlines module, currently in beta form, My Yahoo! also becomes a web-based aggregator. It captures non-Yahoo! content and can display your choice of syndicated RSS feeds from tens of thousands of sources on the web—including vlogs.

note

I should stress that at the time of this writing, such technology was still being developed in beta form.

After you install and run the RSS module and enter edit mode, you have a couple options for finding content. One is to search for content by keyword (for example, "Soccer") or for the specific source or web site (such as NPR or CNN) you want to add. My Yahoo! will try to locate a relevant RSS URL that you can add to the aggregator's subscription directory with the click of a button. It works this way for weblogs as well. Alternatively, if you know the exact RSS URL for the content you seek, you can simply type or paste it and click the Add button.

Yahoo! Podcasts

Yahoo! Podcasts (http://podcasts.yahoo.com), shown in Figure 10.3, lets you search its directory of podcasts by keyword. You can also listen to podcasts online, right away, and subscribe to them right then and there. You can download just one episode of a podcast to your computer or subscribe to the podcast to receive them all. Yahoo! Podcasts even lets you publish your own basic podcast. This is a site you must visit (Yahoo! is renowned for its extensive directories), and it will soon be a bona fide competitor to iTunes. Competition is good for everyone in the podosphere.

Figure 10.3 Yahoo! Podcasts is rapidly adding podcasts to its already extensive directory of web resources.

DTV

A non-profit entity called Participatory Culture (http://participatoryculture.org) has produced a product called DTV (short for Digital TV). DTV is essentially a free and open source broadcasting platform based also on the open standards of RSS and BitTorrent. DTV lets users subscribe to digital video channels and download content as it becomes available. (Sound familiar?) Channels are usually RSS feeds with video enclosures. At this time, DTV features more than 100 free Internet TV channels. In addition, vlog producers can post their content on DTV's open channels page; any existing RSS feeds with video enclosures are compatible. You can also add channels created by indie video-makers and professional broadcasters alike. Alternatively, if you add a web site URL into the DTV app, it will troll that web site to look for videos. The app supports Creative Commons licenses, which can be useful if you wish to re-use or tweak video content for your own purposes. Finally, DTV is integrated with a bookmarking site called del.icio.us, enabling DTV users to build a channel that looks for certain del.icio.us tags for video. If an individual creates a link to a video with that del.icio.us tag, DTV will automatically capture that video.

note

At the time of this writing, a Windows version of DTV was in the works for imminent release, along with a related and fully functioning web site. Right now, it runs on Macs, and uses QuickTime 7 to run videos that are in QuickTime format.

del.icio.us

del.icio.us (no www. prefix) is a social bookmark manager that lets you bookmark web sites and categorize them with keywords. It's different from browser bookmarks in that you can share your collection among your own browsers as well as with others. What makes del.icio.us "social" is that it lets you see and subscribe links that others have collected, and also shows you who else has bookmarked a specific site in which you are interested. It's essentially a shared-interest sharing site. You can also use del.icio.us to locate files that contain a certain tag, such as "cat" or "tree" or what have you. (Check out the web site for the nuts and bolts of how tagging works.)

Open Media Network

Vlog producers can post their work on Open Media Network (http://www.omn.org), which offers an array of free programs that are displayed in a basic program guide. The site automatically delivers programming that you select on the schedule you specify. Those using Open Media Network can watch the video on the site on several pieces of hardware, including PCs, certain iPods with video functionality, digital televisions, and some SmartPhones.

Finding and Subscribing to Vlogs

For viewers of vlogs, special RSS aggregators exist (or are under development) to help capture video content. These include the following:

- **Mefeedia (http://mefeedia.com).** This commercial online video service has created a video or vlog aggregator. It acts like Bloglines and other standard podcast aggregators, but for vlogs. Feed subscribers are notified whenever a new video is posted, and the video, which can be viewed in iTunes, is downloaded automatically. This is possible in large part to ANT aggregation technology, which functions like TiVo for vlogs. Mefeedia's basic services are available free of charge; for-fee enhanced services are currently under development. At the time of this writing, Mefeedia is was available only for Macs, but a Windows version is in the works.

- **Google Blog Search (http://google.com/blogsearch).** Search is the name of the game for Google. It follows, then, that although it's a late entry, it will apply its expertise in any area—like vlogging and podcasting—that experiences rapid growth. Indeed, in mid-September 2005, Google began testing a search service for weblogs. For now, if you go to www.google.com/blogserach, you'll see Google's GOOG database, which includes syndicated weblog posts. At the time of this writing, however, it did not support commercial news web sites, weather, or stock quotes. It likewise did not include aggregation of vlogs posted on weblogs, but the buzz is that Google is planning to add this functionality soon. Keep a sharp eye out for developments from Google in this sphere.

The Future of Mobile Devices

Less than 20 percent of podcast audiences use non-portable means to listen to their programs; the vast majority do so on-the-go. What's needed is a device that lets listeners go to a WiFi hotspot, like Starbucks, and download a subscribed podcast to their mobile device. Of course, as I showed you in Chapter 8, RSS aggregators for mobile devices already exist; they just need to be integrated with WiFi to close the tech gap. I believe that the wireless handset industry is poised to do this in 2006.

In 2006, I also expect hardware manufacturers to ramp up development of even more mobile devices that enable users to view video or vlogs on them. It's true that mobile devices for viewing digital video now exist, but none were geared specifically to podcasting or vlogging per se—until Apple came along in late 2005 and unleashed another groundbreaking surprise with its video iPod. (I discuss this amazing device in the following sidebar). As for other portable video players on the market, you have to hack them to make them work for vlogs.

Apple Video iPod

In mid-October 2005, Apple unveiled its new video iPod player and latest version of iTunes to support downloading TV programs. This development is what most video podcasters have been waiting for: the ability to download on a portable device videos residing in a podcast directory—in this case iTunes. It is one of the first big podcast players to use RSS to syndicate video feeds!

The new video iPod, compared to its predecessor, has more memory (30 gigabytes instead of 20 gigabytes) and is a bit thinner. Its video screen is 2.5 inches diagonally and the resolution is very sharp. It's pleasing to the eye despite its small size. Of course, this is not the only video player game in town; I profiled another video-capable MP3 player in Chapter 9. The video iPod, however, is unbeatable as to design and aesthetics, which are Apple's strengths. It is also easy to use.

This iPod's seamless integration with the new version of iTunes lets you access legal and reasonably priced videos. For example, thanks to a partnership with ABC TV, iTunes broadcasts for the video iPod include *Lost* and *Desperate Housewives*. In addition to a growing list of offerings from ABC, you can quickly access music videos, syndicated TV shows, movie trailers, and some Pixar short films.

Apple does not earn much from the podcasts it carries. But by aggregating podcasts and channeling people to the iTunes music store, it creates a good opportunity to sell more iPods and songs. Now, by introducing and being a repository for video as well, Apple has expanded its potential market. To put things in perspective, people love music and a good music CD will move about 400,000 copies. In contrast, a popular TV show draws up to 35,000,000 viewers. It's clear that Apple is setting the stage to become a full blown media company. These are pioneering times for podcasting and vlogging. It will be very exciting to see how new video-based business models and technologies unfold.

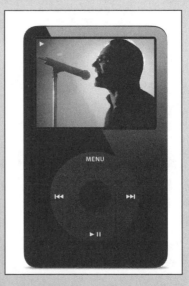

Apple's video iPod, shown in Figure 10.4, comes in 30-gigabyte and 60-gigabyte models. The latter can handle up to 15,000 songs or up to 25,000 photos. It also supports up to 150 hours of video. The video iPod has up to 20 hours of battery life—five hours longer than its predecessor. Moreover, at under half an inch thin, the video iPod utilizes about 40 percent less space than its predecessor. Downloads from iTunes Music Store can include selections from over 2,000,000 songs, 25,000 podcasts, and 2,200 music videos (see Figure 10.5). You can download them to your Mac or PC and then sync them to your video iPod.

Figure 10.4 Apple's recently-introduced video iPod breaks new ground in the world of video podcasting.

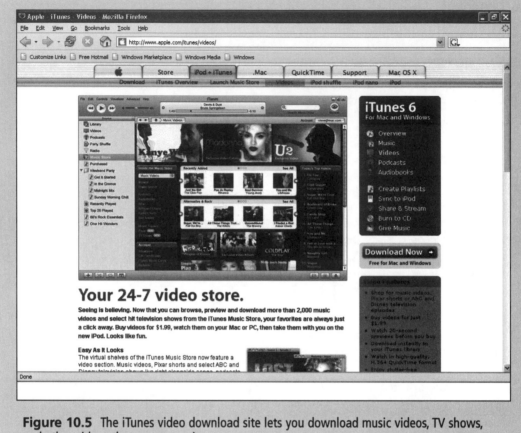

Figure 10.5 The iTunes video download site lets you download music videos, TV shows, and other videos that you can enjoy.

Skype and VOIP Moblogging

Skype is a VOIP (voice over Internet protocol) network that works across different networks. With VOIP networks, voice packets are routed from subscriber to subscriber with help from a free desktop application. In addition to talking to other subscribers, free of charge, Skypers can use the company's SkypeOut and SkypeIn services to connect with traditional telephone numbers for a fee. VOIP is also highly conducive to rich media apps.

So what does all this have to do with podcasting and vlogging? Well, in September 2005 eBay acquired Skype for a tidy $2.6 billion. Why? I'm guessing it's so that eBay members can use the service to view video of products for sale on its platform, along with text and audio descriptions. That means you can look for Skype to roll out support for podcasts and video. Also look for these services to come in a mobile, or moblogging, version.

Satellite Radio and Podcasting

Satellite radio is a fantastic service. It lets you enjoy what you want to hear—when you want to hear it. That said, it is costly. That's why podcasting is attractive: It's free. Podcasting becomes even more attractive if you can convert a satellite radio show to a podcast, syndicate it, and distribute it for free. But wait—that's illegal, isn't it? XM Satellite Radio and Sirius Satellite Radio certainly think so. In fact, to make their point, these companies are pursuing legal action against a company called TimeTrax, described in the following sidebar.

On the other hand, anyone wishing to tape satellite radio may suggest that doing so isn't so different from using a cassette tape to recorde a hit from an FM station. Sure, it's technically illegal, but it's practically accepted, as long as content is not resold. No doubt, the debate will be endless. In the meantime, XM and Sirius plan to roll out TiVo-like devices to allow listeners to pause and rewind live broadcasts.

TimeTrax

TimeTrax (http://www.timetraxtech.com) is a software app for use with satellite radio feeds from XM Satellite Radio and Sirius Satellite Radio. It lets you "capture" (XM might call it something else) more than 120 satellite radio channels, including talk, news, music, and comedy. You can record content in MP3 or WAV format for replay on your computer and, ultimately, on your portable device. It has a 10 event scheduling function that lets you set recording times. The company offers a basic software package for $45 and a more enhanced one for $130.

Internet Radio and Podcasting

Companies like Applian Technologies, makers of Replay Radio (http://www.replay-radio.com), have cropped up to enable you to record Internet radio broadcasts. These radio broadcasts—which are neither traditional radio nor satellite radio in nature—are online, making them an ideal source for syndicated content. (As always, you must be aware of copyright issues when recording Internet radio broadcasts.) To capture various syndicated shows, you use Replay Radio's built-in podcast aggregator. You can use the software to record to to MP3, WAV, WMA, OGG, and AAC audio formats, and the program supports Windows, Real, and other media players. Applian also sells a package called Replay Video to help you produce vlogs; both apps sell for $50 per package.

note

Replay Radio also lets you record XM Satellite Radio broadcasts.

Using Advertising to Parlay Your Podcast or Vlog into a Business

If your podcast or vlog becomes a hit, you may be able parlay it into a commercial or semi-commercial enterprise. Specifically, you can use services such as Google AdSense or BlogAds.com to find companies interested in advertising on your blog. If you use Google AdSense, you'll earn a small commission each time a visitor clicks an ad placed on your weblog. If the ad receives lots of clicks, it can add up quickly. With BlogAds, you earn revenue on the basis of maximizing visits to your weblog.

The Future of Podcasting

One major theme of this book is the ongoing convergence of podcasts, vlogs, and weblogs. This can also be viewed as a convergence of audio, video, and print media. Although this convergence of communication platforms and media formats is already happening in the here and now, the technology behind it has not been perfected. More needs to be done. As further advances are made, more and more podcasts will likely be multimedia-rich; podcasters will be empowered to create more compelling audio and video broadcasts, with print content added for good measure.

Moreover, improved feed capture systems that more fully embrace the exciting world of video weblogs will underpin podcasts of the future. Podcast directories will add filters to help users separate uplifting messages from those that border on the absurd. Yahoo! and Google's recent forays into podcasting represent a strong indication that we will soon be able to collect, rank, and filter podcasts, as well as help podcasters get their best messages out. For example, filters as they now appear in a typical Yahoo! message board will be employed to rate podcasts and vlogs. Better search tools will become available to help you find podcasts using classic keyword search techniques.

I also believe that podcasts will eventually take their place alongside mainstream radio, satellite radio, television, newspapers, magazines, DVDs, and other forms of news and entertainment. The podcast share of this media pie will continue to grow. The fuel behind this growth will be easier-to-use technology and compelling and diverse content—both of which are already currently underway.

Some might say that the best audio content still resides with traditional radio and satellite radio. After all, the people behind these broadcasts are paid professionals who know more than a bit about broadcasting! All too often, however, traditional radio content remains stale, preformatted, scheduled, and peppered with far too many irrelevant commercials. In contrast, podcasts represent the content you want, where you want it, and when you want it. Even advertising within a podcast will likely be relevant to the topic of the podcast.

As the future unfolds, you'll see creativity explode into a new golden age of individual broadcasting. Sure, the content is created by amateurs, but podcast productions will likely improve in quality over time. Those that do not get better will drift away as filters and other mechanisms kick in to separate the good from the bad.

New uses for podcasting will continue to emerge. Although traditional radio broadcasters are currently resistant to podcasts (perhaps because they feel threatened by it), some will begin to selectively release certain shows as syndicated podcasts—as long as doing so serves their economic interest. For example, podcasts may represent good promo opportunities for other shows or events that they regularly broadcast and for which they have lucrative sponsorships.

Other fascinating applications of podcasts and vlogs will include indie film and musical productions. Novelists will be able to create audio plays to extend their own reach. Churches will make available their sermons. Government agencies will use their web sites to podcast public service announcements. Companies will issue podcast manuals that describe how their products should be used. Stock analysts will send out real-time audio reports to paying clients. Heretofore unheard-of podcast advertising models will emerge.

As you can see, the possibilities are endless. Take time to think about other ways that podcasting can be used. Explore your interests, and don't be surprised to find out that there is probably some room for one more podcast about that interest!

PART FOUR

APPENDIXES

APPENDIX A

RESOURCES

The purpose of this appendix is to provide an at-a-glance overview of some podcasting-related web sites and resources. This appendix is far from exhaustive, simply because the number of podcasts—and the technology behind them—is growing so quickly.

My approach is not to describe each and every web site indicated in this appendix, although I do describe some. Where it makes sense to do so, I have grouped resources under generic headings. In the case of some resources with unique features, I have added commentary. Take the time to browse through some of the sites that catch your interest. You'll get an even better idea of what podcasts are all about.

Podcasting-Related Web Sites and Directories

Many of the web sites in this section represent organizations and people that are the pioneers of podcasting. Others in this list are simply catching on fast... *really* fast!

- **Allpodcasts.com** (http://www.allpodcasts.com) enables podcasters to browse feeds by category. The site features an RSS feed validator for your own script. That means if there are any problems with the feed you submitted for validation, it will give you a helpful message identifying the problem.
- **Audio.weblogs.com** (http://audio.weblogs.com) has several podcast links and lots of information about podcasting.
- **blinkxtv** (http://www.blinkx.tv) enables you to search the web for video using plain-language search terms and allows you to set up a smart folder for searching topics while not connected to the Internet. This web site is profiled in Chapter 10, "The Leading Edge of Podcasting."

- **BlogExplosion** (http://www.blogexplosion.com/podcast) enables you to stream your podcast audio and video weblogs to the Internet. It cannot play all Internet radio streams, requires a Macromedia Flash player (downloadable from the web site) and only plays "canned" MP3 files (that is, files already exported to MP3) Nonetheless, it epitomizes the morphing of podcasting into a multimedia form.

- **Bloguniverse** (http://www.bloguniverse.com) is a weblog directory and tool resource, with links. It makes it easy to add your site, and to search for sites under lots of topics.

- **Digitalpodcast.com** (http://www.digitalpodcast.com) lists podcasts by category, facilitates searches, and enables you to upload your own script and to get your podcast rated. The site also maintains a list of podcast forums for discussions of all things podcasting.

- **Engadget** (http://podcasts.engadget.com) has a lot of useful articles and entries about the podcasting industry, and about other technologies.

- **gigadial.net** (http://www.gigadial.net) allows you to create and subscribe to podcast-powered feeds from your favorite podcasters. The home page lists about 30 of the most recently updated feeds.

- **idiotvox** (http://www.idiotvox.com) is a well-organized site with podcast reviews from listeners, and its podcasts are sorted into categories. You'll need to have software from the site's list of compatible applications in order to update and organize your podcasts, but it provides dozens of download links. It makes it easy to list your podcast, requiring only a reciprocal link.

- **Indiepodder.org**, a.k.a. iPodder.org (http://www.ipodder.org), is a decentralized, categorized directory of links to podcast feeds. It maintains podcasts in a list of folders and links to recently updated podcasts.

- **The Internet Archive** (http://www.archive.org) is the World Wide Web's library—a non-profit organization established for the purpose of offering permanent access to historical collections in digital format.

- **iPodderX** (http://www.ipodderx.com) bills itself as a competitor to iTunes, and is a popular site among some user groups. It has many features iTunes lacks including the ability to turn text into audio podcasts. Although the company asserts that it will soon be coming out with a version for Windows, the software currently it requires MacOS X 10.3.5 or better, and iTunes. To use the service, you have to download the company's software for about $25.

- **iTunes** (http://www.apple.com/podcasting) has a podcasting web site that provides an easy upload and download process.

- **MySportsRadio** (http://www.mysportsradio.com) is a production of the Sports Podcast Network, a raucous sports-focused site with lots of sports news and opinions.

- **Odeo.com** (http://www.odeo.com) lets you browse by topic or by tag and is a multimedia-friendly podcasting site. It is described more fully in Chapter 7, "Hosting and Promoting Your Podcasts."

- **Open Media Networks** (http://www.omn.org) proclaims that it is "the future of public TV and radio." The site receives video and audio from more than 25 public TV and radio stations. It also enables you to upload your own feed with a drag-and-drop interface. This site is multimedia-friendly.

- **OpenPodcast.org** (http://www.openpodcast.org) is a dynamically generated podcast creator. The web site indicates that it seeks short segments (under five minutes is suggested), which will be included in a feed as they are received. Think of it as an unmoderated call-in show.

- **Penguinradio** (http://www.penguinradio.com/podcasting) "strives to free the Internet from the shackles of your PC," and maintains a long list of podcasts, updated daily. The site is divided between pages catering to U.S. and U.K. audiences.

- **Pocketcasting.com** (http://www.pocketcasting.com) is podcasting tailored for the pocket PC. It provides pocket PC podcasting news, and facilitates RSS feeds from websites specifically designed for handhelds. It exemplifies how podcasting has morphed into a mobile activity.

- **Podblaze.com** (http://www.podblaze.com) focuses on usability. The site asserts that "We make it easy to get your podcast on the web in blazing speed." Podblaze has free listener accounts, and has some commercial podcasting and distribution services.

- **Podcast.net** (http://www.podcast.net) bills itself as "The Podcast Directory," and it does maintain a comprehensive list of podcasts. It also provides links for getting podcasting software and accepts suggestions for new subject categories.

- **Podcast411.com** (http://www.podcast411.com) maintains resources for podcasters, including tutorials, as well as the obligatory directory of podcasts.

- **Podcastalley.com** (http://www.podcastalley.com) proclaims "Free the Airwaves," and it does a lot to facilitate just that with a directory of resources for podcasters. The site maintains a list of regularly updated feeds, as well as a Top 10 list, and a random list for those willing to take a ride on chance.

- **The Podcast Bunker** (http://www.podcastbunker.com) says "We're about Podcast Quality, not Quantity!" and provides podcast previews, calling itself the "Home of the 30-second Podcast." *TIME Magazine* called it one of the 50 Coolest Websites of 2005.

- **Podcastcentral** (http://www.podcastcentral.com) provides a list of resources for you to "do it yourself," links to download podcast software, and a list of feeds.

- **PodcastExpert** (http://www.podcastexpert.com) has a lot of know-it-all information about podcasting.

- **Podcasthost.com** (http://www.podcasthost.com) is a site maintained by a community of podcasters, and boasts a clearinghouse of how-to stuff, news, and forums about podcasting, in addition to a directory of podcasts.

- **The Podcast Network** (http://www.thepodcastnetwork.com) is a comprehensive site about podcasting.

- **Podcasting Avenue** (http://podcasters.blogspot.com) discusses podcasting and other trends in a weblog format.

- **Podcastingnews.com** (http://www.podcastingnews.com) has a list of podcasting-related jobs in addition to podcasting news and other resources.

- **The Podcasting Station** (http://www.podcasting-station.com) is a simple and elegant site. It states that "the goal of The Podcasting Station is to enable you to find podcasts with minimal effort." It features links to tools, a tutorial, news, and an MP3/MIDI resource site.

- **Podcasting Tools** (http://www.podcasting-tools.com) features a home page that notes "This site is a comprehensive podcasting resource detailing everything you need to know about Podcasting." It provides a number of resources, including useful graphics and other tools, as well as a directory of podcast forums.

- **PodcastPickle.com** (http://www.podcastpickle.com) calls itself "The World's Best Podcast Directory." That may be a tall and overstated claim, but the site does have a lot of resources, as well as Pickle gear.

- **Podcast Shuffle** (http://www.podcastshuffle.com) is a free and advertisement-free podcast directory built and maintained to support the podcast community. It maintains a directory indexed by subject as well as a Podcast Shuffle page that shuffles your podcast selection every 10 seconds.

- **Podfeed.net** (http://www.podfeed.net) provides a place for listeners to read and write reviews and to share podcasts, as well as featuring a podcast directory.

- **Podfeeder** (http://www.podfeeder.com) has its own podcast-listening software—with a freeware version and a commercial version—and an interesting index; the bigger the link, the more feeds in the category. You can add feeds, too.

- **Podnova** (http://www.podnova.com) claims among its developers some people who've been involved in podcasting since the beginning. The site is designed to make it easy to find and listen to podcasts.

- **Podscope** (http://www.podscope.com) is the first and only search engine that creates a "Spoken Word Index" for the entire content of podcasts—enabling the user to find the exact content that interests him or her—a technology that is also applicable to video blogs and personal videos. Podscope crawls the web looking for podcasts and creates an index against every word, thereby making the contents searchable. The user can search on a term, generate a list of results ranked by a variety of methods to find the most relevant podcast, and click to play or to download. Podscope is covered further in Chapter 10.

- **PublicRadioFan.com** (http://www.publicradiofan.com/podcasts.html) features program listings for hundreds of public radio stations around the world. The site maintains an index of podcasts, sortable by title or by subject.

- **RSS Digest** (http://www.bigbold.com/rssdigest) is all about RSS technology.

- **The RSS Network** (http://www.rss-network.com) makes it easy to find and to publish RSS feeds.

- **Singing Fish** (http://www.singingfish.com) is an audio/video search engine. It enables you to select files from a check-box menu.

- **Sportpodcasts.com** (http://www.sportpodcasts.com) is a sports-oriented site with a simple and elegant presentation. It has a subject-oriented directory, a forum, and other resources.

- **Technorati** (http://www.technorati.com) is a powerful tag-driven search site oriented toward weblogs more so than podcasts. Nonetheless, it's noteworthy due to its sheer size and possible usefulness in finding podcasts since podcasts may be found in some of the included weblogs. It is currently tracking two million tags.

- **Yahoo! Podcasts** (http://podcasts.yahoo.com) is a recent entry in the podosphere. Rest assured that when the good folks at Yahoo! enter an Internet space like podcasting, it's because they believe in the potential of this trend and in the underlying technology behind it. You can use one of Yahoo!'s most notable features, its directory tool, to browse its growing directory of podcasts. You can also listen to podcasts right away online (if you like it, you can subscribe), and you can download just one broadcast to your PC or Mac or subscribe to them all. Finally, Yahoo! Podcasts can help you publish your own no-frills podcast.

Podcasting Software: Aggregators

These applications are desktop- or web-based. Each has a common feature that captures podcasts and other feeds you wish to listen to. Many are discussed in Chapter 8, "Podcasting Software." Most aggregators in the following list have a few more features that set them apart from the rest.

The following aggregators were introduced and discussed in Chapter 8:

Aggregator	URL
iPodder	http://ipodder.sourceforge.net
iPodder X	http://ipodderx.com
iPodder.NET	http://ipodder.net
iTunes 4.9	http://itunes.com
jpodder	http://jpodder.com
Nimiq	http://nimiq.nl
Now Playing	http://brandon.fuller.name/archives/hacks/nowplaying/
Playpod	http://iggsoftware.com/playpod
PocketRSS	http://www.happyjackroad.net
Pod2GO	http://kainjow.com/pod2go
PoddumFeeder	http://tucows.com

The following software resources, organized by category, are related to podcasting, but most were not mentioned previously in this book. They may be better or worse than those programs that received a nod, or do things that are a bit different from the aggregators I discuss in this book.

Desktop News Aggregators

Desktop aggregators reside on your desktop. They get syndicated content for you, manage your subscriptions, and help you sync with your MP3 device. Some desktop aggregators look like web browsers; others look like email programs. They require a bit more work on your part to operate.

For All Operating Systems

Aggregator	URL	Description
Bitty Browser	http://www.bitty.com	Applets display a virtual web browser within a frame on a web page. Can also display podcast, RSS, and ATOM feeds.
BlogMatrix Sparks!	http://www.blogmatrix.com/sparks_main	Includes a podcast recording feature.
NewsFeed	http://home.arcor.de/mdoege/newsfeed	An RSS/RDF/ATOM reader written in Phthon/Tk. Supports voice.
NewsMonster	http://newsmonster.org	An RSS aggregator that runs on an open-source web browser.
RadioUserLand	http://radio.userland.com	Integrates with a weblog editing tool.
Sage	http://sage.mozdev.org	A lightweight RSS and ATOM feed reader extension for the Firefox web browser.
ThinFeeder	http://thinfeeder.sourceforge.net	A simple RSS/ATOM aggregator developed in Java.

For Windows

Aggregator	URL	Description
All Headline News	http://www.allheadlinenews.com/reader	Delivers RSS and is preconfigured with popular news feeds. Lets you add RSS feeds and set preferences. Content includes news, financial data, and more; premium content is available for a fee.
Attensa	http://www.attensa.com	Delivers newsfeeds into Microsoft Outlook. Includes browser toolbars for Internet Explorer and Firefox that simplify the process of adding and managing subscriptions. Supports attachment of podcast files.
Awasu	http://awasu.com	Multi-featured, customizable, and extensible using an embedded Internet Explorer or non-Firefox browser.
Custom Reader	http://www.customreader.com	An aggregator you can brand as your own and customize to your preferences. Includes full statistical usage analysis.
GreatNews	http://curiostudio.com	Feature-filled, but not a memory hog.
Net Newz	http://www.net-newz.com/en/welcome.php	Available in English and French.
NewsAnts	http://www.newsants.com	A Chinese podcast aggregator with a news web site search tool that converts HTML to RSS. It has tons of links to Chinese newspapers. China's population of Internet users has surpassed 100 million and is the world's second largest after the United States, which has 130 million.
NewsBar	http://www.stelmarski.com/NewsBar	News is shown on your desktop in the same scrolling manner that news networks use on TV.
WinRss	http://www.brindys.com/winrss/iukmenu.html	When a podcast site is updated, it summarizes the feed as a Windows tool tip.
Wizz RSS	http://www.wizzcomputers.com/WizzRss.php	A Firefox extension supporting all versions of RSS, ATOM 0.3, and podcast feeds. Also supports Mandrake Linux 10.1.
wTicker	http://www.wticker.org	Feature-filled podcast aggregator including mail notification, SSL security, stock tickers, and article read-outs. Customizable with SQL scripts, and can run on a memory stick.

For Mac OS X

Aggregator	URL	Description
Ensemble	http://pyxis-project.net/ensemble/index.php	Japanese RSS/ATOM news reader with OPML-import capability. (Click the translation icon.)
MiNews	http://www.js8media.com/minews	Aggregator for Mac OS X.
NetNewsWire Lite	http://ranchero.com/netnewswire/#lite	Freeware edition of the commercial NetNewsWire program (ranchero.com/netnewswire).
NewsMac	http://www.thinkmac.co.uk/newsmac	Multi-lingual RSS reader with Palm and iPod sync capability.
News Reader	http://www.benkazez.com/newsreader.php	Displays news feeds in a nice dashboard widget.
RSSOwl	http://www.rssowl.org	RSS/RDF/ATOM newsreader in Java with an intuitive graphic user interface.
Safari RSS	http://www.apple.com/macosx/features/safari	Built into Mac OSX 10.4.

For Unix

Aggregator	URL	Description
akregator	http://akregator.sourceforge.net	A KDE RSS/ATOM aggregator.
Feedisto	http://normo.org/projects/feedisto-modules	A module choosing interesting RSS links with text search. Supports both online and offline browsing.
Lektora	http://www.lektora.com	Integrates with Firefox within the browser.
Liferea	http://liferea.sourceforge.net	A GTK/GNOME aggregator.
Olive	http://freshmeat.net/projects/olive	Provides a chronological view instead of the more common site-oriented view of news stories.
PenguinTV	http://penguintv.sourceforge.net	A simple but powerful multimedia aggregator that downloads enclosed media in podcasts and video blogs.
Raggle	http://www.raggle.org	A console RSS aggregator.
Snownews	http://kiza.kcore.de/software/snownews	A text-based RSS newsreader.
Straw	http://www.nongnu.org/straw	An RSS/RDF/ATOM aggregator for GNOME, written in Python.

Online News Aggregators

Online aggregators are aggregators that reside on the Internet rather than on your desktop, but have aggregator functionality. They are typically hosted on ISP servers or on mega-portals like My Yahoo! The work of finding podcasts is done mostly by them, but things may be controlled by them as well. Examples of this control may include incorporating a limited number of features the aggregator has, and forcing you to use their interface, with which you may not be familiar. Choice of content may be limited and registration is likely required. The entries in this list could be free or may represent a paid service.

Free Online News Aggregators

Aggregator	URL	Description
BigBlogZoo	http://www.bigblogzoo.com	Categorizes nearly 100,000 feeds.
Bloglines	http://www.bloglines.com	Owned by Ask Jeeves (http://www.askjeeves.com), this is a service for subscribing to news feeds and to publishing weblogs using your feeds. Supports many languages and moblogging.
Everyfeed	http://www.everyfeed.com	Presents many feed-finding forms such as directories, a search engine, and personalized feeds.
FeedBucket	http://www.feedbucket.com	A no-frills RSS aggregator.
Feeds2Read	http://feeds2read.net	An RSS feed reader and directory supporting several languages.
FeedShake	http://feedshake.com	A simple and very usable interface that lets you sort, filter, merge, and limit multiple RSS feeds and podcasts.
fluctu8	http://fluctu8.com	Supports podcasts in RSS and ATOM, as most aggregators do. Also supports MP3, OGG, and FLAC audio formats for clear audio.
iNews Torrent	http://www.inewstorrent.com	Submit news articles or RSS feeds to any of this site's channels. Broadcast your own news channels and create a personal selection of news channels. Submit feeds from weblogs.
Kinja	http://kinja.com/	Web-based RSS/RDF/ATOM reader and weblog portal. Collects news from selected web sites.
LiveJournal	http://www.livejournal.com	A blogging site with news aggregation. Several other sites are highly integrated with LiveJournal and its code.
NewsIsFree	http://www.newsisfree.com	A newsreader with tools to browse and search for podcasts. The Premium Services option offers advanced features such as news clipping, click tracking, news alerts, and news archives.
NewsXS	http://www.newsxs.com	News aggregator and RSS-feed generator. Supports many European languages.
Morenews.be	http://www.morenews.be	Read news from newspapers, weblogs, and magazines and create your own personal page here. You can add RSS newsfeeds as well.

Aggregator	URL	Description
My Yahoo! RSS	http://my.yahoo.com/s/guest-promo.php	My Yahoo! added a lot of new features including news aggregation (add any RSS feed to your page) for podcasts, video and images. It is convenient if you're a Yahoo! subscriber. It does have what its more functional podcasting competitors don't—$2.5 billion in net cash waiting to be used for enhancements!

Commercial Online News Aggregators

Aggregator	URL	Description
All Headline News	http://www.allheadlinenews.com	Provides professionally aggregated RSS and JavaScript news feeds from the web, print media, TV video broadcasts, and radio. Supports moblogging and interactive applications. Content like news, weather, and stock data is delivered in real time via an XML feed. Compatible with JavaScript for richer multimedia.
YellowBrix	http://www.yellowbrix.com	Aggregates news from thousands of top news sources. Categorizes and downloads feeds in real-time through XML script.

Software to Create Podcast Productions

In this book, I profiled Audacity as a tool to record, edit, and enhance podcasts, but there are others:

Software	URL
Adobe Audition	http://www.adobe.com/audition
GarageBand	http://www.apple.com/garageband
iPodcast Producer	http://www.industrialaudiosoftware.com/products/index.html
Mix Cast Live	http://www.mixcastlive.com
Propaganda	http://www.makepropaganda.com
Sound Byte	http://www.blackcatsystems.com/software/soundbyte.html
Sound Recorder for Windows*	http://www.microsoft.com
Soundtrack Pro for Mac	http://www.apple.com/finalcutstudio/soundtrackpro
Sparks! 2.0	http://www.blogmatrix.com

*To open Sound Recorder, click Start, select All Programs, select Accessories, point to Entertainment, and then click Sound Recorder. Try it. With your mic hooked up, it takes only seconds to create a quick track.

RSS Feed Creators to Upload Usable Podcasts

Propaganda, iPodcast Producer, and Sparks! 2.0 (listed in the preceding section) also come with RSS feed creators. I introduced these applications in Chapter 7, "Hosting and Promoting Your Podcasts." The following are stand-alone apps.

Software	URL
Feeder	http://www.reinventedsoftware.com
FeedForAll	http://www.feedforall.com
Live365 for streaming	http://www.live365.com/index.live
Nicecast for streaming	http://www.rogueamoeba.com/nicecast

Podcasts of Interest

Most of these podcasts are created by individuals; others are commercial in nature. They are organized by category; categories in podcast directories are even more specific. This short list represents $1/1,000^{th}$ of one percent of the podcasts out there in the podosphere. Add the related vlogs, and the figure is much higher. The purpose is to show you what is available, how podcasts are being used, and what they look like.

Entertainment, Leisure, and Sports

Podcast	URL
AssistiveMedia	http://www.assistivemedia.org
Audible.com	http://www.audible.com
AudioBooksForFree.com	http://www.audiobooksforfree.com
Audiobooks Online	http://www.audiobooksonline.com
Canadian Broadcasting Corporation	http://www.cbc.ca
Harry Podder	http://harrypodderpodcast.blogspot.com
My Sports Radio.com	http://mysportsradio.com
National Public Radio	http://www.npr.org

Money and Finances

Podcast	URL
Debt Podcast	http://debtpodcast.blogspot.com
Exit 50	http://www.exit50.com
The Indie Analyst Show	http://www.indieanalyst.com
Investibles	http://investibles.blogspot.com
Landed.fm	http://www.landed.fm
Pro Money Talk	http://www.promoneytalk.com
TheBizCast Podcast	http://thebizcast.libsyn.com

Technology

Podcast	URL
Digital Off Ramp	http://digitalofframp.blogspot.com
iLounge	http://www.ilounge.com
stuFF mc	http://www.stuffmc.com
Make Magazine	http://makezine.com
TechNewsRadio	http://www.technewsradio.com

Health

Podcast	URL
HerbalEd.org	http://www.herbaled.org
The Home Spa Goddess Show	http://hsgshow.blogspot.com
MARINA's Body Sculpting & Stretch	http://www.marinaspodcast.com/highnrg_podcasts
MommyCast	http://www.mommycast.com
The Nursing Station	http://www.thenursingstation.org
Strength Radio	http://www.strengthradio.com

Spirituality

Podcast	URL
ChristianPodcasting.com	http://www.tfc.edu/radio/podcasting
ChristianTuner	http://www.christiantuner.com/programs/podcasting.aspx
Rabbi Garfinkel's Podcasting Network	http://homepage.mac.com/rabbigarfinkel1/podcasts

Online Legalities

Creative Commons–licensed content is available at http://www.creativecommons.org; you can learn more about the organization at this site. ASCAP Internet license agreements are discussed at http://www.ascap.com/weblicense.

APPENDIX B

GLOSSARY

A

AAC Advanced Audio Coding is a digital compression algorithm that reduces the size of digital music files. It is commonly used with Apple's iPod players. Although it has better sound dynamics than the MP3 format, it is still part of the MPEG (Motion Picture Experts Group) standard-setting body.

ADPCM Adaptive Differential Pulse Code Modulation is a fast 16-bit file format using lossy (in the compression process, a small amount of data is lost) compression.

ADSL High-speed connection offered by phone companies in many areas of the country. Also known as DSL.

AIFF and AIFF-C Audio Interchange File Format. This format was developed by Apple Computer Corporation to store sounds in the data element of a file. Macintoshes can play and record AIFF files. Common data extensions for AIFF files include .aif, .aiff, and .aifc.

ActiveSync An application that synchronizes digital files between a PC and PDAs (personal digital assistants) and other mobile devices running Microsoft Windows mobile operating systems.

aggregator An application that obtains and profiles feeds from podcasts and weblogs. It also handles feeds from commercial news sites and video weblogs, or *vlogs*. It usually compiles a number of user-specified XML format feeds (of which RSS is a part) into a user-friendly web page, client application (like iPodder), or device (such as an MP3 player). Aggregators are evolving as key built-in features of commercial web sites like My Yahoo!, web browsers, media players (like iTunes), and email clients. Aggregator or similar features (non-XML) can be found in cell phones that let you download audio to a weblog (known as *moblogging*). Aggregators are also found in hardware like TiVo and software like Replay Radio. They can reside on a personal computer or online.

analog A wave that continuously varies in strength and/or quantity. Digital, on the other hand is a series of 1s and 0s, or on and off states.

analog ripper Converts analog signals from cassette tapes, vinyl, or radio to WAV files.

analog-to-digital converter Converts sound waves from their analog format (what you hear with your ear) to a digital format (what the computer can understand).

application A piece of software that tells hardware, such as a computer or SmartPhone, what to do.

attenuation The total or partial reduction of the level of a signal.

attenuation threshold Suppressing sound above a certain level.

audio tracks Individual songs or cuts on an audio CD.

B

BitTorrent A peer-to-peer file distribution protocol. With BitTorrent, files are disassembled into smaller fragments, sent through the Internet, and then reassembled on the computer of the person or application requesting the information. If a piece cannot be found, each peer member's server takes advantage of the best connection to find the missing pieces. This speeds up the data-gathering process and is why BitTorrent is great at handling large volumes of data such as big podcasts and long vlogs.

blog Also known as a *weblog*, which is a short form of *web* and *log*. A blog is a web site of pages where content is updated periodically. Content is posted as a web journal entry using software applications. The content can vary considerably and include one or more of written text, audio podcasts, music, video without sound, or video with sound. A blog is also an essential platform or online home where all of these file types may reside. It makes sense for them to reside on a blog because a written explanation of what the file contains is a logical starting point.

blogging The process of posting a text journal entry (to your own weblog page) or contributing a comment or response as a visitor (to another person's weblog). Highly related to this is podcasting (creating or listening to audio on a weblog), vlogging or video blogging (creating or viewing video on a weblog), and photo blogging (creating or viewing pictures on a weblog). Weblogging, podcasting, vlogging, and picture sharing can be done from a computer or on the go (also referred to as *moblogging*). Moblogging is a method or channel of blogging, not a type or form of blogging. Essentially, you can blog words, as well as an array of multimedia including voice, music, video, or pictures. You can also essentially create a personal "newspaper."

bootleg recording The unauthorized recording of a live concert, CD, cassette tape, record album, or musical broadcast on radio or television. Also known as a *pirate recording* or *underground recording.*

burning The process of writing information to a CD.

C

client An application or piece of software.

codec Short for COder-DECoder. An application that transforms one digital format into another. For example, a WAV audio file can be transformed into MP3 format via codec.

compression mode The process that determines the quality and format of the finished digital file. Depending on the method used, modes can be *lossy* or *lossless*—keeping or losing audio quality.

copyright The legal right to control how a song, lyric, program, book, or other piece of intellectual property is reproduced, tributed, and sold. Songs in particular can have multiple copyrights—one for the author of the music, one for the author of the lyrics, and one for the musician or band performing the piece.

CPU The central processing unit is the brains of a computer, PDA (personal digital assistant), laptop, or other electronic device that has applications and programs requiring the processing of information in a logical (programmed) way.

cut An individual song or piece of music on a track.

D

decibel A common expression of sound measurement and a measurement of a sound:power ratio.

device In the context of podcasting, any hard-drive- or flash-memory-based piece of hardware, including a digital music player.

digital audio Sound or music that is stored as a series of bits rather than by a continuously varying (analog) signal.

E

equalization The term for adjusting the relative output of frequencies in a given range to give a more balanced sound.

equalizer A hardware or software device that lets you filter specific frequency ranges (equalize) the audio output to your speakers.

F

flash memory A form of RAM (Random Access Memory) that retains digital data when the power of the device on which flash memory resides is turned off. Flash memory can be built-in or removable. It is quickly gaining in storage capacity to the point it now rivals hard drives. Most MP3 players and SmartPhones now use flash memory because it supports miniaturization. There are no moving parts within flash memory.

frame The smallest "slice" of data you can play or manipulate in a track being recorded. The term comes from movie and video production and frames of films.

FTP File Transfer Protocol is a standard, protocol, and channel by which large files can be transmitted over the Internet. It is typically secured, but can also be unsecured.

H

hard-drive memory A way of storing data on a hard drive that has moving parts, much like the hard drive on your home computer.

hyperlink A strand of code in a document (that can be hidden or revealed in a web browser) linking to another resource, such as a web page with an RSS or other feed, or any other online document.

I

IDE Acronym for Integrated Device Electronics. An inexpensive and popular interface for PC hardware and devices. IDE has largely been supplanted by EIDE, which can handle more devices in a single computer. *See also* EIDE and SCSI.

iPod A line of MP3 players from Apple Computer.

iPodder An aggregator (software or client) that downloads podcast audio files directly to your computer and/or MP3 player.

iTunes Apple's Mac- and PC-based media player that plays MP3s, AAC files, and other audio formats.

L

licensing Contracting for the right to perform, record, distribute, and/or digitally transmit a copyrighted song or other work.

line-out jack Bypasses any amplifier built into the sound card so you can connect the sound card to an external amplified source.

M

media player An application that plays multimedia including music, videos, and podcasts. Windows Media Player and iTunes are two of many examples. Some media players play sound *and* video; others play sound *or* video.

mix A combination of multiple tracks to create a finished song that can be heard on a CD or an album.

mixer A device that creates several different versions of the same song depending on the volumes, tempos, and effects chosen in the mix. The individual tracks are then combined into a final mix that usually has only two tracks (stereo).

moblogging A method or channel of blogging, podcasting, vlogging, and picture sharing. It refers to *the way* blogging and such is done, not *what* is done. It uses mobile portable devices like cell phones, not desktop computers.

morphing Adding effects, such as reverb, that transform the way the MP3 file sounds.

MP2 One of several related standards for storing audio and video.

MP3 Abbreviation for MPEG 1, Layer 3, which is the portion of the MPEG standard that specifies how audio files are stored. It is a type of digital compression that is used to reduce the size of music files while maintaining quality. MP3 compression is part of MPEG compression.

MP3 file A digital audio file created using lossy compression techniques that conform to the MPEG 1, Layer 3 standard. MP3 files are relatively small—about 1 megabyte per minute of audio—but also provide near CD-quality sound.

MP3 player A device that plays files (podcasts or music) in MP3 format.

MP4 One of several related standards for storing audio and video.

MPEG The Motion Pictures Expert Group is an organization that sets standards for digital data compression. Recently adopted standards include MPEG Layer 5 and JPEG2000 for videos and pictures. MPEG compresses large video files (and the audio or podcasts within them). MPEG audio files can be created using Layer 1, 2, or 3. Standard MP3 files use Layer 1, the most compressed of the layers. Layers 2 and 3 provide greater quality at the cost of a larger audio file. MPEG 1, Layer 3 files typically have a sampling rate of 44.1 kilohertz.

N

noise Anything that obscures a signal.

normalizing The process of setting various frequency ranges so that the tracks sound more normal.

O

Ogg Vorbis (or OOG) Not an alien planet. It is an open-source file compression format that works like an MPEG codec. Similar but superior in sound quality to MP3.

OPML Outline Processor Markup Language creates files for RSS and is conducive to multimedia.

P

peer-to-peer (or P2P) A computer network that uses individuals' online computers as a proxy to a formal network run by a broadband company. Peer-to-peer maximizes the usefulness of a critical mass of computers to speed up the information-gathering process. If more computers are accessible, it follows that the likelihood of finding data online also increases, hence the faster speed of information retrieval.

piracy The unauthorized and illegal duplication or distribution of copyrighted material. This material may be a music CD, radio show, or other broadcast. Piracy of material belonging to others often involves some form of financial gain. Also known as *bootleg recording*.

player A type of software that plays MP3 or other audio or video files.

plug-in An application that is "plugged" into an existing program (like Firefox) to add to a program's functionality.

podcast A digital audio broadcast that can be transferred to a portable digital music device like an iPod or other MP3 player. It can also be listened to on a desktop or laptop computer, PDA (personal digital assistant), mobile phone, SmartPhone, BlackBerry, and other MP3-capable mobile devices.

podcaster A person who listens to or creates podcasts. A participant in the realm of podcasting, or *podosphere*.

podcasting The process of posting an audio entry (usually to your own personal or commercial weblog page or sometimes to just a standard web page) or listening to the podcast audio on a weblog. Highly related to this is *blogging* (posting a text journal entry to your own weblog page or contributing to another person's weblog with comments), vlogging, or video blogging (creating or viewing video on a weblog), and photo blogging (creating or viewing pictures on a weblog). Podcasting, weblogging, vlogging, and picture sharing can be done from a computer or on the go (also referred to as *moblogging*). Moblogging is a method or channel of blogging, not a type or form of blogging. Essentially, you can blog words, as well as an array of multimedia including voice, music, video, or pictures. You can also essentially create a personal "radio broadcast." Podcasting in a vlog is still essentially podcasting in that you are still conveying a personal audio message.

podcatcher An aggregator that is limited to podcasts. Current aggregators may catch a lot more than just podcasts, so this term is being used less.

poditorial A term coined by John Hedtke to describe a podcasting editorial.

podmercial A term coined and trademarked by John Iasiuolo to describe a podcasting commercial.

podosphere Indicates the realm or domain within which people listen to and create podcasts. It is the podcasting world.

preamp A preamplifier that, in the context of podcasting, typically powers the microphone. It is a hardware device or a program that sets the level of sound before it is amplified. Hardware preamps are often used to boost and filter the signal of a turntable prior to the signal being amplified. Preamps provide filtering at the source of the audio signal.

public domain Intellectual property of any kind that may be freely copied, performed, and distributed. Intellectual property can become public domain by having the copyright expire or by a declaration by the copyright owner(s) that the material is in the public domain.

Q–R

QuickTime A video format from Apple used for multimedia files. QuickTime movies usually have the extension .mov.

RAM Random Access Memory stores information like computer programs and data. The CPU manages the dynamic flow of information to, from, and within RAM. It's a holding area, canvas, or table where all data is placed and is arranged by your computer as it was programmed to do. Unlike flash memory, RAM memory is lost when power is down (although technically it may be recovered by your computer with special applications).

RealAudio Another popular file format for sound and video. RealAudio files are compressed to minimize their size, but they are not as compressed as MP3 files.

RSS Really Simple Syndication is a standard or protocol designed mostly to download podcasts. The RSS feed is the actual link to the podcast or other file type. The RSS script allows a file to be downloaded on a subscription basis, so users get the new file when it is updated.

S

sampling Reading sound waves at regular intervals and storing the information in a digitized file.

sampling precision The amount of information stored about a sample. Typical rates are 8-bit and 16-bit. 8-bit sampling will give up to 256 different levels, while 16-bit sampling gives up to 65,536 different levels. In general, the more frequently you sample and the greater the precision, the more closely the digital version will resemble the audio version.

sampling rate The number of times per second that the sound card samples the sound being converted. Typical sampling rates for audio are 11 kilohertz, 22 kilohertz, and 44 kilohertz. One hertz (abbreviated Hz) is a single cycle per second, so a sampling rate of 44 kilohertz means that the computer is sampling the sound 44,000 times every second. The more often the computer samples the sound, the more of the sound the computer "hears."

SCSI Small Computer System Interface, pronounced "scuzzy." An interface between computers and devices that is not as common on Windows computers as it is on Macintosh computers, where it is a standard.

SmartPhone Usually associated with a Treo SmartPhone, but also applies to any other phone that has all of phone, web browsing, email, messaging, and photography or video camera capability. Used for vlogging.

speaker-out jack Lets you plug the sound card into a set of unamplified speakers and run them off the sound card's internal amplifier.

streaming Playing sounds and video in real time while you download. Particularly useful for reproduction and distribution of radio broadcasts.

streaming media Multimedia file streamed directly from a web site to a computer. Content is downloaded in real time as it is streaming instead of being saved in computer memory for later use.

T–U

track Entire songs (whether MP3 files, WAV files, or original cuts from vinyl or CDs). Old industry jargon from radio DJs and the music business. When speaking of mixing and audio production, however, the term refers to a single signal or set of signals in an unmixed recording, such as the lyrics track, the drum track, or the bass track. These tracks are then mixed into the completed song.

underground recording Also known as a *bootleg recording*.

URL Uniform Resource Locator. The address of a web page.

USB Universal Serial Bus. A common connection method for connecting computers to portable digital devices to exchange electronic files. USB 2.0 is even faster.

V

VBR Variable Bit Rate. VBR maximizes the quality of the audio but does not limit the size of the resulting MP3 file. Not all MP3 players can handle MP3 files recorded using VBR.

vlog A form of podcasting that integrates audio and video. The process of creating and posting a video (with or without sound) to your own weblog page or viewing that video as a visitor to another person's vlog. Highly related to this is podcasting (creating or listening to audio on a weblog), blogging (posting a text journal entry to your own weblog page or contributing to another person's weblog with comments), and photo blogging (creating or viewing pictures on a weblog). Vlogging, podcasting, weblogging, and picture sharing can be done from a computer or on the go, also referred to as *moblogging*. Moblogging is a method or channel of blogging, not a type or form of blogging. Essentially, you can blog words as well as an array of multimedia including voice, music, video, or pictures. You can also essentially create a personal "TV or news broadcast."

W–X

WAV Denotes *WAVEform*, which is a Microsoft audio format.

weblog Also known as a *blog*. A combination of *web* and *log*. A blog is a web site of pages where content is updated periodically. Content is posted as a web journal entry using software applications. The content can vary considerably and can include one or more of written text, audio podcasts, music, video without sound, or video with sound. A blog is also an essential platform or online home where all of these file types may reside. It makes sense for them to reside on a weblog because a written explanation of what the files contain is a logical starting point.

XML Extensible Markup Language. A programming language that is an umbrella standard under which RSS operates. More podcasts now have XML links than they do RSS links.

INDEX